THE COLORING BOOK JOURNAL: A 52-WEEK DEVOTIONAL

WRITTEN & ILLUSTRATED BY: SHONTICE BUTLER

Copyright © 2021

Hardback ISBN: 979-8-218-64622-6
Paperback ISBN: 978-0-578-81295-3

Atlanta, GA

Cover & Layout Design: Start Write Publish & Andromeda GFX

Interior Artwork: Shontice Butler

All rights reserved.

No part of this publication may be reproduced, distributed, or transmitted in any form or by any means, including photocopying, recording, or other electronic or mechanical methods, without the prior written permission of the publisher, except in the case of brief quotations embodied in critical reviews and certain other noncommercial uses permitted by copyright law.

Dedication & Thanks

I dedicate this devotional to everyone who is desiring to grow deeper in their relationship with God. This is a dark world we live in and more people need the light that results from such a decision. This decision to follow Jesus closely will come with trials and tough daily decisions, so if no one else tells you, I'm proud of you for saying, "yes."

Keep going. Galatians 6:9

A special thank you to the following people for being a part of the process of creating this devotional. Your encouragement and help was, and always will be, much appreciated.

May God bless you all:

Alexis, Ashley S., Ashley J., Aunt Barbara, Chelsea, Courtney, Dad, Erica, Ja'Terria, Jennifer, Jynelle, Lauren, Llewellyn, Mom, Ms. Ronda, Shenell, and Mrs. Tyonna.

Table of Contents

INTRODUCTION 6
   Note from the Author 6
   Prayer 9

JANUARY 11
- ☐ Is God's word really written in the Bible? 12
- ☐ Be Still and Know 21
- ☐ Beacon of Light 27
- ☐ Primary Concern 33

FEBRUARY 40
- ☐ The Path to Purity 41
- ☐ Do you love Jesus? 48
- ☐ Faith OVER Feelings 55
- ☐ Seek God 61

MARCH 68
- ☐ Mountains and Valleys 69
- ☐ No Time for Negativity 75
- ☐ Affirmation 81
- ☐ Be a Good Steward 91
- ☐ Shine On! 98

APRIL 105
- ☐ Time with God 106
- ☐ One Way 111
- ☐ Finished Work 116
- ☐ Deeply Loved 122
- ☐ Time of Reflection: Part 1 130

MAY 135
- ☐ Pray Without Ceasing 136
- ☐ Testimony 142
- ☐ See God, Experience God 149
- ☐ Snatched Thoughts 155

JUNE 161
- ☐ God Knows 162
- ☐ Overflow 173
- ☐ Resist 178
- ☐ Choose this Day 184

JULY 192
- ☐ Peace in Chaos 193
- ☐ Lean Not 199
- ☐ Get Up! 205
- ☐ You be You, Let God be God 210

AUGUST 214
- ☐ Order over Chaos 215
- ☐ Run the Race 223
- ☐ The Love of God 228
- ☐ Crafty with Purpose 234
- ☐ Time of Reflection: Part 2 241

SEPTEMBER 246
- ☐ Plans, Plans, Plans! 247
- ☐ Broken Jars 254
- ☐ Tell Your Story 263
- ☐ Ablaze 269

OCTOBER 273
- ☐ Vision 274
- ☐ Obey 282
- ☐ Altogether Beautiful 290
- ☐ The Great Escape 296

NOVEMBER 301
- ☐ Deeply Rooted 302
- ☐ God is With You 308
- ☐ Don't Tap Out! 316
- ☐ Unreliable Faith 326

DECEMBER 333
- ☐ Pressed 334
- ☐ Blank Canvas, Clean Slate 340
- ☐ Worth the Wait 348
- ☐ Chosen by the King! 358
- ☐ Time of Reflection: Part 3 365

END OF JOURNAL MESSAGE 370

ADDITIONAL BLANK PAGES 371

FULL ANSWER KEY 377

APPENDIX A: TO CONDEMN OR NOT TO CONDEMN? 438

APPENDIX B: THE LAW OR GRACE? 439

APPENDIX C: THE TRINITY 441

APPENDIX D: DELIVERANCE 443

APPENDIX E: EVANGELISM 447

APPENDIX F: FASTING 457

YEARLONG CHRONOLOGICAL BIBLE READING PLAN 461

BIBLIOGRAPHY 465

BOOK SUMMARY 466

Introduction
A Note from the Author

Welcome to the Coloring Book Journal (CBJ)! I wrote this journal for anyone to pick up and make their own. But this one, this one right here, is just for you! Once purchased, write your name on the front cover as you would in school (no matter how long ago that was).

This journal is now your personalized devotional. I was motivated to create this engaging devotional to encourage as many people (including you) as possible to consistently spend quality time with God by studying His word, getting to know Him, and putting His word into practice. This journal isn't meant to be a daunting homework assignment to get a good grade on nor is it another thing to add to your religious checklist. The CBJ is all about creating a meeting place for you and your Creator, so go through each scripture at your own pace and let the Lord take you on a fun journey of coming to know Him more deeply. If you didn't know, God has desired to meet with you your entire life (and even before you were born) because He loves you, wants you to know Him, and He wants to know you. Being that He has revealed Himself to us through Jesus and the Bible, reading it, asking His Holy Spirit to help you understand it, and applying it to your life will cause eternal change; all it takes is spending time with Him and surrendering. Prayerfully, the CBJ will be a tool to help set those moments up for you as you seek after God throughout the year. I pray you encounter Jesus in new and refreshing ways. Yalla(let's go), below is some info on what to expect from the CBJ!

Although this looks like a composition notebook and is called a journal, it is, in fact, a devotional in which you will be challenged to read various scriptures and answer questions to help you go deeper into what you're reading. Each week's devotional is called a "journal entry." With four journal entries each month, there's one for each week, each also accompanied by a coloring page for added fun!

There are various ways you can complete each journal entry:

- *Complete the journal entry in one sitting (note: some are longer than others) and reflect on the scriptures and takeaways throughout the week*
- *Complete this journal throughout the week, marking where you stop and picking back up the next day (highly recommended)*
- *A mixture of both options based on the week*
- *Color at your leisure*

Bonus option:

- *Make copies of the coloring page, share them with a young believer of any age, and discuss the scriptures and/or the topic as you complete the journal entry*

No matter how you approach completing your journal entries, be sure to go deep each week as you reflect on and revisit scripture and takeaways from each entry.

Here's a few tips for studying the Bible:
- *Always pray before starting, inviting the Holy Spirit into your time. I've supplied a sample prayer after this intro if you don't feel confident in praying yet (Sidenote: just talk to God like he's a respected friend)*
- *View studying the Bible as getting to know God more deeply rather than as a chore*
- *Start small by deeply studying a single verse in addition to doing your journal entry*
- *Research who the author of the given book of the Bible was and who the original audience was for big picture context*
- *Read surrounding chapters and/or verses so that you can gather more background for the passage at hand*
- *When defining words in scriptures, first find the word in HEBREW if it's in the Old Testament or GREEK if it's in the New Testament (Biblehub.com is an excellent online resource, Blue Letter Bible App, or invest in a physical copy of Strong's Exhaustive Concordance Bible)*

Typically, in devotionals, the author gives you their interpretation and commentary for a particular topic, accompanied by scripture. However, in this journal, it is the opposite. You will read the scriptures and answer various questions first for yourself, and at the end of your devotional time, you can look at the answer key in the back to discover what I saw in the scriptures. Feel free to discuss these answers with others to hear what God shows them in the text. If you happen to disagree with my responses or simply want to discuss, feel free to send me an email at DISCUSS.CBJ@GMAIL.COM and let's chat.

Each journal entry ends with a Let's make it personal(LMIP) section. Use this section to assess your life concerning the scriptures and apply the Word of God directly to it. Occasionally, there is a Selah Moment in various journal entries, these sections are for you to pause and reflect on the topic or scripture at hand. The LMIP and Selah Moment sections do not typically have right or wrong answers in the answer key as the answers are based on your personal thoughts or experiences.

You will also find a Worship Playlist with various genres of music exalting Jesus at the very bottom of various journal entries. The songs mentioned are songs I thought would go perfectly with the topic at hand. Search them on your favorite streaming platform and listen for the connections. You can also find a compiled playlist I've created on our YouTube channel: @moveandseek!

Lastly, every four months you will find a Time of Reflection sheet in which I urge you to take a day to sit with God and reflect on all He's done, the state of your heart, and where you are mentally and spiritually.

Well, that's all I have. Enjoy.

With Love,

Shontice

Prayer

Father God, I thank you for this time that you've allowed me to read your word and spend time with you. As I draw closer to you during this time, Lord, I invite your Holy Spirit to speak and minister to be through your word. Holy Spirit, open my eyes so that I may see all you would have me to. Open my ears so that I may hear and understand all you are saying. Clear my mind so that I am free of all distractions and can focus on you, Lord. Soften my heart so that I can receive what you have for me at this moment and let go of whatever is within me that is not like you. I want to know you better, God. Show me who you are, who I am, and what you desire of me.

In Jesus' name I pray,
Amen

STOP, DID YOU READ THE INTRO?

I know, I know, who reads the introduction to a book? I'm the same way, but there's important information there so that you can get the best out of your time using the CBJ as you study the Bible. If you read it, great, keep going. If you skipped those couple of pages, go back and take five to ten minutes to read over it.

January

Is God's word really written in the Bible?

I don't know who owns this journal - you could be a believer of Jesus Christ or your parents could be raising you in a Christian household, but you haven't truly put your faith in Jesus yet(that was me for a long time). You could be one investigating who Jesus is on your own or could be a part of a different faith and proclaim another religion. You could even be an Atheist or Agnostic who doesn't yet believe that God is even real or is just there but not active in our lives. No matter who you are or where you fall in that spectrum of people, let me stop here and say, "Heyyyy! Thanks for picking up this journal; I pray it blesses your life." If you read the intro, I've already formally welcomed you, but I rarely read the introductions to books before I wrote my own, so boom, there's another welcome, but I highly recommend you pause here and go read the intro. I digress.

Without this initial topic, you cannot go any further in this journal and receive the fullness of it. As, without the belief that the Bible is truly God's word, the things written in it don't hold as much weight as they should. There are many other beliefs about who God is and many other religious texts in the world. Thus, without this belief and understanding that the Holy Bible is God's preserved word, this entire journal would be obsolete and meaningless. Not only that, but our faith in God (Yahweh, Jesus) altogether would be obsolete because let's face it, we weren't there from the beginning to see God form the Earth and we weren't there walking with God as He walked on the Earth through Jesus. So, let's get to the bottom of it - is God's word really written in the Bible? How can we be sure that this book called the "Holy Bible" is the real deal? Are you ready? Let's start with some basic facts.

How many Books of the Bible are there?
The Bible has 66 books.

Who wrote the Bible on paper?
The Bible was physically written by about 40 different men, in different time periods, and of different backgrounds/professions.

How long is there between the first book of the Bible written (Genesis) to the last book (Revelation)?
1450 B.C - A.D 95 (so roughly 1,546 years timespan)

Read 2 Timothy 3:16-17 and Romans 15:4 below.

> *All Scripture is God-breathed and is useful for instruction, for conviction, for correction, and for training in righteousness so that the man of God may be complete, fully equipped for every good work.*
>
> *(2 Timothy 3:16-17)*

> *For everything that was written in the past was written for our instruction so that through endurance and the encouragement of the Scriptures, we might have hope.*
>
> *(Romans 15:4)*

1. Based on the scriptures above, what is the purpose(s) of the Bible? What is it useful for?

....
....
....

2. What does scripture say about the creation of the Bible? Who is it ultimately inspired by? (Hint: Read 2 Timothy 3:16 in NLT & ESV translations)

....
....

Why are there different versions of the Bible?

Short answer: The various versions of the Bible are simply translations of the Bible from Hebrew/Greek to English and other languages. Although they are different in expression (because no language is the same and some translators used different techniques) they're from the same source, God Himself (2 Timothy 3:16-17) and across translations, the essence of the word of God is unchanged.

Longer answer: Being that the God of the Bible is the Creator of all peoples and He died for all(John 3:16), He doesn't hinder anyone from coming to Him. Scripture also says that people from every nation will be before the throne of Heaven(Revelation 7:9) and that we are to store the word of God in our hearts(Deuteronomy 6:6-9). Therefore, everyone needs to have the opportunity to hear and understand what God says is true. Thus, the Bible has been translated into over 700 languages and counting! The original languages of the Bible are Hebrew, Greek, and some Aramaic portions. Throughout the CBJ you will see me suggest certain translations like "KJV", "NLT", "ESV", "AMP", etc these are various English translations of the Bible and they can be found on the Bible app or online(if you don't have access to these, no worries, the Bible you have is just fine). The reason each of these English translations' wording differs is due to the evolution of the English language over time, the technique used for translating, and access to early manuscripts.

3. *Do a quick search - Define "prophecy".*

....

....

....

Within the Bible, one could find a plethora of prophecies which have unfolded and come to pass. The ones that have not still have time to be made manifest being that life is still going. Do a quick search to see for yourself the various prophecies in the Bible that were foretold well in advance and then came to pass.

In Jesus Christ alone, there are hundreds of prophecies written in the Old Testament (B.C) days that were, in fact, fulfilled when Jesus hit the scene in 6 - 4 B.C, until His death and resurrection around A.D 33.

The image below is an infographic that gives a visual representation of the Old Testament's prophecies telling of the coming Messiah, Jesus, with a line connecting it to where Jesus fulfilled it in the New Testament.

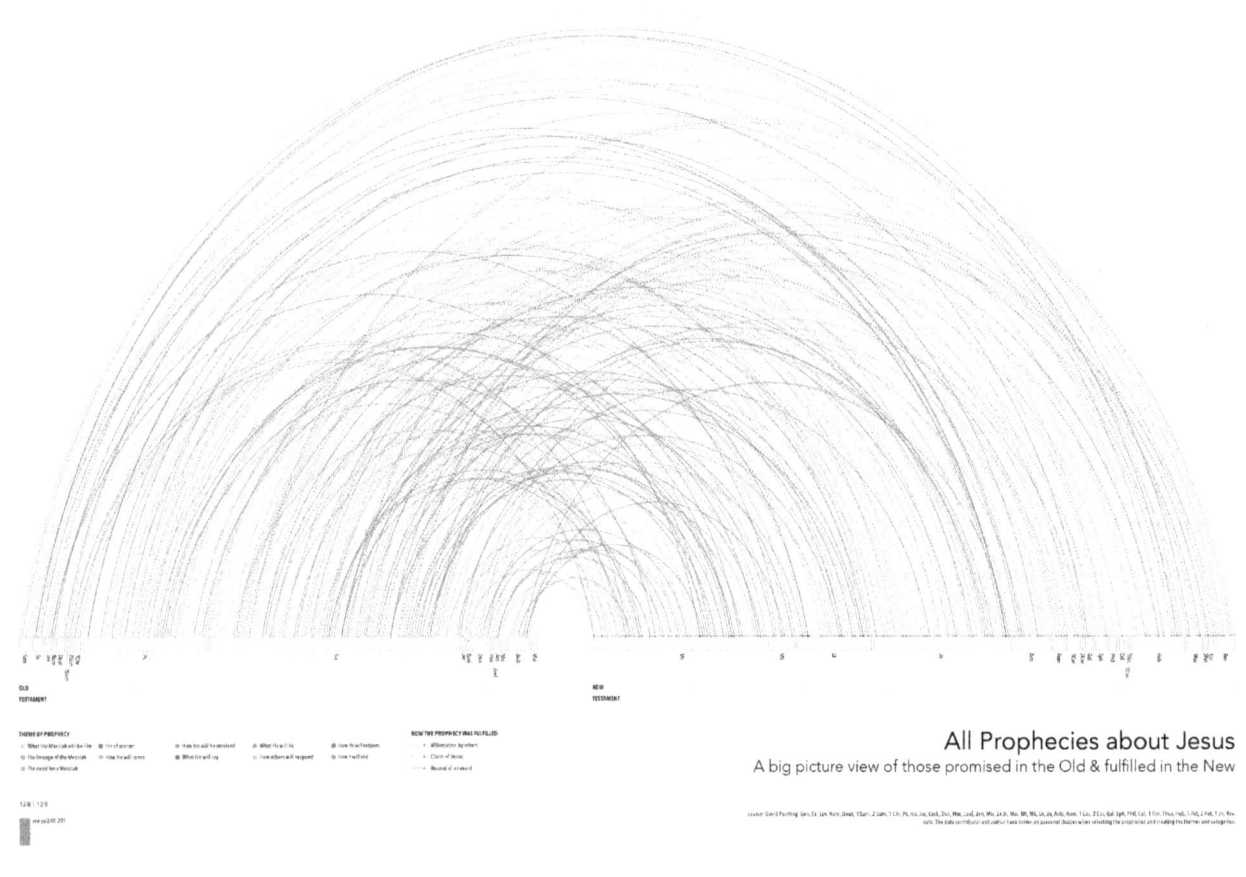

Image from The Infographic Bible: Visualising the Drama of God's Word © Karen Sawrey 2018, 2019.

According to a renowned site for answering questions about the Bible, gotquestions.org:

"One scholar, J. Barton Payne, has found as many as 574 verses in the Old Testament that somehow point to or describe or reference the coming Messiah. Alfred Edersheim found 456 Old Testament verses referring to the Messiah or His times. Conservatively, Jesus fulfilled at least 300 prophecies in His earthly ministry."

To try to convince you (if you aren't already) of the sureness of the Bible being God's word, I could go on and on about the following things:

- *The God of the Bible (God the Father, Son (Jesus), and Holy Spirit) transforming lives, making Himself known, and conquering many battles for people.*
- *The scriptures still being relevant to this day, although it was written centuries ago, and, where other texts would be outdated, it is still alive, active, and meaningful.*
- *People being healed in the name of Jesus.*
- *People giving their lives to the God of the Bible and having personal testimonies of being transformed into totally new people with new desires and hearts.*

I could even quote the scripture, which states, "All Scripture is God-breathed (inspired by God)..." going on and on with truth and words from this holy book. However, for a skeptic to hear what people say based on personal testimonies and to hear what the Bible says about the Bible won't quite hold up. Since I've presented some internal and sentimental facts, let's also take a look outside of the Bible for its validity.

Time

Let's start with the very topic of time and how history is told with it: B.C & A.D.

4. Do a quick search - what does "B.C." stand for? (not be confused with B.C.E)

....

5. Do a quick search - what does "A.D." stand for? (Hint: it's not "After Death"). What does it mean in English?

....

6. With these two abbreviations being used and accepted to mark moments in WORLD history, what do you think that says/means for the validity of Christ and the ONLY Holy Book in which points to and informs us about Him in His fullness, the Bible?

....
....
....

Preservation

Many people try to discredit the Bible because it's been translated and duplicated by humans many times, but you'd be surprised at how well preserved the Bible is; it's kind of like God was protecting it or something. Hmm, that's something to think about.

One way to test the accuracy of ancient texts is by comparing the amount of time between the original text and the copy; this is called the "Bibliographical Test." The closer the duplicated text is written to the original, the better. Guess what? The New Testament surpasses expectations. Aforementioned authors wrote the original Greek New Testament between A.D 50 - 100, and transcribers wrote the copied manuscripts in A.D 130, only a 50-year time gap. In comparison, many other ancient and well-accepted texts have hundreds and thousands of years between the original and the copies (McDowell & Jones, 2014); this points to the urgency, need, and reliability of the New Testament scriptures and the Bible as a whole.

Speaking of, the Old Testament has a great rate of preservation too. When historians discovered the Dead Sea Scrolls in 1947, they had their hands on the oldest known Old Testament texts dating back over 1,000 years from the duplicated versions they had. After comparing the originals of the Dead Sea Scrolls to the scriptures they had access to in the Bible, they came to find that although there was a significant time difference, there were no errors or changes that changed the meaning of the text!

I don't think you understand how significant that fact is, so let's give it some context! Have you ever played the game "telephone?" Someone creates a phrase and whispers it to someone, and that person whispers it to another person, and so on. Imagine playing this game with 1,000 people.

7. What would you expect to have happened to the original message? Would it be the same as it first started? Why?

....
....
....

In a way, the game of telephone shows the grandeur of the Bible's preservation as unlike our game, the Bible had NO significant changes from the original text to the duplicated text after a 1,000-year time gap. WOW! That's preservation at it's finest.

Archaeology & History

With the specific locations of various places mentioned in the Bible, the Bible serves as an ancient map for historians in mapping out the early world and also helping archaeologists discover new findings and artifacts that have preserved the ancient world. Below are a couple of those findings.

Egypt

Many believe that Ramses II is the Pharaoh mentioned throughout the beginning of Exodus and who Moses had to consistently toil with to let the people of God, the Israelites, be released from his rule (Exodus 8:1). Ramses II's reign was between 1279–1213 B.C. He was known to be one of the most powerful, architectural (he built many monuments unto himself and other gods), and militant Pharaohs (Rattini, 2019). With such a personality and reputation, it is not hard to assume why the record of the Israelites victory over Pharaoh is not recorded within the reign of Ramses II (Isbouts, 2018) as legacy and reputation meant a great deal. However, during the reign of Merneptah, Ramses II's son, he inscribed Israel's name into a stone called the Merneptah Stele, marking his victory over Israel during a battle in 1207 B.C. Thus, exposing their existence in history and their independence later in life (Reinsch, 2018).

Jericho

According to historians, Jericho was a well-fortified city with walls that stretched almost 12 feet high and 6 feet wide. Historians also record, "Jericho fell in the 16th century around 1573 B.C when an earthquake violently destroyed it. Charred wood found at the site suggests that the remains of the city were burned. Buried food supplies also suggest that it was not captured following a siege." (Ramos, 2016)

> **Note:** Historians have discovered physical evidence of Jericho's walls; however, some archaeologists' findings predate the time period in which it is recorded in the Bible.

Read Joshua 6:15-24

8. How does the statement above and scriptures you read relate to each other? What similarities do you see?

....

....

....

So, there you have it, internal, external, and sentimental facts pointing to the validity of the Bible. And if none of that is enough evidence for you, then you can always rely on faith, and that's not a bad option either, for "blessed are they that have not seen, and yet have believed." (Jesus, A.D. 33, John:20:29)

Worship Playlist: *"Is He Worthy? (Live)" by UPPERROOM, Aaron Tedeschi, & Ashley Bailey*

Be Still and Know

How easily are you shaken? When tests and trials come, are you still like Jesus on the boat during a terrible storm (Mark 4:37-38), or are you like the sailors on the boat with Jonah, running rampant (Jonah 1:4-5)? As we grow to know who God is, we will grow in our faith, and thus, our level of stillness during tests and trials will increase as well. Ready to add to your faith tank?

Read Isaiah 40:25-28

1. Is God limited in His power and abilities? What do these verses say about that?

....
....
....

2. Define "sovereign" as a noun and adjective.

....
....
....

3. Based on Isaiah 40:25-28 and the definition of "sovereign," fill in the blank:

God is ....

Read Psalm 46

4. What adjectives and actions describe God in the text?

....
....
....

5. What is stillness? What do you think stillness looks like?

....
....
....

6. What's the opposite of stillness? What do you think that looks like?

....

....

....

7. What's the purpose of a 'fortress'? Notice that God is described as a "fortress" twice, what do you think this means?

....

....

....

8. Being that God is everything mentioned in Psalm 46, why are we able to "be still" even in the midst of trouble, suffering, and challenging circumstances?

....

....

....

Let's take a look at a man of God who experienced many tests, trials, and suffering.

Read Job 1:1-12, Job 2:3-7, and Ezekiel 13:23

9. Before Satan could test Job, what did God have to do first? In Ezekiel, what do you notice God had the power to do?

....

....

....

10. How does this show the sovereignty of God?

....

....

....

11. *Why did God allow Job to go through such tests?*

....

....

....

12. *Where was God while Job was going through these many tests? (Job 2:3)*

....

....

....

Read Job 1:13-22 and Job 2:8-10

13. *After much of what Job cared about was taken away, how did Job respond?*

....

....

....

14. *Using Job 1:21 and Job 2:10, what did Job understand about himself and God? How do you think this helped him to praise God during these circumstances still?*

....

....

....

Read Job 29:1-6, Job 30:1, and Job 30:24-31

15. *At this point, Job has endured these tests and trials for some time. How has Job's attitude shifted? What caused him to no longer "be still" as you saw earlier?*

....

....

....

Read Job 38:1-13 and Isaiah 40:25-31

16. How do you see the sovereignty of God?

> **Hint:** *Think about what Job's vs. God's answers to the questions in the text would be*

....
....
....

Read Job 40:1-5 and Job 42:1-6

17. How did Job respond to the sovereignty of God?

....
....
....

Read Job 42:10-17

18. What did God do for Job that no man could ever do?

....
....
....

Selah Moment:

Read James 1:2-4 a few times before answering the questions below,

"Consider it pure joy, my brothers and sisters, whenever you face trials of many kinds, because you know that the testing of your faith produces perseverance. Let perseverance finish its work so that you may be mature and complete, not lacking anything."

What do you notice? How do you want to live after reading this?

....
....
....

Let's make it personal

When tests and trials come your way, how do you respond? Is your response in the same still manner as Job was in the beginning chapters (distraught but trusting God and being still)? Or do you respond in the way Job did in the latter chapters (questioning God, allowing arrogance and comparison to creep in, etc.)?

....
....
....

Knowing the sovereignty of God and all that He's able to see and do, how does that bring about added comfort for you now when we go through tests and trials? Knowing these things, how are you now able to be still?

....
....
....

Just as Job, remember, every test and trial you go through doesn't mean God is punishing you. So, instead of choosing a victim mindset when times of trial and suffering come, choose to see it as an opportunity to see God move mightily, strengthen your faith as you lean on Him to make it through(Song of Solomon 8:5), refine your character, and/or as an opportunity to let Satan know that although trials come, your faith will not be shaken. So, strive after enduring every test and trial with great stillness and grace, knowing that the God in Heaven you serve is sovereign and will help you make it through. Jesus warned us that we'd have trials, so brace yourself by keeping your faith, being still, and knowing who your Almighty God is and what He's capable of. Lastly, take note that being still doesn't mean you must be fake happy as you endure trials. Expressing your struggle(not complaining) to God and a trusted friend is good. As we see in Job's life, said honesty deepened his relationship with God because he was open and vulnerable allowing himself to be humbled where he needed and encouraged in the end.

Worship Playlist: *"Peace" by Bethel Music & We The Kingdom*
"Endure" by Sarah Jueres ft. Montell Fish
"Gravity" by Anike & Jordan L'Oreal

Beacon of Light

When studying the Bible, knowing the context and background are essential in order to read the scriptures as God intended. Before reading today, do some research on who the audience is in the book of Isaiah. Reading the surrounding chapters also helps to give more insight into the text you are focusing on. Today, start by reading Isaiah 1 & Isaiah 59 to see the state of the people God was initially speaking to, as this will help you with today's study of God's word.

1. While reading Isaiah 1, 58 & 59, what did you notice about the people and God?

	The group of people mentioned	God
Isaiah 1		
Isaiah 58-59		

2. Who is the audience?

....

....

3. What's the purpose of the text?

....
....
....

Additional Biblical context: As we see laid out in various scriptures(see Galatians 3, Romans 8, and Romans 11 to start) those whose faith is in Jesus, have been grafted into the family of God along with believing Israelites because of Jesus' victory on the cross and pouring out His Holy Spirit thereafter. Thus, we too have become descendants of Abraham and will obtain various promises of God. This however does not mean we(disciples of Christ, the Church) replace the natural-born descendants of Abraham that God made His original promises to(the Jews). Just as an adopted child doesn't replace the natural-born children of foster parents, but instead, they are added to the inheritance because they are now one with the family. Thus, due to our adoption, we share in the promises of God, namely eternally inheriting the promised land of the kingdom of God as heirs with Christ. Being so, when we read about how God dealt with Israel, we can get an understanding of how He sees us as His children and how He operates as a Father, Savior, God, and friend.

Let's make it personal: Part 1

In what areas of your life do you see yourself in Israel?

....
....
....
....

Read Isaiah 60:1

4. Define "arise." (Remember to look it up in a Hebrew concordance because this is an Old Testament word)

....
....

5. Think backward. If the command to arise is given, what must have been the state of the people prior?

....
....

6. After reading Isaiah 1, 58 & 59, explain why Israel needed to be commanded to "arise."

....

....

7. Although Israel had turned against the ways of the Lord, based on what you see is to come, did God give up on them or did He choose to steadily pursue them? Circle one.

        God gave up on them   *God pursued them*

8. What is the light mentioned in verse 1?

....

Read Isaiah 60:2-3

9. Who is the light? (See John 8:12 for additional support)

....

10. What will cause the darkness that is mentioned? What does this suggest about the timeframe of this prophecy coming to pass? (See Zechariah 14:3-9, Matthew 24:26-31, and 2 Peter 3:9-15 for support)

....

....

Read Matthew 22:1-14, Revelation 19:6-9, Ephesians 5:25-27, and 2 Peter 3:9-15

11. Pay attention to how God speaks and what He does in the above verses(note: this may be shown through a story or the words of a disciple inspired by God), what's God's heart and desire for all people?

....

....

12. In the end, Jesus will shine and reign victoriously(Isaiah 60 and Daniel 2:44-45), what must happen for us to remain with Him after the deep darkness consumes the world? (See Isaiah 1:27-28 for additional support)

....

....

As you saw today, God won't relent. He loves you and the world at large. He's constantly in pursuit of you. How are you responding? Will you arise before it's too late?

January

Let's make it personal: Part 2

Take inventory of your life. Put a check next to the things you see evidence of in your life and an "X" next to things you don't see in your life:

__ I am a part of the bride of Christ (you've repented and confessed with your mouth and believe in your heart that Jesus is Lord of your life and Savior of your soul after dying and resurrecting three days later)

__ I allow the Bible alone to determine how I live; I live a holy and godly life

__ I am repentant and ask the Lord for forgiveness if I sin and mess up

__ I spend time with God through prayer and studying the scriptures

__ I thank God and rejoice for all He's done for me

__ I am a light of Christ in the world (Jesus is on display for others to see based on how you live; you strive to make disciples)

What things do you need to work on? Take time to pray and ask God for help in those areas. I also suggest you turn to someone more mature in their faith and ask them to help you in these areas. Also, be sure to take time to celebrate all the ways you have done well too! These are great victories as times get darker.

....
....
....
....
....
....

The coming redemption of Israel and the total cleansing of the world hasn't happened yet, but today can be the day of salvation for you. If you'd like to accept Jesus as Lord and Savior so that the light you learned about this week won't only be outside of you, but within you as well, take time now to pray and express these things to God. Below is a sample prayer, feel free to add to it and make it personal for yourself.

> *Father God, I have sinned and fallen short of your glory. I have lived in this dark world and joined in by _____(insert any sins that come to mind). Lord, I repent of these things and every other sin I've committed knowingly and unknowingly. I now desire to be filled with your light and Holy Spirit. I confess with my mouth and believe in my heart that Jesus died on the cross to pay the penalty my sins earned. I also believe that on the third day, He rose from the dead and conquered death so that I might do the same. In Jesus' name, Hell no longer has victory over me from this day forward. Thank you Jesus for your loving kindness and saving grace. Hallelujah, I am free from the bondage of sin and shame! Father God, I accept, welcome, and profess Jesus as Lord over my life. My life is no longer my own, I place it in Your hands. May my life have greater meaning as I vow to pursue Your will over my own for my life. Soften my heart, open my eyes, and transform me from the inside out to be all you've called and chosen me to be. Help me to be the light of Christ in this dark world. In Jesus' name, I pray, Amen!*

Worship playlist: *"Getting Ready" by Maverick City & UPPERROOM*
"Mighty to Save" by Hillsong

"...and He will give you all you need from day to day if you live for Him and make the Kingdom of God your primary concern."

Matthew 6:33 (NLT)

Primary Concern

It's the beginning of a new year. Many people typically use this as a marker for new beginnings, new habits, and new opportunities. Before you flood your calendar and create your list of many goals, have you ever taken the time to see what God's ultimate desire and goal is for you? Let's take the time to explore this idea and see what God says we should make our number one goal in life and what the promises are for those who achieve said goal.

Today's journal entry is a little different. It's called "scripture dissection." There are various ways to read scripture: you can read it as a whole, like reading a book, you can break down passages, or you can pay close attention to a single verse and study it by breaking it apart, that's scripture dissection. When using this study method, I like to first read the scripture and surrounding scriptures for context a few times before doing anything. I then annotate various parts of the scripture to help highlight key things and make them stand out.

Remember, it's always important for you to pray before reading as the Holy Spirit is the one who can give you more in-depth insight than your natural eyes and mind could ever see or understand. So, take this time to pray and ask God to allow His Holy Spirit (that lives within you if you're saved) to open your eyes to see what He would have you to and that you'd receive divine revelation as you study and interpret His word. May your time with God be fruitful, in Jesus' name.

Read Matthew 6:24-34

1. Pay close attention to Matthew 6:24-25. Why does Jesus say you should not worry about everyday life?

....

....

....

2. Why does Jesus instruct you (as a believer) not to worry about day-to-day things? What examples does He give to further His point?

....

....

....

3. What does Jesus say is the cause of worry?

....
....
....

4. Who does Jesus say thoughts of worry are meant for? Why do you think this is?

....
....
....

Now that you have context, focus on verse 33 on today's activity page and "dissect" (annotate) it by following the instructions below. I've made it simpler for you by already outlining everything, you just have to trace it with the colors you assign. A huge part of scripture dissection is reflecting on what you're annotating, the questions below help you with that. Start by picking a colored highlighter for each of the sections below:

Color	Part of Speech
	Nouns/Pronouns (words that are circled in the activity)
	Verbs (words that are boxed in the activity)
	"Will" (Promise sentence starter) Highlight the promise this color too
	"If" (Stipulation sentence starter) Highlight the stipulation this color too

Circle the pronouns

5. Who is "He"/"Him" that is spoken of?

....

6. In the context of the scripture, who is "you" referring to (believers or unbelievers)?

....

Put a box around the verbs

7. What actions are for God to do? What actions are for you to do?

....

....

....

> *Hint: Pay attention to the verbs next to He/Him for God's part vs. verbs next to "you" for your part*

Put a squiggly line under the word "will"

Highlight the promise

   (TIP: when the word "will" is used, we know a promise is coming afterward)

8. What is the promise?

....

....

....

Now cross-reference (using other scriptures in the Bible that relate to help you go deeper in understanding) the promise by reading Philippians 4:19

9. What similarities do you notice between Matthew 6:33 and Philippians 4:19?

....

....

....

Double underline the word "if"

God's promises often come with some form of stipulation that requires something for the promise to come to pass. Highlight the stipulation.

(TIP: when the word "if" is used, the words following are typically the stipulation).

10. What stipulation does God say you must do to hold up your end of the bargain?

....
....
....

11. What is the Kingdom of God? (See Daniel 6:26 and Matthew 3:2 for additional help).

....

12. Define "primary."

....
....

13. What does it mean/look like to make something your primary concern?

....
....
....

14. How can you make the Kingdom of God your primary concern in life?

....
....
....

Remember, God sent His one and only son to die for you so that you can enter into a personal relationship with Him. Don't take this relationship for granted, and don't waste this opportunity to get to know God intimately. Just as your earthly relationships require you to spend time with people, your heavenly relationship with God requires quality time too. In fact, He deserves top quality.

Let's make it personal

Think about your day to day routines/actions. What things do you put your time towards weekly? Use the prompts or create your own and record the number of hours you put towards each task daily. Then, multiply it by 7(or however many days a week you do the task) to get your weekly total.

> *NOTE: There is no set time for how much you seek after God; this is just a snapshot to show you where your priorities are based on how you spend your time*

After you have your totals for the week, create a pie chart showing you a visual of how you spend your time.

Social Media	_____ min/hrs daily	× **7** =	_____ min/hrs weekly
Work	_____ min/hrs daily	× **7** =	_____ min/hrs weekly
Fitness	_____ min/hrs daily	× **7** =	_____ min/hrs weekly
Clubbing/Partying	_____ min/hrs daily	× **7** =	_____ min/hrs weekly
Playing games	_____ min/hrs daily	× **7** =	_____ min/hrs weekly
Reading your Bible	_____ min/hrs daily	× **7** =	_____ min/hrs weekly
Praying	_____ min/hrs daily	× **7** =	_____ min/hrs weekly
Helping others	_____ min/hrs daily	× **7** =	_____ min/hrs weekly
Being with Community	_____ min/hrs daily	× **7** =	_____ min/hrs weekly

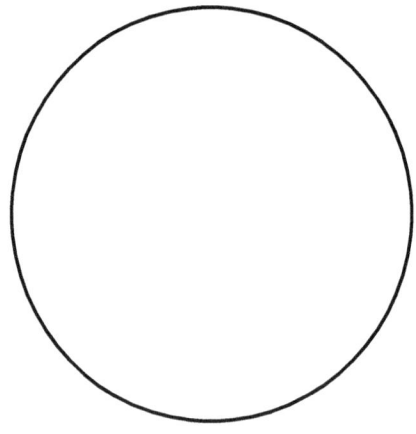

On your pie chart, color the Kingdom-focused tasks one color and the Non-Kingdom focused tasks another color. Evaluate your responses and the pie chart. Based on what you see, is seeking the Kingdom of God and living righteously your primary concern?

....

If so, how can you continue to or grow deeper? If not, what things do you need to shift, do less of, or incorporate God into to make the Kingdom of God your primary concern? (ie. You can pray at work, or share the gospel at the grocery store, etc.).

....
....
....
....
....
....
....
....
....
....

Some of the beautiful things about God is that He is merciful, loving, and omnipresent. Meaning, He forgives your misdeeds, cares deeply for you without you even doing a thing (He just loves you for you), and He is everywhere. If you are a believer, do not allow these traits of God to enable you to get comfortable and do nothing for God. Instead, allow them to spur you on to choose this day to press in this year to be more in tune with Him, seeking after Him daily and finding ways to share Him with others. Why? As a believer it's what you've agreed to do in following Jesus and making Him Lord, there's promises attached as you've read this week, and God is worthy of your time for He is a Holy and omnipotent (all-powerful) God who deserves and requires honor and obedience. He also simply desires to be with you and know you. Be sure to also repent of any wasted time, disobedience, idolatry(anything we put before God becomes an idol), etc.

Worship Playlist: *"Make Room" by Jonathan McReynolds*

February

The Path to Purity

Read Psalm 119:9-11

1. How can a young person stay on the path of purity?

....

....

2. Define "purity."

....

....

....

As the definition you found probably suggests, purity is most often thought of regarding sexual purity. Many people know that having sex before marriage is a sin (fornication/ sexual immorality) and thus would make him/her "impure." However, many people don't know why sexual immorality is a sin and the damage it causes. Many people also don't realize that sexual purity isn't the only purity that we need. Today you will look at each of these sides of purity and their importance.

Read Leviticus 18, 1 Corinthians 5:1-2, Romans 1:21-27, and Matthew 5:27-28

3. Is God general or specific about what sexual immorality is? What is it?

....

....

....

Read 1 Corinthians 6:15-20, Colossians 3:5, Song of Solomon 8:4, and Matthew 5:29-30

4. What are you told to do regarding sexual immorality? What verbs stand out?

....

....

....

5. According to 1 Corinthians 6:15-20, why should you uphold the standards you mentioned above?

....

....

....

Read Genesis 2:24-25, Genesis 4:1, Genesis 24:58-67, and 1 Corinthians 7:1-9

6. God created humans with sexual desires. Thus, the urge for sex is natural. However, when does God say sex is permitted?

....

....

....

To further get the point across, notice in Genesis 2:24, God says husband and wife shall become one flesh. This "oneness" is also mentioned in 1 Corinthians 6:16 when God urges us through Paul to not have sex with prostitutes because it results in the same oneness of a husband and wife. Therefore, in the eyes of God, everyone you have sex with is technically your spouse now. This reality is greatly debated amongst people, but scriptures clearly show the truth: Sex is not only for marriage, it is a marriage ceremony.

Selah Moment:

Quickly read Exodus 22:16-17

How is the seriousness of pre-marital sex in the eyes of God displayed?

....

....

Read Leviticus 18:24, Hebrews 13:4, 1 Corinthians 6:12-20, and Matthew 7:6

7. Why is it important to stay sexually pure?

....

....

....

Let's make it personal: Part 1

Are you sexually pure? Remember this includes your thoughts too. If so, what's keeping you that way? If not, why?

....
....
....
....
....
....

If you aren't currently sexually pure but want to be, all it takes is a choice to get started. In this next section, you will see just what that is. If you are currently sexually pure, I celebrate your decision, as it can definitely be challenging. However, this next section on purity is still for you as there are many other sins we can so easily be entangled in and thus need purity.

Read Hebrews 9:13-15, Isaiah 1:16, and 1 John 1:7

8. What must you be purified of?

....
....
....

Read Isaiah 53:5-6, 1 Peter 2:24-25, Ephesians 5:25-27, and Hebrews 9:15-28

9. Why are you able to be purified?

....
....
....

Read Revelation 22:14-15 (ESV)

10. Who will be able to enter into the gates of Heaven? (Take note of who will not make it in)

....

Read Revelation 7:13-14, Isaiah 1:18, and Hebrews 9:22

11. What do you think "wash their robes" means?

12. How does "washing their robes" relate to purity?

Read Isaiah 1:18-20, Mark 1:15, John 3:16, and 1 John 1:6-9

13. How can people "wash their robes"?

14. Using the scriptures you've read today and Hebrews 12:14, who will NOT be able to enter into the gate of Heaven?

Let's make it personal: Part 2

What sins do you find yourself continually falling into? What sin issues do you see in your life?

Do you desire to turn away from these things? How can you take steps to choose purity?

Think practically. For instance, if you struggle with sexual immorality, choosing not to talk to the opposite sex after a specific time of the night, or when you have the urge to have sex, calling a friend who could hold you accountable, etc.

Don't be fooled by the schemes and lies of religions and tactics of this world; there's only ONE way for us to be cleansed (purified) of sin, and thus, there's only one way for us to get to Heaven, as stated in John 14:6. Without being made holy, righteous, and purified, you will not see God in Heaven. As you studied today, all it takes is a decision to repent, believe, and receive Jesus. No longer do you have to sacrifice a goat, nor do you have to pray hail Mary's, you don't need to burn sage for hours, you don't have to turn to a priest to be a mediator and confess your sins to him to be made right with God(although confessing your sins to your believing friends/community for accountability and prayer is important, see James 5:16). None of that purifies your soul; only the blood of Jesus does. He is the ultimate sacrifice and mediator between you and God. By repenting, placing your faith in Jesus, receiving the Holy Spirit, renewing your mind, and obeying God's word, you are purified of your sin and are on the path of righteousness.

Have you made that decision? Have you entrusted God with your life? Have you accepted Jesus as Lord and Savior? If not, with sincerity, take this time to pray and confess to God. Below is a sample prayer. Feel free to add anything else in it you'd like to say to your Heavenly Father:

> "Father God, I admit that I am a sinner and have fallen short of your glorious standards. I no longer desire to continue to live in this way. I know Your word is true and believe that Jesus died on the cross to pay the penalty for my sins, but He didn't stay there because, on the third day, you raised Him from the dead so that I can be free from this bondage of sin. So, Father God, please come into my life. I accept Jesus as Lord and Savior, and I lay down my own life to pick up the life you created me to have. I humbly and freely accept your Holy Spirit to lead and guide me for the rest of my life. In Jesus' name, I pray, Amen."

Coloring activity: *On today's coloring sheet, in the top (left) triangle, write down various sins that you've committed. Afterward, color the entire background of that triangle red (representing the blood of Jesus). On the other side of the line that has "Jesus Christ" written, leave the background of the triangle white, but write down words that describe how God sees you now as you are holy and blameless in His sight (hint, I just gave you two words you could use; read 1 Peter 2:9, Romans 5:10, Colossians 1:21-23, and John 15:15 for help). The completed sheet represents what happens if you have placed your faith in Jesus and are saved. The blood of Jesus covers every sin and God makes you clean.*

Worship Playlist: *"Worth the Wait" by: Franchesca*
"Pure" by Abbie Gamboa
"Clean" by Natalie Grant
"Wash Me Clean" by Bryan Terrell ft. Chris West

Do you love Jesus?

Would it be easier to go to work at a job you loved or at a job you just did for a paycheck? Would your work be more meaningful for you at a job you loved or at a job you just did for a paycheck? Let's see how Jesus feels about the topic.

Before you get started, remember, context is everything. The more background you have, the better you'll understand scripture. Today you will be looking at the life and love of Peter, one of Jesus' disciples, but before we get to the point, let's investigate Peter's life a little to gain greater context.

Read Matthew 4:18-22

1. Who were the first men Jesus called to be "fishers of men"? What was their original job?

....

....

2. How did they respond to Jesus' call to follow Him?

....

....

....

Read Matthew 16:13-16

3. After following Jesus for some time, who does He proclaim Jesus is?

....

As you can see, Peter followed, trusted, and got to know Jesus intimately throughout His entire ministry on Earth. He saw Jesus do miracles, preach the good news, and do countless other things that weren't recorded in the Bible (John 21:25). Peter was a loyal follower of Christ.

Read Matthew 26:33-35

4. How does Peter plan on showing his loyalty to Jesus?

....

5. Knowing all things, what does Jesus say and know Peter will do?

....
....
....

Read Luke 22:54-62

6. What happened in the text?

....
....
....

> Selah Moment:
>
> Do you think Peter's shortcomings, mistakes, and failures meant he didn't love Jesus? What do you think was going through Peter's head in those three moments? How do you think he felt?
>
> ....
> ....
> ....
> ....

Read John 21:15-17

Important context: This chapter of John happened after Jesus had already died on the cross and was raised from the dead, so this entire encounter happened after Peter denied Jesus three times as you previously read.

7. What does Jesus ask Peter three times?

....

8. Define "love". Remember, when defining words in scripture, define the word in the original language, New Testament words were originally in Greek. I suggest using Biblehub.com

The greek word for this form of love is "agapaó", define that.

....

....

9. How does Peter respond to Jesus' question?

....

....

....

10. In the original Greek, the form of "love" Peter responded with was "phileó". Define phileó.

....

....

11. What's the difference between the love(agapaó) Jesus spoke of versus the love(phileó) Peter spoke of? Which does God prefer most? (Hint: what did Jesus constantly ask about?)

....

....

....

Selah Moment:

Why do you think Jesus kept asking Peter the same question?

....

....

....

....

Read John 14:15-24

12. What does Jesus say is required if we love Him?

....

....

13. Using what you've learned, what form of love is Jesus speaking of? Circle one.

               Agapaó   OR   Phileó

14. What does Jesus say God will do for you if you love Him in this way?

....

....

....

Read Matthew 7:21-22, Matthew 22:1-14, and Matthew 25:31-46

15. Will everyone make it into Heaven("inherit the Kingdom")?

....

16. Who will make it into Heaven? Who won't make it into Heaven?

....

....

....

....

....

Read Matthew 22:34-40

17. What is the greatest command of God?.

....

....

After studying Peter and Jesus' exchange and other scriptures, I believe Jesus wanted to wake Peter up to the reality that to love God requires affectionate friendship AND sacrifice. Henceforth why he kept asking him the same question and gave commands afterward. Peter thrived in the area of phileó for Jesus but lacked in agapaó. Similarly, the Pharisees thrived in agapaó but drastically lacked in phileó. Seemingly, without both, one will not inherit the Kingdom of God.

Let's make it personal

More than anything, God desires preferential and sacrificial love. He wants you to prefer Him above all, thus this will look like something and goes beyond mere feelings. Although God desires this kind of love from you, He will not force you into it, but He has invited you into such a relationship with Him. Will you accept the invitation to not only love Him with your affection, but with your sacrifice and actions? That looks like denying yourself and what your flesh desires and choosing God's will and way over everything.

So, ..., (insert your name), do you love Jesus?

If your answer is no, do you desire to? How can you grow to love Jesus the way He desires?
For a moment, think about it in terms of falling in love with a significant other. What would it take to fall in love with him/her? (ie spending time with him/her) Similarly, apply these things to Jesus. Remember, just as falling in love with people is a process, the same applies to Jesus, as an intimate relationship isn't built overnight. Write your thoughts below.

....
....
....
....
....
....
....
....

So, did Peter love Jesus? Certainly. Jesus just wanted to cultivate in Him a deeper level of love. Loving God the way He desires is a balance of passion (oh to be lovesick for the Lord is beautiful) and preference, preferring God's ways over all else. Have you ever heard of the five love languages? I'm convinced that they missed one as God's love language seems to be obedience and quality time.

As you saw this week, Jesus knew Peter would deny him, yet Jesus still loved him and called him deeper in their relationship. By the grace of God, your mistakes don't count you out, but God is calling you to go deeper with Him. After studying this week, if God has shown you that you do not truly love Him, I urge you to take the necessary steps to grab a hold of Him. Remember, falling in love is a process but you're not in it alone. In prayer, ask God to make Himself and His love known to you in new ways. Ask Him to search your heart and comb out the patterns in you that hold you back from truly falling for Him. If your love for God is strong, pray that the fire on the altar of your heart would be all-encompassing and would never burn out and pray for others. Selah.

Worship Playlist: *"No Greater Love" by Rudy Currence & Chrisette Michele*
"More Than Anything" by Anita Wilson
"More Than Anything" by Sunday Service Choir

Faith OVER Feelings

In moments of insecurity, feeling alone, afraid, distant, and any other number of overwhelming emotions, you must know what God says, and you must have faith that God's word will not return to Him void. Unlike your fleeting and fickle feelings, God is definite. Let's take a look at scriptures that are sure to combat your thoughts and feelings.

Read Psalm 139:1-4, Colossians 1:13-17, and John 11:4-6

1. At times, you may feel that God is far away from you, He's hands-off, and is completely detached from what you have going on. What do these first few verses help you to know about the true character of God?

....

....

....

Read Psalm 139:5-6

2. In times of feeling lost, confused, and without purpose, in this text, what comfort can you find in knowing this message from God?

....

....

....

....

Read Psalm 139:7-12

3. There may be times in your life where you feel like running from what God has for you or, fleeing out of fear, you may desire to isolate yourself and hide. Or, maybe you find yourself feeling rejected or isolated by friends or family. What truths can you know and remind yourself about God that can pull you out of those dark places of your mind and circumstances?

....

....

....

Read Psalm 139:13-16

4. Often, you may not feel special, or you may allow your insecurities to blur the way you see yourself. In those moments, you may feel like God formed you incorrectly, or you may feel like a mistake. But what does this section of scripture tell you that you should know about the ways of your Creator and Heavenly Father?

....

....

....

Read Psalm 139:17-18, Isaiah 55:6-8, Genesis 1:26-27 & 31, and Psalm 8:3-9

5. If you ever feel surrounded on every side by anxious thoughts, if your mind is ever consumed with lies and you feel inadequate or incapable of thinking a better thought. If you don't know what to do or don't know what to think about yourself, another person, or a situation, based on the scriptures, who can you turn to in your time of need? How do you know you can trust this source to have a solution?

....

....

....

Read Psalm 139:19-22

> **Disclaimer:** *Jesus ate with and hung around sinners (Mark 2:16-17) as He came to save them and how can you save someone you're not willing to sit with? Jesus also gave us the template on how to live now that He had come into the world to redeem it; He said to, "love your enemies and pray for those who persecute you"(Matthew 5:44). So these verses in Psalm 139 are not license to ostracize or judge people who are living in the world. It is, however, a heart and action check for yourself and others who proclaim Jesus as Lord. While in the company of unbelievers, what do your actions look like? Do you blend in?*

6. At various points in life as you walk with Jesus, you may still have friends or will cross paths with people who live worldly lives full of sin and no repentance(note: be precautious of not becoming self-righteous and looking down on said people; remember how far the Lord has brought you), this may cause you to feel torn, peer pressured, confused, or like an outsider. Based on David's words in this scripture, how does God view such lifestyles and what will His final judgment be if no change happens in an unrepentant person's life?

....

....

> *Selah Moment:*
>
> *Pause here and pray for any friends/family/acquaintances that come to mind who have not given their lives to Christ. Write their names down and commit to praying for them this week (TIP: Pray for them as you'd want someone to pray for you). Also, ask the Lord who you are to sit with as He did to love them well and be His light amongst them. Don't force or make up an answer, be led by the Holy Spirit.*

Read 2 Peter 3:1-10 and John 3:16-18

7. Why is it important to take Psalm 139:19-22 seriously? What's coming?

Read 2 Peter 3:11-18, Matthew 5:13-16, Ephesians 5:15-21, and 1 Corinthians 9:19-23

8. Knowing what's coming, how should you live?

Read and write out Psalm 139:23-24

9. It's very easy to feel as though you've got it all together and end up in an arrogant place although God desires you to be humble. What prayer did David pray to keep him humble and exposed before God? As you write these verses out, sincerely pray it too.

....
....
....

Read Luke 15:16-20, Acts 3:18-20, and Matthew 6:14-15

10. Living in this world, you may find yourself caught up in sin and/or trouble due to mistakes you made. This may cause you to feel imprisoned, closed in, and unable to find relief. But what does the word of God say about these things?

....
....
....

Read Joshua 1:9, Isaiah 41:10, Isaiah 43:2, and Matthew 28:18-20

11. As you do the will of God, you may feel like He is not with you and has left you to figure it all out on your own. What can you know for a fact is true about God?

....
....
....

Let's make it personal

Describe how you have been feeling about God lately. What have been your thoughts about him? How have you been experiencing Him? (ie has He felt distant or close? have you been angry with Him or are you pleased? etc, be real and honest)

....
....
....
....

If those feelings/thoughts are negative, find some scriptures to combat them or find someone in the Bible who may have felt the same way via a simple Google search; if those feelings are positive, fantastic! Take this time to rejoice, thank God, and find some scriptures that confirm how you see God at this moment.

Although you may feel a certain way, if it is not a feeling that can be backed up with scripture (truth), I urge you to sit with God about those things. Process every thought and feeling with Him, express your frustrations or pain, wait for God to respond, then hold your feelings up next to truth found in scripture. As you do this, I believe the Lord will help you through it and lead you into His truth and comfort. The words of the Bible, though written by man, are inspired by God and can be trusted. Our hearts are deceptive and imperfect and thus our thoughts and feelings are fleeting, but God's word and character are fixed and spotless. Knowing scripture is your greatest weapon. Have faith and trust God. Be encouraged.

Worship Playlist: *"What A God(Live)" by SEU Worship, ONE HOUSE, Kenzie Walker, Chelsea Plank, & Roosevelt Stewart*

Seek God

More than your hand for service, God wants your heart. By giving Him your heart first and foremost, He can do a lot more than if He only has your hand for service. Not only does having a heart for God help with your relationship with Him, but it also helps with your earthly relationships with people.

Read Psalm 37:4

1. Define "delight." (Remember the TIP for defining words in scripture)

....

....

> Selah Moment:
>
> What do you think it looks like to "delight yourself in the Lord"?
>
> ....
>
> ....
>
> ....
>
> ....
>
> ....

2. What does this show about God's desires?

....

....

....

Read John 14:21

3. How does Jesus say you can truly tell if someone loves Him?

....

....

....

February

Let's make it personal: Part 1

Do you agree with this sign of showing love? Would you believe that bae truly loved you if he/she didn't do what you asked of them? Would you believe that bae loved you if he/she did what you hated?

....

....

Based on Jesus' standards and the way you live, do you love God? Do you delight in Him?

....

....

....

Read Psalm 119:9-16 and Joshua 1:8

4. To follow commandments, as Jesus stated, one must first know the commandments. According to scripture, how can you get to know the commands of God?

....

....

....

Read Mark 12:28-33

5. What is the greatest commandment?

....

....

6. What's the second greatest commandment?

....

....

With such an order, we not only see the order of importance but the fact that without first loving God, it is impossible to truly love your neighbor (anyone on this Earth) with 1 Corinthians 13 love. For instance. If you can't love a God who is perfect, provides for your every need, is always there for you, is extremely patient, and literally gives you breath, how do you expect to love a flawed human being? With that in mind, I pray you are more motivated to seek after

God more fervently in order to know and love Him more deeply!

Let's make it personal: Part 2

Refer back to your answer to the opening question. How would you feel if bae (or future bae) sought after you second or third to another person?

....
....
....

More than likely, you'd be upset! How do you think God feels when/if you primarily give your time and attention to other things (idols/gods[1]) instead of Him?

....
....
....

Read Exodus 34:14, Deuteronomy 4:23-24, and Isaiah 64:4-12

7. How does God feel about you turning to other things (gods) before Him?

....
....
....

Read Matthew 6:19-24

8. What's the danger of seeking other gods?

....
....
....
....

---

[1] idols/gods are not limited to other religious gods, but anything you give your allegiance to based on how you spend your time, give your atten-tion, idolize, etc. For instance, Instagram, food, people, and self, can be gods.

Read Jeremiah 29:13-14, Psalm 1:1-2, and Matthew 6:31-34

9. What does God promise for the one who seeks after Him first and foremost?

....

....

....

10. Compare the following set of scriptures to each other. Record what you notice in each section of scripture in the table below.

Isaiah 64:5, Joel 2:12-13, Ephesians 2:8-9, and Micah 6:6-8	Isaiah 29:13-14, Isaiah 64:6, and Matthew 7:21-22

11. Which side of the chart is what God desires? What do you notice is predominantly on that side of the table?

....

....

....

Read Luke 10:38-42

12. What did Mary do?

....

....

....

13. What did Martha do?

....

14. Who was Jesus more pleased with? Explain why.

15. Based on the array of scriptures from today, what does God desire most from you?

Know that although it's great to be like Mary, sitting before the Lord and basking in His presence, it's also great to be like Martha and desire to work for the Lord and serve Him. Jesus said Martha was busy or distracted with much serving, so be sure to find a balance and always strive to start from a place of rest and sit with Jesus in prayer and worship.

Let's make it personal: Part 3

Who are you most like in this season of your life, Mary or Martha?

Rate the quality of your time spent with God on a scale of 1-10. What would make it better?

How do you view God? Do you view Him as a loving friend who wants a relationship with you? If not, what would help?

February

....

....

....

As you seek after God and come to know Him fully, He will transform your heart, mind, and your perspective on life will be shifted. Thus, it is after you have first sought after the heart of a perfect God that you can adequately and enjoyably do work for Him and be prepared to love others well in their flaws and all. So, begin to enjoy God and sit in His presence.

Worship playlist: *"Know You" by: Koryn Hawthorne ft. Steffany Gretzinger*
"I Wanna Know You" by Dante Bowe

March

Mountains and Valleys

God is the same God while we are on mountain tops and in valleys. Meaning, God is the same God when we are going through good times and bad times. His character doesn't change, and thus your trust in Him doesn't have to change just because your circumstances have changed. God will make a way in some form or fashion. For, the Lord is your Shepherd, He will lead you, guide you, care for you, and be with you always.

Read Psalm 23:1-4 (AMP)

1. Where does it say that God will be as you walk through the "valley of the shadow of death?"

....

2. What's the purpose of the rod and staff?

....

3. Do you have to be fearful or worried as you walk through dark times? Why?

....

....

....

Let's make it personal: Part 1

How does it make you feel knowing that God is with you even at your low points?

....

....

....

....

Read Romans 8:28-29

4. What's the promise made in these scriptures?

....

5. Who is this verse and promise exclusively for? Who does God work things together for?

....

....

6. How many things does God promise to work together in this scripture?

....

7. Who does God want you to be transformed in the image of?

....

Read Romans 8:14-17

8. Jesus went through great suffering in His life on Earth, especially when He was on the cross. But, He was then glorified in His resurrection. If we are to be transformed into the image of Jesus, what must we also go through?

....

9. What will we also share with Jesus in after suffering for a little while?

....

10. Ultimately, when will we share in the glory of Jesus? (John 14:3, 2 Corinthians 4:13-14)

....

....

Read Romans 8:35-37, 1 Peter 5:10, Galatians 6:9, and John 16:33

11. Although you will go through moments of suffering, what is promised?

....

....

....

Read 2 Corinthians 4:16-18

12. What does Paul say they've committed to refrain from doing in verse 16?

....

13. How are the troubles believers go through described?

....

14. Knowing these troubles are only temporary (especially compared to eternity), what does verse 18 suggest?

....

....

....

Read James 1:1-4

15. How does James say you should react to trials and troubles? Why does he say that?

....

....

....

As you live life, you will inevitably go through moments of suffering, aka "valleys," so don't run from them or think less of yourself because you're experiencing hardship. Instead, remember that God is still the same God as He is during mountaintops in those valley moments too. God knows all and sees all, and He will be with you as you grow through (yes you read that correctly, "GROW " through). Keep your focus on Him, endure, and learn along the way. Before you know it, you will be on the other side, stronger in faith, and more refined than ever.

Let's make it personal: Part 2

In February, you reflected on your love for Jesus. How have you seen growth in your relationship with Him since then?

....

....

....

....

....

....

What struggles have you been going through lately?

....
....
....
....
....
....
....

How well have you been trusting God to get you through it (i.e., not being anxious and worried, but having faith that God will see you through it)? Rate yourself on a scale of 1-10 and explain.

....
....
....
....
....
....
....

I know the trials and tests may be hard and your hands may be tired of being on the plow, but if I can, I want to encourage you that the trouble will not last always. I wish I could tell you when the specific trials and tests you're going through will be over, but I can't. All I can say assuredly is this: God is a good Father and He will not forsake you. Be encouraged today, and believe afresh that what you're enduring won't be forever! Pray, cry, talk to friends you trust, take a breather, and keep pressing on. When all you can see are the trees and trials of the valley, remember that God is with you always and WILL make a way just as He did for the Israelites as they stood in front of the Red Sea(Exodus 14:21-22), many others in the Bible, many people present day, and likely even you. As you're going through, ask the Lord to remind you of His faithfulness from past seasons. If you feel He hasn't been faithful, ask Him to show you where He was during the storms of your life. If you feel abandoned by God, express that to Him and wait for His reply; I know He will reveal Himself and bring you a fresh perspective. Lastly, again, I implore you to learn and grow through the tough times knowing that all things work together for the good of those that love the Lord. And keep your faith, love, and gaze fixed on Him (Psalm 121). Selah.

Worship Playlist: *"I Look to You" by: Whitney Houston*
"Never Would've Made It" by: Marvin Sapp
"Intentional" by: Travis Greene

No Time for Negativity

There is a widespread belief that you very well may be your own worst critic, from possibly comparing yourself to others, having extremely high standards for yourself, or people not treating you the same as others. All of these things would cause anyone to feel less of themselves. So, if that is you, you're not alone. However, it's not good enough for us to address the issue without seeking a solution. The God in Heaven who created you thinks highly of you and loves you dearly. Instead of believing the lies of your negative thoughts, what others have to say, or what Satan tries, dump that and believe what God says. Today, you will focus on the dumping stage.

Read Proverbs 18:21 and James 3:3-12

1. What do these scriptures warn you about?

....
....
....

Read Exodus 3:7-8 and Numbers 13:1-2, 25-33

2. What did God say about the land?

....
....
....

3. What report did the majority of men bring back about the land?

....
....
....

4. What did Caleb believe? (Use Numbers 14:6-9 for more detail)

....
....

5. What did the majority of the leaders believe?

Read Numbers 14:1-4

6. Whose report was spread throughout the camp and believed: Caleb's or the other leaders?

7. What did the Israelites do in response to the bad report of the majority of the leaders?

8. Did they think negatively or positively about themselves and God?

9. Did they believe what God said or what people said?

Read Numbers 14:10-13

10. How did God feel about the way the Israelites were acting? Why?

The Israelites' poor thinking of themselves not only stopped there, but in their disbelief and negative thinking, it also showed their disbelief in God as well. They not only believed they were too weak, but they also believed that God wasn't strong enough or powerful enough to allow them to prevail either. Such thinking and unbelief infuriated God after all He'd done for them (tip for Bible study: pay attention to the things that upset and delight God and live accordingly). For context, read the book of Exodus to go on a journey of seeing the provision of God for the Israelites.

Read Numbers 14:20-25

11. What happened to the majority of the Israelites? Why?

....

....

....

12. What happened to Caleb? Why?

....

....

....

> **Selah Moment:**
> How do you think the Israelites' situation would have been different if they dumped their negative mindset and had taken up Caleb's positive mindset and belief in God?
>
> ....
>
> ....
>
> ....

Read 2 Corinthians 10:3-5

13. What are we to do with thoughts that contradict who God is and what He says?

....

....

....

Read Philippians 4:8

14. Describe the type of things you should think about.

....

....

Do you see the power of your thoughts and beliefs? What you think and believe leads to your words and actions, thus affecting how you live. So, choose wisely whose report you believe! You can choose to believe negative thoughts and worldly-minded people OR you can choose to believe the report that God says in His word, by His Spirit, and kingdom-minded people(like Caleb). I urge you to care more about God's thoughts in every area of your life than the thoughts of people who live according to their flesh (Isaiah 55:7-9). Depending on your life experiences, this may be more difficult and you will have to work at this, but it is possible and the Lord is willing to walk through this process with you. He is a friend who sticks closer to you than a brother and He promised to not leave you or forsake you (Luke 7:34 and Hebrews 13:5). Having healthy and meaningful criticism when you aren't doing well is good, but repeating negative statements over yourself is not beneficial, healthy, or godly. Do not ignore the voice of God! Just as with the Israelites, God has great plans and desires for you eternally and presently. Don't allow a negative perception of yourself (or God), lies, or unbelief to cause you to miss out. Fight to believe God! Fight to believe His words! Fight to deny your flesh and live by the Spirit of God! "Today, if you hear His voice, do not harden your hearts". (See Hebrews 4:7-11)

Let's make it personal

What negative things (trash) do you think or say about yourself and/or others? Write them down.

Based on James 3:5 and the account of the Israelites, we see the power of the tongue to alter the direction of one's life or states of matter. What direction is your life going if you continue to think and speak the trash you listed above?

....
....
....
....
....
....
....

In closing, if you've become accustomed to thinking or speaking negatively and bad habits are beginning to form, take this time to pray and ask God to tame your tongue, and take the thoughts that aren't like God captive(2 Corinthians 10:5) and focus on truth instead(Philippians 4:8). Ask God to show you how He views you and every situation you find yourself in. Ask Him to help you renew your mind (Romans 12:2) and to help you in whatever areas of unbelief you have(Mark 9:23-24). Just like anything, renewing your mind is a process and this is just the starting point.

Coloring activity: *Write single words on the pieces of trash that best describe the negative thoughts and words you are officially dumping. It's time to empty that trash from your mind, heart, and mouth.*

What do you see when you look in the mirror?

Affirmation

The power of life and death is in your tongue. The ability to praise and curse God is in your tongue. The power of good and evil lies in your tongue. In the last devotional, hopefully, you chose to cancel out the lies (trash) that you once thought and/or said. However, the job is not complete. Anyone who's ever been on a diet can tell you, you can't just take the french fries away; you have to also replace it with something better for you, like veggie straws or baked sweet potato fries with cinnamon and a honey glaze. Failure to do this would easily cause you to go back to the french fries in a heartbeat. It's the same here. It's not enough to just dump and block the negative thoughts that are no good; you have to also fill yourself up with what's good and true for lasting change and to fight back.

Read Ephesians 6:17-18

1. What are the offensive weapons God has given you? What must you do to use these weapons effectively?

....

....

Read Matthew 4:1-11

2. What do you notice Jesus says each time He addresses Satan's lies?

....

3. For Jesus to be able to have so many comebacks for Satan's lies, schemes, and misinterpretation of scripture, He had to first know the Word of God for Himself. How do you think you can get to know God's word better to have the proper weapon to fight against Satan's lies?

....

....

....

Ready to add some scriptures to your toolbelt to fight back against the lies of Satan?
As you read in the previous devotional, you have great power in your tongue. Let's refresh your memory of the benefits of speaking and believing God's word(life) rather than death.

March

Read Numbers 13:25-33, Numbers 14:20-24, and 28-30

4. What does Caleb do that's different from the leaders and Israelites?

....

....

....

5. How does Caleb's fate differ from the rest of the Israelites?

....

....

....

Read Proverbs 18:20-21(AMP) below:

"A man's stomach will be satisfied with the fruit of his mouth; He will be satisfied with the consequence of his words. Death and life are in the power of the tongue, And those who love it and indulge it will eat its fruit and bear the consequences of their words."

6. What do these verses say will happen whether you speak life or death?

....

....

As you continue this week's journal entry, it's important to know that the Bible isn't about you, your parents, or your friends. The Bible is about God's redemptive story of how He has prepared the way for us to be completely reconciled to Him through Jesus. However, when scripture is used in context (pay attention to the author, audience, and purpose), you can learn a lot about God's design for you as one of His chosen people (if you have given your life to Christ). For instance, in places in scripture where God is addressing the Israelites, His first chosen people, some Gentiles, or His children, you can come to find what God says and thinks about you as you also carry this title.

Using your favorite translation of the Bible (NLT, NIV, AMP, & ESV are my faves), read, write out, and dissect(highlight essential parts) each verse so that you can more easily see what God says about His people. Then, write an affirmation that includes parts of the scripture in it. Use the example below as a guide. Starting affirmations with "I am..." is a typical template, but feel free to change it up. I also suggest you write affirmations that declare who God is based on the verse you're reading. For example: "God is merciful and loves deeply.

TIP: Reading the entire chapter, or at least the surrounding verses, will give you context for the verse at hand.

Example:

Write and dissect Ephesians 2:4-5 (NIV)

"But because of his great love for us, God, who is rich in mercy, made us alive with Christ even when we were dead in transgressions—it is by grace you have been saved."

me

Affirmation(s):
I am greatly loved by God.
I am alive in Christ.
God's grace has saved me, not my works (Ephesians 2:9).

Your turn! Try it with a little help:

Write and dissect Ephesians 2:10 (NIV)

"For we are God's handiwork, created in Christ Jesus to do good works, which God prepared in advance, for us to do."

First, pray and ask God to reveal Himself to you in His word. Pray that God would open your eyes so that you can see and receive the revelations of His word that He would have you to understand.

Dissecting

- *In this verse, Paul was talking to believers in Ephesus, so circle the pronouns associated with believers (which includes you), i.e., we, us, our. By doing this, you will know which things can be associated with you or not.*

- *Highlight or put a box around any nouns, verbs, or adjectives used to describe believers.*

- *Want to get really fancy? Find anything that may be hidden; things that may not be explicitly stated (don't force it or make it up, as that's how people end up with false doctrine and lies). You can also find other verses you know that relate to the topic of the scripture at hand. For instance, Genesis 1:26 goes well with this scripture, so you can include that verse in your affirmation.*

Affirmation(s):

- *Using the words you've highlighted, create an affirmation/decree. One way is to begin with "I am," but you can start however you'd like*

I am ....

I am ....

....

....

Try it again with a little less help:

Write and dissect Ephesians 2:18-22 (NIV)

"For through Him, we both have access to the Father by one Spirit. Consequently, you are no longer foreigners and strangers, but fellow citizens with God's people and also members of his household, built on the foundation of the apostles and prophets, with Christ Jesus Himself as the chief cornerstone. In Him, the whole building is joined together and rises to become a holy temple in the Lord. And in Him, you too are being built together to become a dwelling in which God lives by His Spirit."

Affirmation:

I am ....

I am ....

I am ....

I am ....

....

....

Got the hang of it? Try these on your own.

Write and dissect 1 Peter 2:9

....

....

....
....
....

Affirmation(s):

....
....
....
....

Write and dissect Songs of Solomon 4:7

> *(Note: Remember context- Songs of Solomon is a collection of poems King Solomon wrote about his wife (bride). This scripture relates to you because you are a part of the "Bride of Christ," aka the Church. (Ephesians 5:25-27)*

....
....
....
....

Affirmation(s):

....
....
....
....
....

Write and dissect 2 Timothy 1:7

....
....

Affirmation(s):

Write and dissect Romans 8:37–39

Affirmation(s):

Write and dissect Isaiah 54:17

Affirmation(s):

....

....

....

....

....

....

....

Look at you exegeting the scriptures! As always, you can take a look at my answers in the back, but know that you may have found more than I did! God's word is living and active, so God may reveal even more things to you the next time you read those verses. As long as you read the scriptures in context, your affirmations are probably spot on! Share them with a friend and speak them over yourself until you believe it!

Let's make it Personal

Ready to take it up a notch and do some research? Find scriptures that talk about areas you wrote in your last journal entry about negative thinking. For instance, if you "dumped" anxiety, find scriptures that talk about peace. You can use Google, or in the back of your Bible, there may be a concordance of words with their scripture reference next to it.

Refer to last week's journal entry. In one word, what did you "dump" last week? Write that where it says "Topic" below and then find scripture that opposes that negativity.

Topic: ....

Write and dissect ....

....

....

Affirmation(s):

Topic: ....

Write and dissect ....

Affirmation(s):

Now that you have affirmations founded on the word of God, you're more equipped to fight and win the battle of your mind. When negative thoughts come your way, remember, rebuke them in the name of Jesus and as Jesus did, use the word of God to fight back. Recite these affirmations as often as needed. Once you begin to believe them, you'll come to find that the battle of your mind is already won because no lie of your enemy, Satan, or negative thought trumps God's word.

Read Ephesians 1:17-19a and sincerely pray it over yourself by making it personal for you with any specific things that relate to you. Feel free to write your prayer in the space provided.

> "I keep asking that the God of our Lord Jesus Christ, the glorious Father, may give you the Spirit[a] of wisdom and revelation, so that you may know him better. I pray that the eyes of your heart may be enlightened in order that you may know the hope to which he has called you, the riches of his glorious inheritance in his holy people, and his incomparably great power for us who believe..." (NIV)

....

....

....

....

....

....

....

....

In closing, take time to pray and switch your way of thinking beginning now. Then as you go about your days, if the lies and negative thoughts come, recognize them, take them captive, and speak the truth you've found in the word of God instead. Doing this constantly is how you will renew your mind and be transformed. Feel free to add to or take away from this prayer:

> *Father, I want to believe what You say about me and others. I repent for agreeing with the lies of Satan and come out of agreement with them. Lord tear down every stronghold that is not of you. I desire to think as you do and to believe what You say alone. I repent for thinking and saying (insert statements from last week's journal entry and any others you've thought of; do this one at a time) _____ and instead I accept and believe what You say, for you say (insert the truths you've found this week in Scripture to counteract the lie; do this one at a time) _____. Lord, please rebuke every lie and attach me to You instead. I want to believe you and think your thoughts, Jesus. Transform my mind, Father God. Thank you for all you've done for me. I humbly accept your thoughts. I want to fix my mind on things that are above as you command in your word. May your will be done in my life as it is in Heaven. In Jesus' name, I pray, Amen.*

Worship playlist: *"Lovin' Me"* by Jonathan McReynolds
"Who You Say I Am" by Hillsong Worship
"Sound Mind" by Melissa Helser

Time well spent

MONDAY

TUESDAY

WEDNESDAY

THURSDAY

FRIDAY

SATURDAY

SUNDAY

Be a Good Steward

When you think of a "good steward," what comes to mind? Did an excellent flight attendant come to mind? Although they are known as "stewardesses," that's not quite the direction this plane is flying today. Did money come to mind? If so, this is a step in the right direction. People often think of stewardship in terms of how well they use the money they have. Today, you will look into how you steward an often neglected commodity that is very precious and can't be bought. Its length is uncertain, and yet it is fleeting: TIME.

1. Define "stewardship."

....

....

2. Based on the definition you found, what do you think makes someone a "good steward?"

....

....

....

Read Matthew 25:14-28

Please take note that this parable is a literal representation of what the kingdom of Heaven will be like (see Matthew 25:1). However, we can also learn the principle of the fruits of stewardship when we read Jesus' teaching figuratively as well

3. Who were the good stewards? How do you know?

....

....

....

4. Who was the poor steward? How do you know?

....

....

....

5. What was the difference between the master's response to the good steward and the poor steward?

....
....
....

Let's make it personal: Part 1

Now that you've seen an example of good and bad stewardship let's relate this to time. What do you spend most of your time doing?

....
....
....

Should you spend the most time on what's most important or what's least important?

Most important **Least important**

That question may sound like it has an obvious answer, but if you take inventory of your life, you may come to find that you aren't following this pattern; if you are, great job! Keep it up! Let's see what God says about how you should best steward your time.

Read Psalm 39:5-6, Job 14:5, and James 4:13-15

6. What do these scriptures say about time?

....
....
....

7. Knowing the things above, why is it important to be a good steward of your time?

....
....
....

You've already determined that you should spend more time on what's most important. To know what's most important and how to steward your time well, you must make sure that your priorities are in check.

Read Matthew 6:33, Matthew 22:36-40, and Psalm 27:4

8. What should be your top priority?

....
....
....
....
....

In literature and life, the last words of someone are significant and are held onto dearly by loved ones. The last words of Jesus on the cross were "it is finished," words that still echo until this day as Hell has been defeated, and those that accept Jesus as Lord and Savior can share in that victory. Being that Jesus was resurrected (raised from the dead), He was able to interact with His disciples before leaving the earth. It is during this interaction that you can see yet another set of powerful final words. Take a look!

Read Matthew 28:18-20 and Romans 10:14-15

9. What were Jesus' final words on Earth telling His disciples to do? What does that require of you?

....
....
....

Read Matthew 22:36-40, Luke 10:38-42, and re-read Matthew 6:33

10. As a disciple of Christ, what are the most important things you should be focused on? What should your top priorities be?

....
....
....
....

Read Matthew 24:35-44, Matthew 25:31-46, Hebrews 9:28, and 2 Peter 3:9-10

11. Why is it essential to make matters of Jesus your top priorities?

....
....
....

Read Luke 10:39-42, John 14:21, Romans 12:1, Psalm 2:11-12, Psalm 96:1-4, 1 Thessalonians 5:16-18, and Psalm 51:16-17

12. How can you love God well and seek after Him?

....
....
....
....

Read Job 2:11-13, Matthew 5:43-48, and Romans 12:9-21

13. How can you love people well?

....
....
....
....

Read 2 Corinthians 5:18-21, Acts 2:37-41, Colossians 1:21-23, Romans 5:8-11, Romans 8:1-4, and Romans 10:8-13

14. As you've seen today, two of the priorities of God is for us love one another and make disciples. Sharing the gospel with others is a great way to do both of these tasks! What is the gospel? How are people saved?

....
....
....
....

Let's make it personal: Part 2

How are you currently spending your time each day? Are your priorities in order? Rate yourself. Circle one.

Very Poorly   Poorly   Decent   Well   Very Well

Explain why.

What things are you doing well with your time according to God's expectations?

....
....
....
....

What things are you wasting time on? How can you cut down on these things?

....
....
....

Think about places you frequently go, what you're known for, and groups of people you're around often. How can you use those places, talents, and things as a platform and opportunity to tell someone about Jesus, share the gospel, and inform them of the importance of time not being wasted?

....
....
....
....
....
....

Your time on Earth is very short. Make sure you're spending your time well. Like the parable you read earlier about the talents (money), Jesus, our Master, is coming back. When that time comes, Will you be ready? Will you be found in an intimate relationship with God when Jesus returns? Will others be ready because of your life? The gift of eternal life and face to face communion with God, your Creator, is the end goal. Make daily decisions that will allow you and others to reap such a reward.

Below, write down the names of people you know who are not saved or who claim to be but don't show the fruit of it in their lives. Pray for the salvation of your friends, family, and even strangers that you will cross paths with.

....
....
....
....
....
....

Have you taken the time to develop a true relationship with God? Have you accepted Jesus as Lord and Savior? If not, and if you want to, with sincerity, pray this prayer and add to it whatever you'd like to say to your Heavenly Father:

> *Father God, I understand that the time is close for you to come and judge the world. I know that You will only save those who have confessed that Jesus is Lord and believed that You raised Him from the dead. Today God, I want to make that declaration. Today I confess that I am a sinner and have fallen short of your perfect standards. I repent from my old ways, and today I ask that you give me a new life, that I'd see things differently, and that your Holy Spirit would be within me and operate within my life. I humbly lay down my life and profess that Jesus is Lord over my life. I believe that I am free from the bondage of sin because of His victory over death in rising from the dead. Thank you, Lord, for being patient with me. Help me to lead others to you. In Jesus' name, I pray, Amen.*

Coloring activity: *Write out your daily routine. Remembering that your relationship with God is your top priority, be sure to set aside time where you spend it with Him in reading His word(the Bible), in prayer, worship, and fellowship with other believers.*

Worship Playlist: *"Make Room" by: Jonathan McReynolds*
"My Portion" by: Isla Vista Worship & Mark Barlow
"Love Note" by Abbie Gamboa

So let your light shine!

matthew 5:16

Shine On!

No matter the circumstance, light will always overcome darkness! This concept is established and stated in God's word, and scientists even agree. As a believer, did you know that there's light inside of you? Let's see what happens when you let it shine.

Read John 8:3-12

Note: Some Bible translations denote John 7:53–8:11 as "not in earliest manuscripts." This has led to debates about whether later additions affect the Bible's reliability and if we should read sections that were "added later." After doing some research and seeking advice, I conclude that whether this passage was added later or not, because there are several pieces of evidence that suggest it was an authentic historical event passed down by early Christians and does not alter the Gospel, Jesus' identity, or future events, it is justified and acceptable. The Bible's books were carefully examined and confirmed as divinely inspired in various ways. So, we can trust that all canonized texts will strengthen our faith, shape our character, and increase our knowledge of God. Unlike many ancient writings, the New Testament remains the most well-preserved and historically reliable book of the day. As you read John 8:3-12, take mental note of what other scriptures you're reminded of (this is called cross-referencing) and what biblical themes you see.

1. What caused the Pharisees to bring the woman to Jesus?

....

....

....

2. What were the Pharisees ready to do to punish the woman?

....

3. Did the Pharisees come up with the punishment? Where did they get it from? (Leviticus 20:10)

....

....

....

4. What is Jesus' response to the Pharisees?

....

....

....

5. How did the Pharisees respond? Why?

....

....

....

6. Besides the woman, who was the only one who didn't walk away?

....

7. Being that Jesus was the only one remaining with the woman, what do you think this implies?(See 2 Corinthians 5:21 for help) What did Jesus choose to do with such power/authority?

....

....

....

Leviticus 20:10 says, "'If a man commits adultery with another man's wife--with the wife of his neighbor--both the adulterer and the adulteress are to be put to death." Aside from them conveniently leaving the man behind, the Pharisees were correct in their assumption of the punishment of death. However, God was doing a new thing in the earth through the concept of grace. To read more on how we've moved from being held under the law (Old Testament) to the law of grace (New Testament), read more about it in Appendix B.

Read John 1:1-18 and John 8:12

8. Who is the source of light?

....

9. What is the light?

....

Read Romans 8:1-4

10. Why was it necessary for Jesus to come into the world for you to have light (life)? Why wasn't simply following the laws of Moses as the Pharisees mentioned enough?

....

....

....

Read Mark 1:15, Luke 11:11-13, and Acts 26:15-23

11. How do you receive the light (life)?

....

....

....

Read John 3:19-20, Acts 26:17-18, Romans 6:23, and Matthew 25:41

12. For light to be beneficial, there must be darkness. What is the darkness of the world? What happens to those who live in that darkness?

....

....

....

> Selah Moment: Pause and reflect on the scriptures you've read, especially John 8:12. How does your life measure up? Based on the scriptures, do you have the light of Christ? Or have you loved darkness more? Examine your mind, heart, and actions

Read Matthew 5:14-16

13. Upon receiving the light of Christ, what are you to do with the light that is within you?

....

....

....

Read 1 John 1:5-10

14. Why is it essential for you to allow your light to shine and walk in the light

....

....

....

Read Acts 26:19-20, 1 Thessalonians 5:8-9, Hebrews 12:1-2, and Ephesians 5:8-20

15. Practically, what does it look like to allow your light to shine and live in the light?

....

....

Read Daniel 12:2-3, Romans 6:23, Matthew 25:34, and Revelation 21:3

16. What reward will you reap if you do not give up and keep your light shining?

....

....

....

....

....

Read Matthew 10:26-33, Galatians 1:10, and John 12:42-43

17. What are a few ways you could "hide your light under a basket"?

....

....

....

Read 2 Corinthians 6:14

18. We have all sinned and fallen short; however, once you've given your life to Christ, a transformation begins to happen. No longer are you bound to sin, so your old lifestyle no longer will fit you as you start to grow out of your old self. However, in that time of your old life, you will have made friends who did those same things that you now are beginning to see as detestable or are striving to get away from because God hates it. If those friends weren't willing to honor and accept your new lifestyle or if you must compromise your faith in anyway for them(idolatry), what will be necessary for you to do?

Testimony: In college, before being serious about Jesus, I partied and drank a lot. After surrendering my life to Jesus, I saw the battle of choosing my old life vs my new one. So, I asked the Lord to remove anyone from my life that would influence me to go backward. By the next semester, the main two people I'd turn to for partying left my college. In other relationships I had to be bold to set boundaries myself.

....
....
....

Disclaimer: This may be hard, especially as a new believer, but speaking from personal experience, if you allow God to separate you from what you once knew, it will drastically help your faith, commitment, and the vibrance of His light shining through you. Don't love your life so much that you lose it. Lose it so that you can gain oh so much better for you(Matthew 10:39).

<u>Let's make it personal</u>

Rate how brightly you've been letting the light of Christ shine in your life through how you live. Color in the amount of stars you believe represent your brightness. Explain.

☆ ☆ ☆ ☆ ☆

How can you shine brighter? (ie. What sins or struggles trip you up most and dim your light? What people do you need to part ways with? How can you let these go practically after confessing and repenting? Look back at #15 and make a practical list specifically for your life.)

....
....
....
....

....

....

So, you, child of God, filled with light amid a dark world, times will be hard walking with Jesus, especially if others around you are choosing otherwise. But remember what God is saving you from, what's to come if you endure well(Matthew 25:23), and that other believers are walking out this life with you(1 Peter 5:9). Yes, the darkness you once lived in may have been fun and entertaining, but as Jesus said, what is it to gain the world but lose your soul?! Know that believers everywhere are enduring just as you are, and you are not alone. Keep your faith, pray, and fight. Fight to keep your light shining. Please know that if/when you're weak and struggling, God can be made strong within you and help you to endure. So in moments that your light is challenged, cry out to Him for help in those moments of struggle. You're not meant to do this life alone, the Holy Spirit will be your help in times of trouble, and he will help you fight to keep the lights on. Also, be sure to find a solid Christian community of friends(even if it's just one of two people) to reach out to for support. If for some reason you find yourself vulnerable and you fall back into the darkness you once lived in, come to your senses(Luke 15:16-19), repent(run back to the Father), dust yourself off, and shine on.

Worship Playlist: *"Shine" by: Tobe Nwigwe*

Time with God

In God's word, Jesus tells us that if we want to be one of His disciples (followers), we must deny ourselves (put our desires second to God's), and follow Him (live according to the teaching of God, following in the footsteps of Jesus and becoming more like Him each day). This is the standard that Jesus set, but how can we do any of this if we are not spending time with Him? Today you will take a look at what it means to be devoted to God.

Read Matthew 6:24

1. Define "devoted."

....

....

2. What does it look like for someone to be devoted to a sport, craft, etc.? How much time do you expect they'd spend?

....

....

....

Let's make it personal: Part 1

Looking at how you live your life, what are you devoted to? Who are you devoted to?

....

....

....

Read Acts 2:42-47, 1 Corinthians 9:24-27, and Matthew 16:24-27

3. What do you think it looks like to be devoted to God?

....

....

....

Read Matthew 7:15-21

4. How are people able to decipher who God's people are and who aren't God's people?

....

....

....

Read Matthew 7:21, 2 Timothy 3:16-17, and John 15:1-10

5. Why is it important that we be devoted to reading God's Word and spending time with God?

....

....

....

Read Acts 17:1-34

6. Compare and contrast the people of Thessalonica and Berea. Write what you notice about each town under the town's name. If you see any similarities, write them in the section titled "both."

Thessalonicans	Bereans	Athenians

All of Them

7. Which town was more devoted to God? How do you know?

....
....
....

8. How can you be more like the townspeople of the town that was most devoted to God?

....
....
....

Read Mark 6:45-46, Luke 5:15-16, Matthew 26:38-42, and Luke 2:41-49

9. What do you notice about Jesus' devotion to God in each of these pieces of scripture?

....
....
....
....
....
....

Read Psalm 34:4-22

10. What rewards and provisions does God promise to those devoted to Him and are constantly turning to Him?

....
....
....

Let's make it personal: Part 2

After reading Psalm 34:4-22, How are you impacted by these verses? What do they do for you?

....
....

As you read today, there are great rewards when we are devoted to God and give Him our time. God has also given us many examples of people who have shown us how to be devoted to Him. However, God doesn't just want our actions, He wants our hearts (Isaiah 29:13), and in spending your time with Him, your heart will come to know Him better and grow more and more for Him. Remember, what you give your time to most is what matters most to you! Truly put God first.

Rate your devotion to God on a scale of 1-5, looking back over all you've read and studied this week. How can you improve? (Sample answer in back)

Worship Playlist: *"He Has Time" by: Common Hymnal & Jamie MacDonald*

One Way

The 21st century has been both a blessing and a curse. On the one hand, we see how people are more accepting of each other, and there are many freedoms. However, on the other hand, the push for a polytheistic (the idea that there are many gods) society is also very prominent. People are dabbling and experimenting with all kinds of paths to a "spiritual life" in the efforts to grow closer to "God." Unlike this idea of there being many paths, God's Word, the Holy Bible, states something very different. If you genuinely want a relationship with Him, Jesus gives us clear instructions and guidelines.

Read Matthew 7:13-14 (NLT)

1. What gate gives us access to the Kingdom of God (Heaven; eternal life)? Describe it.

....
....
....

2. What gate gives us access to Hell(destruction)? Describe it.

....
....
....

3. Which gate is the most popular? How do you know?

....
....
....

> Selah Moment:
>
> What do you think "the gate to Heaven is narrow" means? Why do you think it's narrow?
>
> ....
> ....
> ....

April

> *What do you think "the gate to Hell is wide" means? Why do you think it's wide?*
>
> ....
>
> ....
>
> ....

Read 1 Corinthians 6:9-11, Colossians 3:5-8, Galatians 5:19-21, and Revelation 22:15

4. List all of the things that can lead to the destruction of a person (death; eternal separation from God; Hell).

....

....

....

....

....

....

5. Based on these scriptures, why is the gate to Hell wide?

....

....

....

Read 1 Corinthians 6:11, John 14:1-6, and Romans 6:23

6. List all of the ways that can lead a person to God (eternal life; Heaven

....

7. Based on these scriptures, why is the gate to Heaven so narrow?

....

....

....

....

Let that sink in. Jesus is THE way and the ONLY way to God. Narrow is the gate. Have you chosen His way? If not, do you want to? Remember, it's the ONLY way to eternal life in Heaven with God. It's the only way to truly draw closer to God(the Creator of the universe and everything in it) while you live in this world. The great thing is that God has not made it difficult for us to get to Him. All it takes is a choice.

Read Romans 10:8-13, Matthew 16:13-19 and Proverbs 3:5-6

8. What do you have to do to be saved (gain eternal life and be able to enter into the Kingdom of God, Heaven)?

....

....

....

Let's make it personal

After today's devotional, you have seen the two paths that are available. How does your life measure up? Are you living a life of sin on the wide highway to Hell? Have you accepted Jesus Christ as Lord and Savior and live accordingly? Or do you feel like you're a mixture of both worlds? (If so, read Revelation 3:15-22. Is it a good space to be in the middle/mixture of both? What do you want to do about that?)

....

....

....

....

....

....

....

So, who do you say Jesus is? Is He the only way to God? Is He the SON(one with Him) of the God? Is He the Savior of the world? If you need more time to investigate this, that's okay. Take time now to pray and ask God to reveal who He is to you. If your answer to all of the above questions is yes, do you realize you are in need of Jesus to rescue you from your sin and this world? Do you want Him to? If so, know that He's rejoicing at this revelation you've gained and are ready to surrender to. Take time now to pray and express all of these things directly to Him. Below is a sample prayer you can use, but make it personal to you, speak sincerely and directly to your Heavenly Father who loves you so much that He sent His only Son to die in your place.

> "Father God, I need you! I admit that I am a sinner and have fallen short of your glorious standards. I no longer desire to continue to live in this way. Today, I confess that Jesus, you are the Son of God and you are the savior of the world. I put my faith and trust in You and You alone. I renounce every other way that I've sought after to reach you God. Put me on your narrow path, Lord. I repent for taking the wide path by _____ (insert any other ways you tried to get to God or reach spiritual enlightenment in the past). I know Your word is true and believe that Jesus died on the cross to pay the penalty for my sins, but He didn't stay there because, on the third day, you raised Him from the dead so that I can be free from this bondage of sin. So, Father God, please come into my life. I accept Jesus as Lord and Savior, and I lay down my own life to pick up the life you created me to have. I humbly and freely accept your Holy Spirit to lead and guide me for the rest of my life. In Jesus' name, I pray, Amen."

If you have just accepted Jesus as Lord and Savior today, ALL OF HEAVEN REJOICES, and I am cheering for you! Yayyy! You're now on the narrow path. It won't be easy because temptation is all around you, but you will have the Holy Spirit who will help, lead, and guide you if you allow Him to. If you slip up and feel like you're veering off of the narrow path, repent (go to God in prayer and sincerely apologize for the wrong you commit) and turn back to God's way of living. Be sure to also get connected in a true Bible-teaching commuity(if you don't have this in your area, check online and consider starting a bible study group of your own), seek after getting baptized, and continually grow intimately with God (ie. invite Him into your day, talk to Him honestly and vulnerably about what you're going through, think about Him while you're at work, playing basketball, or grocery shopping, meditate on scripture, and sing praises to Him). Again, having at least a small group of friends/people who have also decided to follow Jesus is so important. Can't find a community like this? Maybe the Lord would have you to start one out of your own home (pray and ask Him for direction)."

Worship Playlist: *"Only Way" by: Franchesca*
"Proverbs 3(Tablet of Your Heart)" by Todd Dulaney
"One Name(Jesus) [Live]" by Naomi Raine

What does "finished" mean?

What is "it"?

"it is FINISHED."

John 19:30

April

Finished Work

*I*n a portion of the Jewish community, some do not believe that Jesus was the savior, and thus, we are still waiting for God to send the prophesied (foretold) King who would rescue them(and the whole world). Today, you will get to search the scriptures for yourself, comparing the Old Testament scriptures(written hundreds of years before Jesus came to earth) to what was written about Him in the New Testament(written in the period of Jesus' death and resurrection on earth). Having this knowledge is important because the finished work on the cross hinges on who Jesus is. So, before you look at what Jesus did, let's take a look at a few prophecies and the fulfillment of them to discover who Jesus was. Is He the prophesied King? Using the table below, read the scriptures that are side by side and write the prophecy stated in the scriptures on the left side and how it was fulfilled on the right side of the table.

Prophecy	Fulfillment
Micah 5:2	Luke 2:4-7
Zechariah 9:9	John 12:12-16
Psalm 22:18	John 19:23-24
Exodus 12:46 (Read Exodus 12:7,12-14 to better understand what the Passover is)	John 19:31-36 (Read John 1:29 and 1 Corinthians 5:7 to understand Jesus as a lamb)
Zechariah 12:10	John 19:34-37

> *Selah Moment: What have you noticed? What conclusions can you draw about who Jesus is based on the scriptures? What questions do you have?*

Based on the facts of scripture, it is evident that Jesus is the Savior of the world that God promised. However, it is also a fact that many do not believe this yet, including some of those mentioned in the Bible. Whether you believe Jesus is the One or if you find yourself in the group that doesn't yet believe, take a look at John 10:22-42 for Jesus' words on the topic.

Read Leviticus 16:1-6, Isaiah 59:1-2, Matthew 27:45-51, 2 Corinthians 3:12-18, and Romans 5:11-15

1. Why did Jesus have to be sacrificed?

Read John 19:30

2. What were Jesus' last words?

The Greek word for "it is finished" is "tetelestai." It has been said that in Jesus' day, when someone paid off their debts, "tetelestai" would be stamped on the documents to state that the debt was "paid in full."

April

Read 1 Timothy 2:5-6, Isaiah 53:4-5, Hebrews 4:14–16, and Romans 8:3-4

3. If the above historical statement is true, why does it make sense for Jesus to say "tetelestai" upon His death on the cross? What was finished and thus now made possible?

....
....
....

Read Romans 6:1-7, Colossians 3:1-17, Ephesians 4:22-24, John 3:16-21

4. With tetelestai being Jesus' last word, what does this mean for:

...your salvation?	(See Ephesians 2:8 and Isaiah 1:18-20)	...your past?	(See Romans 6:5-7)
...your identity?	(See Ephesians 2:18-19 and Romans 8:16-17)	...your present?	(See Romans 6:1-2 and Ephesians 4:22-24)
...your authority?	(See Luke 10:17-20)	...your future?	(See Colossians 3:3-4 and Revelation 22:12)

Read John 1:9-13

5. Knowing all of the above scriptures, what is the main thing required of you? Do you have to clean yourself up and be your own savior first? Explain.

....
....
....

I know last week I presented you the opportunity to confess Jesus as Lord (as you will see, there are many times I present said opportunity throughout this journal as I pray that people who have never believed in Jesus will get their hands on a copy, so I feel led to ask again this week.)

Have you accepted Jesus as both Lord and Savior? The evidence of this answer will show in how you live.

> **Quick story:** I gave my life to Christ when I was in High School at one of my mom's longtime friend's funeral. However, this decision was not followed up with any action of "putting on a new self" or really seeking after an intimate relationship with God, so over time I allowed the cares of the world to creep in that many high school teenagers go through, my frehsman year of college (whoa chile, that was a hot mess), plus a lack of seeking God on my own, it was all a recipe for disaster of not truly living for or with Jesus. Later in the summer of my freshman year, heading into my sophomore year, God encountered me during worship as we sang "How He Loves" by David Crowder Band. In that moment, God's love for me was highlighted and I was suddenly aware of the depth of God's love. However, God also simultaneously revealed to me that my love for Him was superficial like that of one of my ex-boyfriend's love towards me. This moment was so convicting and from that moment I was revived and decided to rededicate my life to Jesus and seek after Him wholeheartedly. Was it easy? Definitely not. Did I mess up? Oh lots of times(I still mess up in various ways currently). But one thing has remained since that moment, I have not turned back and I'm more surrendered to Jesus today than any other time in my life.

I have no idea why I'm telling you this in this moment, but if it's ministering to you and you relate, I urge you to press in and seek God afresh. Recommit your life to Jesus today. If you've never given your life to Christ, but desire freedom, desire the debt of your sins to be covered, if you desire to be one with God, and truly come to know Him, stop and pray a prayer of surrender, repenting of your sins, confessing that Jesus is Lord, and believing in your heart that God raised Him from the dead allowing the DEBT OF YOUR SIN TO BE PAID IN FULL, allowing the work to be FINISHED. If you want guidance in this moment with God, go back to last week's journal entry where I have supplied a sample prayer.

Selah.

<u>Let's make it personal</u>

For as long as you need, but try for at least 30 minutes, put on some worship music, and just sit with Jesus, praising and worshipping God! Thanking Him for all He's done and for being who He is: a redeemer, savior, sustainer, protector, and much, much more!

To help you with your time of prayer and worship, below, write down various attributes of God that you've noticed in your life or read in the Bible (the word of God). Also recall moments of His faithfulness and goodness.

....

_____
_____
_____
_____
_____
_____
_____
_____
_____
_____
_____

With there being a lengthy timespan between Jesus being written about (prophesied) and actually stepping onto the scene, it is hard to negate that Jesus is, in fact, the Messiah and Son of God. Now that you have seen that Jesus is the Savior God promised and He died on the cross for your sins, accept it and walk confidently in your faith, knowing that God keeps His promises and has made a way for you to be with Him presently and eternally through Jesus Christ our Lord.

Coloring Activity: *Answer the questions on the coloring page and reflect on what Jesus did for you!*

Worship Playlist: *"Made a Way" by: Travis Greene*
"Nobody like you Lord" by: Miranda Curtis
"Alpha and Omega" by: Israel & New Breed
"Hallelujah Here Below" by: Elevation Worship
"Most Beautiful" by: All Nations Worship Assembly
"The Blood" by: Naomi Raine ft. Dante Bowe
"Worthy" by Elevation Worship
"I Thank God" by Maverick City

Deeply Loved

Due to the struggles of our present life (i.e., seeing the degradation of the world all around us, being personally mistreated and mishandled by loved ones or hearing of others who have been, and the daily lulls of feeling loneliness), the depth of God's love is one that is hard to believe at times.

Many people have asked the question (or questions similar), "if God is such a loving God, why do people still suffer?" this is a very understandable question. However, as we get to know God through His Word and seek a relationship with Him, seeing, believing, and experiencing His love through moments of suffering is a lot easier. This also makes sense because we then have a fuller understanding of who God is and how He operates in various seasons and times of life. A dating tip I learned from couples is that while you're in the dating phase, it's important to see how each of you responds during good, bad, and sad times for you to know them more completely. Similarly, it is very important for you to know God in this way too. When you're going through times of suffering and storms, how do you relate to God? What does He sound like? How does He speak? You must know God not only in the good times but in the times of struggle too. This week we will take a look to see how greatly loved we are by our Creator. To start, let's learn from a mighty man of God who endured trial.

Read all of 1 Kings 18 and 19

1. How did Elijah relate and connect with God in a time of success and courage? How did God respond?

....

....

....

2. How did Elijah relate to God in a time of threat and persecution? How did God respond?

....

....

....

3. How do you see the love of God expressed? How could things have ended differently if Elijah would've acknowledged God's love in his time of suffering? (See 1 John 4:17-18)

....

....

Read Song of Solomon 2:4, Proverbs 3:11-12, Matthew 9:36, Mark 2:15-17, Matthew 28:20, Hosea 11:1-11, and Malachi 1:1-5

4. How do you see God's love expressed in these scriptures?

Although the Bible isn't about you, you can learn God's character and heart for you because He shows no partiality. For instance, if you're a child of God, when you see how He relates to Israel you can learn how He sees you. If you're not a child of God and rather an enemy of His(no matter how "nice" of a person you may be, this is anyone that's not a child of His and thus doesn't obey Him but lives apart from Him, see James 4:4-10), you can also learn how He sees you as well through the scriptures. So, take time to meditate on these verses, acknowledge, receive, and thank God for His love. If you haven't decided to follow Jesus, I pray these verses will shine light in your heart to see God's great care. You're welcome into His family

Read Ephesians 3:14-21

5. What does Paul's prayer reveal about God and His love?

Read Romans 5:3-5

6. Although it is common for people to think God doesn't exist because of trials, why is it necessary to have times of trials (sufferings) based on the scriptures?

7. Based on the scriptures, why can you have confident hope as you endure trials/suffering?

....

Read John 3:16 and John 16:7

8. What was required for you to have the Holy Spirit?

....

Read Romans 5:7-11, Luke 22:40-44, Matthew 27:32-46, and John 3:16

9. How did God make it evident that He loves you?

....

....

....

> Selah Moment: Jesus was the purest, most holy, and the only truly good person to walk the face of the earth, was He spared suffering? Was His life only filled with sunshine? If He wasn't spared such a fate, how can we, sinful people, expect to be spared? Take time to sit with this thought. How does that impact your view of suffering? Does suffering mean God doesn't love us? Is it cruel of God to allow it?
>
> ....
>
> ....
>
> ....

10. Ultimately, why did God go through the hassle of sending Jesus and sacrificing Him on your behalf? What did God want for you? (verse 10-11)

....

....

....

Read Isaiah 1:1-20

11. What traits do you see in the Israelites in verses 1-15?

....
....
....
....

12. Despite the Israelites behavior in the above verses, how do you see the love of God in verses 16-20 of Isaiah 1?

....
....
....

Let's make it personal: Part 1

Based on the scriptures you've read, do you see yourself in the Israelites or Elijah? Have you ever turned away from God? When you've gone through times of struggle, how did you respond? How would you like to respond differently next time? Explain.

....
....
....

Read Matthew 5:38-48, Matthew 6:14-15, Matthew 18:21-35, John 13:34-35, Ephesians 4:32, and Matthew 22:37-39

(ATTENTION: Please read and pay close attention to each of these verses, they are vital!!)

13. What should our response to God's great love for us be?

....
....
....

April

Let's make it personal: Part 2

Wow, so you've seen the richness of God's love and the righteous requirement He calls us to because of His love. How do you measure up with this? Do you forgive quickly? Do you love your enemies well or do you hold grudges? Take this time to pause and analyze your heart.

....

....

....

If you struggle in this area, have no fear, freedom is possible and you can begin again even now. The last section of this week's journal entry shines light on this.

Read Isaiah 1:27-28(NLT), Jeremiah 35:15, 2 Chronicles 7:14, Acts 2:38 and Hosea 11-14

14. What do you notice God says in each of these scriptures in response to His people's poor actions? What option does He give that would help His people?

....

....

....

....

....

....

....

....

15. Define "repent."

....

....

16. The Hebrew word for "repent" is "shub". Define "shub".

....

....

17. The Greek word for "repent" is "metanoeó." Define "metanoeó."

....

....

No matter the language, the overarching meaning remains the same and God's instruction to repent and be one with Him still stands. He loves you and has made a away for you to be a friend of His(Romans 5:11 and John 15:15). Will you accept? As 2 Peter 3:9 says, because of God's immense love, patience, and grace, He offers the same opportunity of repentance to you as He has done for many others in scripture. However, just as you saw in the verses you read, repentance is a choice. You can choose repentance, or you can continue in your wicked ways, but be mindful of what each choice comes with.

Let's make it personal: Part 3

Who are some people you need to forgive? Do you have any offense against God? Has anyone hurt you that you need to let go of? No matter how much suffering they caused, remember the great love God has poured out on you and take this time to let them go. I know this may be very hard depending on what they may have done to you, but remember God is a just God and vengeance is His NOT yours(Romans 12:19). Do your part and release them. Pray and ask God to help you in this area. List people you need to let go of and forgive below. Then list any other sins you need to repent of and ask the Lord to forgive you of them. (Disclaimer, this may be painful and tears are always okay to be shed. There's so much freedom on the other side of this, don't let satan keep you bound. Be free in Jesus' name)

....

....

....

....

....

....

....

This week you have explored the deep and immense love of God. I pray you to experience this love and pour it out upon those you encounter; even in times of trouble. The love of Jesus Christ is unlike any other the world has ever known. If you look around, times are getting darker and darker, wars are rampant, and sin is at an all-time high in these last days. What's the remedy? The love of God poured out through Jesus and imparted to you through His Spirit. His love prevails even through suffering, His love can turn the hardest and coldest heart into one that is soft and warm, His love transforms, and holds you through every storm. Once received, you have the power to extend this type of love and show the glory of God in this day and age. Will you? Lastly, please know that although God allows suffering and bad things to happen, it doesn't mean He approves or rejoices in any darkness that has been committed against you. If you've been wronged, taken advantage of, or anything in between, ask God to show you how He felt when you suffered, ask Him where He was and wait for His response. Also, know that no evil committed in this life goes unnoticed or undealt with by our Heavenly Father. In the meantime, I pray every hardened and hurt heart be healed and every mind restored, in the name of Jesus. I pray that you will trust again and find peace and freedom in Jesus' name. You will testify of the goodness and redemptive love of God.

Worship Playlist: *"Wreckless Love" by Cory Asbury*
"Jesus What a Savior" by Housefires
"moonflower" by Abbie Gamboa
"too good" by Abbie Gamboa
"Freedom" by Justin Bieber

Time of Reflection: Part 1

Reflect on the past four months of life, then honestly and vulnerably answer the following questions. If you need more lines, use the "additional pages" in the back of this journal!

What are some memorable or important things that have happened in the past 4 months (these can be good or bad, happy, sad, or anyhwere in between)?

....
....
....
....
....
....
....
....
....

What have you been doing well? What do you want to celebrate? What has brought you joy?

....
....
....
....
....
....
....
....
....

April

As you reflect, what main emotions have you felt in the past four months?

....
....
....
....
....

What have you not been doing so well? What are you struggling with? Do you have any fears? Has anything been painful to endure? How do you need help?

....
....
....
....
....
....
....
....
....
....
....

How is your relationship with God? Use the questions below to help you explain.

- *How have you been seeking after Him? Do you think you've "found Him"?(Jeremiah 29:13) How so or not?*
- *Have you felt connected to Him? How so or not?*
- *Are you disappointed or angry with Him? Are you feeling grateful for Him? Do you believe you can trust Him? etc. Take this time to celebrate with Him in the areas you have felt grateful in. Be sure to slow down as you answer these questions and ask the Lord to ease your heart and help you work through any tough areas. Ask Him for His perspective of situations you've experienced and ask Him to show you how He sees you as you've endured. Wait to hear His reply.*

If you need to process some tough emotions or moments, here's a grief cycle model I've followed, you can shorten or change it as you need(timeframe: 1-7 days, depends on you): cry(express emotion) > pray vulnerably (verbally and/or written)

> cry > hear God (be still to listen) > share (tell a trusted and prayerful friend what you're going through) > hear God (be still to listen) > cry > accept what God said > pray (release the situation) > cry > sing praises & thank God as you move on (Psalm 30:1-5).

What deep desires do you have in life right now? How have you seen inklings or ways of them being fulfilled? Do you think they haven't been fulfilled at all? Explain.

(Note: Only God can satisfy our deepest longings, so be sure to take note of how He's bringing fulfillment even if you don't see the physical manifestation of your desires as you imagined. If you don't see Him doing so, take this time to pray vulnerably expressing that, ask Him to open your eyes to see all He is doing, and surrender your desires to Him.)

April

What goals do you have? How are you taking responsibility to reach them?

....
....
....
....
....
....
....
....

How do you feel best supported and cared for by friends and family? On a rate of 1-10, how supported and cared for have you felt by them? Explain.

....
....
....
....
....
....
....
....
....
....
....
....

What God-approved things do you enjoy doing? How often have you been participating in them? How have those moments been for you?

> Note: "God-approved" does not just mean going to church or to church events. It means things that are not against His commands. God also values rest and enjoying life while maintaining our righteousness in Christ, see Ecclesiastes 8, so be sure to take time to just enjoy life with Him

....
....

If you could change one thing about your life right now, what would it be? Why?

> **Suggestion:** *Pray and ask God about this thing. Ask Him for the revelation of why you want it, ask if it's a pure desire to have, and the provision if it's in God's will. Ask God to search your heart and show you the root of your desire.*

What areas of growth do you want to see happen within yourself over the course of the next four months?

NATIONAL day of PRAYER

Lord, I thank you for...

_____
_____
_____
_____

Father, you are so...

_____
_____
_____
_____

Teach me how to...

_____
_____
_____
_____

In Jesus' name I bind...

...and loose...

cover and protect...

In Jesus' name, I pray, Amen.

Date: _____

May

Pray Without Ceasing

Have you ever thought about the fact that because of Jesus, you have direct access to the ears of God? Read 2 Chronicles 7:14, 1 Timothy 2:5, 2 Corinthians 5:18-19, and John 14:12-14 for the proof. So, be mindful of what you pray for and pray without ceasing with pure motives(James 4:3).

In this world we live in, people devotedly pray to various gods. This is nothing new as we see evidence of this in the Bible. However, because we know the one true God, it is imperative that we seek Him in prayer not only on the National Day of Prayer that happens this month, but every day. God is waiting to hear from you! Your voice and relationship with Him matters and has power; don't keep it stored up, don't be silent because of fear or excuses like "you don't know how to pray." Prayer is simply a conversation with your Heavenly Father. Jesus also gave us a template for prayer when he taught His first disciples how to pray,

Read Luke 11:1-13 and Matthew 6:9-13

1. What topics did Jesus mention in His blueprint for prayer?

....
....
....
....

2. What else did you learn about prayer as you looked at Jesus' example?

....
....
....
....

This week's journal entry is a short one because I want to urge you to go deep in prayer this week. One way you can start is by filling in your personalized prayers after the prompts given in the coloring activity. There is also extra space for you to go off script and simply seek after God on your own. Some topics you can pray about are family, friends, coworkers, leaders in your life, the salvation of those in the world, kings and politicians, what's heavy on your mind, your job or future, school, things you're struggling with, your bf/gf/spouse, things you're thankful for and desire to celebrate, and so many other things. You can literally pray about anything because God cares for you(1 Peter 5:7 AMP).

I also want to encourage you to ask the Holy Spirit what He wants you to pray about. After asking, wait for a response. The Holy Spirit could respond to you by showing you an image or a word, you may hear His audible voice, a scripture reference, or someone's name may come to mind, etc. As you get to know how God speaks, you'll get better at discerning and interpreting what He says. Whatever the Holy Spirit reveals, pray accordingly. This is called praying in the Spirit or prophetic prayers. If you have the gift of praying in tongues(1 Corinthians 14:1-5), this is also a form of praying in the Spirit and you should definitely pray this way. If you don't have this gift or if you've never prophesied, ask the Lord for these gifts of His Spirit(Luke 11:!3) and use it in prayer

In the coloring activity, two of the prompts include the terms "binding" and "loosing" (Matthew 18:18-19). Let's take a closer look at what these words mean and how to use them:

> *In seeking the Lord for deliverance and breakthrough, we bind (arrest) the things of darkness, and we loose (release into our lives) the matters of Christ's likeness and light.*

For instance, if you are struggling with pride, in prayer, you could pray:

> *"In the name of Jesus, I bind pride and loose humility."*

If you are struggling with lustful thinking, you could pray:

> *"I bind these lustful thoughts and loose the purity of Christ, in Jesus' name."*

Your turn! Using the table, fill-in various things in your life or the lives of others that you want to pray for God to bind up and then loose in the name of Jesus.

I bind...	I loose...

May

Coloring activity: *Like Jesus often would, get away from the noise of everyday life and take intentional time to sit with God and pray. You can put on some worship or "soaking" music, pace around your room, or even go for a prayer walk, during this time. In this week's coloring activity, I've given you some sentence starters you can use to spark prayer, but remember what you learned about prayer and incorporate them into your time too. As you keep growing in faith and knowing the word, you'll see that your prayer life will continue to grow as well if you're intentional. Lastly, I want to challenge you to commit to praying for at least 15-30 minutes each day this week.*

Worship Playlist: *"When I Pray" by DOE*
"Surrendering to the Presence" by William Augusto
"Into His Presence" by Waldner Worship
"In the Spirit" by Waldner Worship
"Living Waters" by Waldner Worship

May

Testimony

Did you know that you have a testimony (a story of how God has operated in your life)? As the coloring page suggests, each moment of your life is like a new puzzle piece. No matter how tragic or mundane the moment, it has meaning and is needed to complete the puzzle of your life. However, the tragic and painful moments are the ones that sting the most and can be discouraging. But, be encouraged; God can use any and every moment and turn it for your good and the good of others.

Read John 9:1-12

1. Based on the disciples' question, what did they assume the relationship between suffering and sin was?

....
....
....

2. What was Jesus' response?

....
....
....

Disclaimer: *In John 5:6-14, Jesus connects a man's suffering to sin, so such a consequence does happen as a result of sinning, so be mindful of how you live. I'd also like to challenge you to ask God to reveal any generational curses(Deuteronomy 5:9) in your lineage and seek Him for deliverance so that sin cycles will not continue to be passed down.*

3. Define "glorify"(Refer to the Author's Note for a reminder on how to best do so. Matthew 5:16 is a good scripture reference for this word)

....
....
....

4. What did Jesus do for the man?

....
....
....

5. What would have hindered the man's healing?

....
....
....

6. What did the man do as a result of Jesus' healing touch and instruction? How was God ultimately glorified through the man's ailment?(Hint: You will need to read beyond verse 12 to answer this fully)

....
....
....

Read Genesis 37:1-28 and Genesis 39:1

7. Describe Joseph.

....
....
....
....
....

8. What caused Joseph's brothers to sell him into slavery?

....
....
....

9. What person of power and status was Joseph sold to?

....

Read Genesis 39:2-4, 19-23 and Genesis 41:38-41, 53-57

10. While in Egypt, what trends do you notice about the positions that Joseph held?

....

....

....

Read Genesis 42:25, Genesis 45:3-5, and Genesis 47:1-6

11. Due to Joseph's position in Egypt, what was he able to do for his family during the famine?

....

....

....

Read Genesis 45:4-8 and Genesis 50:15-21

12. Although Joseph went through a lot of suffering, how did God show up mightily? Was Joseph's suffering in vain or did it have purpose? Did God's plan for Joseph's life come to past or did the tragedies hinder God's plan? Explain.

....

....

....

....

....

Read Psalm 138:7-8

13. What characteristics of God are prominent in these scriptures?

....

....

....

As you can see, trials and tragedy do come, but if we are willing to surrender to God and allow Him to move and work on our behalf, we will see the purpose behind it all. What the enemy meant for evil, God can turn it for your good and you will then testify of what the Lord has done! Knowing these things, let's now take a look at the power of using your testimony.

Read Revelation 12:7-11

14. . How much power does the blood of Jesus and your testimony have when utilized?

....
....
....

Read 1 Peter 3:14-15

15. You have a unique testimony (a collection of your life encounters and how God pursued you and changed your life). According to the scriptures, what does your testimony give you the ability to do?

....
....
....
....
....

Read 1 Peter 4:12-19

16. So, ultimately, do you suffer in vain? Explain the purpose and peace in your suffering as a disciple of Christ.

....
....
....
....
....

Selah Moment: Is there a difference between suffering because of righteousness (living for Christ) and suffering because of sin? Which is better for you? Explain.

Let's make it personal

Take this time to think about your testimony. What are some of the toughest times you've experienced?

What helped you to endure? How'd you see God move in your life?

How did the circumstance turn out in the end? (ie what lessons were learned, what happened next in life in relation to the event, etc) If it was in the distant past, have you come to see how it worked out for your good? If not, write a prayer to God, asking Him to open your eyes to see from His perspective and ask Him where He was and how He felt when you endured that circumstance. If you're presently struggling and don't see any sight of hope or God, cry out to Him and ask for His help. Pray Psalm 138:7-8 and wait on the Lord. He's moving.

....

....

One way or another, we all go through tough things in life (and there's a greater time of tribulation/trouble the whole world will go through, Matthew 24) and if you are a believer, Jesus foretold that you'd have trials in this world in John 16:33. But, be encouraged because in that same verse, He also said He's greater than every trial and the world itself. Thus, you can rely on Him when you're going through and know every puzzle piece of your life has a purpose. At times it may feel extremely hard to fight because the one hell was made for (Satan and the fallen angels) is the one fighting you and he's honestly good at his job. Yet, I want to urge you to not give up, don't tap out, don't lose faith, don't let Satan win. Call on the name of Jesus, cry, worship, dance, read scripture, ask your friends to pray for you, and do whatever you need to fight to not give up and make it to the other side. Remember, what the enemy means for evil, God can and will turn it for your good. Will you let Him? Keep doing things God's way and you will see. Declare Psalm 138:7-8 out loud over and over until you believe it. If you're not already, you will TESTIFY of the goodness of God

Coloring Activity: *On each puzzle piece, write various things that have occurred in your life that have led you to know God better. Be sure to include the good, the bad, and the ugly. Remember, God tells us in Romans 8:28 that He works all things together for the good of those that love Him and are called according to His purpose.*

Worship Playlist: *"Surrounded" by Upperroom & Elyssa Smith*
"God of Impossible" by 2819 Worship
"i love You" by JUDAH, Dante Bowe, & Aaron Moses
"Stand For Me" by Jonathan Traylor
"Augustus Gloop" by J. Monty

See God, Experience God

There are many ideas about the existence of God. Some believe that there are many gods (polytheists). Others(deists) believe there is a God, but that He simply created the Earth and left it for us to figure out life on our own because He is distant and doesn't engage with us, or that He assigned different "gods" to various regions of the world. While some also believe there is no God at all (atheists). Various people have even said, "if God is real, why won't He do something so amazing that no one can question it?" So, has God shown Himself? Is there only one God or are there many? Let's explore what God has to say about these matters.

Read Isaiah 43:9-21, Deuteronomy 6:4, Mark 12:29-30, and 1 Corinthians 8:4-6

1. What does God make clear in these scriptures?

....
....
....
....

Read Exodus 14:13-23 and Isaiah 43:16-17

2. What Biblical account is God referencing through Isaiah? What mighty thing did God do?

....
....
....

Read Mark 4:35-41

3. What did Jesus do? What resulted afterwards?

....
....
....

4. How did Jesus' disciples respond?

....

Read the following scriptures in order: John 1:1-3, Genesis 1:26, Exodus 3:13-14, and John 8:56-59

5. *Why shouldn't it be surprising that the waves obeyed Jesus?*

....

....

....

As you can see, there is only one God and Jesus Himself proclaims that. So, is Jesus God? What about the Holy Spirit? If so, wouldn't that make it where there are 3 Gods? Whether you've speculated this or not, these are very valid questions. The short answer is yes, Jesus is God, the Holy Spirit is God, and God the Father is God too, but they flow as ONE (having different roles but being of the same "material" and having the same power. See John 14:4-11 and John 10:29-33. A fun way to illustrate how this can be it to think about the states of water: water, ice, and vapor. They all are water, made of the same material but have different roles). Thus there is only ONE God whose name is Yahweh, Yeshua (Jesus), and Holy Spirit (Spirit of truth). For more details on this elaborate phenomena, see Appendix C in the back of the journal.

Read Psalm 19:1 and Romans 1:18-32 (AMP)

6. *Many people struggle with believing in the realness of God and His presence being with us because we can't physically see His form. How do these verses challenge this idea? What has God given us to show His presence and power?*

....

....

7. *Rather than accepting God, what do you notice people did instead? (Also see Exodus 32:1-9)*

....

....

....

....

Read Exodus 20:3-5, Exodus 32:8-11, Jeremiah 7:8-19, Luke 16:13, and Mark 11:15-17

8. How does God feel about other idols/gods being worshiped?

....

....

....

At this point, you have seen that God is real and has shown Himself. You've seen that there is only one God and He has given commands. But how close does He interact with us? Keep reading to find out!

Read Psalm 139:1-10, Jeremiah 1:5, and Jeremiah 23:23-24

9. What does God say about His interaction with people?

....

....

Read 1 Peter 5:6-7(AMP)

10. God is near, but does He care about you and your wellbeing? Explain.

....

....

....

....

Read Job 38-42 (yes, all 5 chapters)

11. What do you notice about God?

....

....

....

....

....

12. Job challenged God, provoking this response. How did Job respond to God?

....

....

Let's make it personal

Have you ever struggled with doubting God's existence? Have you ever directly or indirectly questioned God's authority? (Directly could look like verbally saying your doubts, living them through your actions, or in your beliefs. Whereas indirectly could look like you worrying, having fear of man, or not obeying God) Explain.

....

....

....

How do the scriptures presented today help you combat those thoughts of doubt? Be honest. if they did not help, what questions do you have? Write them below and ask God to show you His truth.

....

....

....

....

....

If you don't struggle with doubt in this area, how can you use these scriptures to help someone who does have doubts?

....

....

....

....

God has been here before the beginning of time. Think about this: the same God who made fragrant and beautiful flowers, the elegant giraffe and powerful elephant, and who perfectly placed the earth in a spot that isn't too close or too far away from the sun making it habitable for humans, plants, animals, and water...this same God who made stars and everything good, also made YOU! And not only did He make you, but He made you in His image and cares about you more than any other creation(Matthew 6:26-33), He wants you to know Him AND He wants to know you and be involved in your life. How will you respond?. I challenge you to be intentional about slowing down and admiring various creations of God and what He's doing on the earth; truly bask in the beauty of God through admiring His handiwork and seeking after knowing Him for yourself. He will reveal so many amazing things about who you are as a result too. As you admire the Lord's creations, please remember, we are not to worship God's creation, nor allow our lives to be determined by these things, or think of them as higher than God. Doing this would make them "gods" and idols (see Romans 1:21-25). God is a jealous God and we should worship and be led by Him and Him alone, not stars (zodiacs), animals, or any other god; the great I Am is almighty

Worship playlist: *"Here as in Heaven" by Elevation Worship*
"So Will I (100 Billion X)" by Live Hillsong United
"I Am" by J. Monty
"Respond" by Travis Greene
"I Am" by J. Monty
"Questions" by Kevin Mayfield

Snatch every THOUGHT and make it OBEDIENT to JESUS CHRIST

Snatched Thoughts

Thoughts are inaudible words to the public, but life-transforming to the one who thinks them. In different moments, seasons of life, times of the day, or simply with certain people, our thoughts are ever-changing. The number of thoughts we can have in our lifetime are infinite and according to scripture, our thoughts hold a lot of power. Thus, with such a vast number of occurrences and power in each one, let's see what God's word says about our thoughts and how we should mind them.

Proverbs 23:6-7 (KJV) says,

"Eat thou not the bread of him that hath an evil eye, neither desire thou his dainty meats: For as he thinketh in his heart, so is he: Eat and drink, saith he to thee; but his heart is not with thee." {NKJV: (For as he thinks in his heart so he is: "Eat and drink," he says to you; but his heart is not with you.)}

1. Based on this scripture, what is more connected with your heart: thoughts or words?

....

2. What does this scripture tell you will truly show one's true self? Thoughts or words? Explain.

....
....
....
....

Knowing how connected your thoughts and heart are, it makes it very important that as a believer, you keep your thoughts in check, and in return, your heart will remain pure as well. This happens as you submit your thoughts to Christ, repent, and replace them with thoughts that align with Jesus when lies come rushing in. However, this can be very hard, especially with a sinful nature and living in this world filled with things to pervert and taint your thoughts. Let's take a look at someone who struggled in this area and learn from him.

Read 1 Kings 19:1-16 (CEV)

3. What caused Elijah to flee and hide?

....

4. What did Elijah call God in verse 10?

....

5. Based on Elijah's actions, did he believe God was who he was proclaiming Him to be? How can you tell his thoughts were actually different?

....
....
....
....
....

6. What was the final result of Elijah's inability to think properly and snap out of it?

....
....

> Selah Moment:
>
> 1. Why was Elijah really in the cave? Desribe what his emotions and thoughts probably were?
>
> ....
> ....
>
> 2. How do you think Elijah's life could've ended differently had he been able to get his fearful thoughts under control?
>
> ....
> ....
> ....
> ....

Read Colossians 3:1-3 and Philippians 4:8

7. What does right-thinking look like?

....

....
....
....

Read Matthew 6:22-23

8. What kind of things will make it harder for you to think purely?

....
....
....
....

Read 2 Corinthians 10:3-6 (NLT) and Ephesians 6:17-18

9. What are your weapons?

....
....
....

10. When dealing with others or yourself, if thoughts that do not align with God come, what are you to do?

....

11. What are some synonyms for "take captive?"

....
....

To take your thoughts captive and make them obedient to Christ, you have to know what God says in His word to grab hold of those thoughts that are lies and trade them with the truth of God's word.

Let's make it personal

Fill-in the chart below as follows.

Left column: *What negative thoughts have you continually repeated to yourself? What flawed beliefs have you accepted about yourself, God, and/or others? Write one in each box.*

Middle column: *Measure those things up to God's word. What does God have to say about you, Himself, and/ or others regarding those things? What scripture combats that negative thought? (See the chart for an example).*

This may require some research of the ANTONYM of the topic of your negative thought.

Here are two ways I suggest for researching:

1. Google it!

    • After you've written the negative thoughts, do a quick Google search for scripture that speak truth (ie. if you're having thoughts of feeling "purposeless", research, "scriptures about purpose").

2. Use a concordance

    • In the back of many Bibles is an alphabetized index of topics in the Bible and their scripture reference. After you've written the negative thoughts, look in the back of your bible for the antonym of the topic of your thought and find verses that combat the thought (ie. if you're having thoughts of feeling "purposeless", find the word, "purpose" in the concordance and follow the scripture references given to find a verse you like and that speaks to you most).

Right column: *Write a new thought based on the truth of God's word. Then, when you catch yourself thinking the negative thought, rebuke it and speak this new thought that's founded on God's truth instead.*

Negative Thought	God's Truth!	My NEW Thought
Ex. I don't have a purpose and my life has no meaning.	Jeremiah 1:5 says, "**Before I formed you** in the womb **I knew you** before you were born, I set you apart; I **appointed** you as a prophet to the nations."	Like Jeremiah, God has known me and created me for a purpose from the beginning.

Wow, who knew our hearts were connected with our thoughts and that our thoughts had so much power? God did, that's who! So be sure to take heed to Proverbs 4:23 and guard your heart! Protect it for from it comes the wellspring of your life. Will your spring be pure and clean water or muddy and salty(James 3:9-12)?

Remember, Satan is the father of lies (John 8:44), thus the negative thoughts must be canceled with the power of God's truth in His Word! So, from this moment forward, remember your authority in Christ and take every thought captive and cancel it out with the truth of God's word. As soon as those thoughts come, recognize it, rebuke, bind it in prayer, and speak God's truth instead. Before you know it, you'll be believing what God believes in no time! There is a great reward for followers of Christ: immense authority is one (Ephesians 6:12 & Luke 10:19), remember it and use it to fight against your enemy, Satan.

Coloring activity: *In the thought bubbles, write your NEW thoughts from the LMIP section about yourself, God, and/or others. Be sure to color them for an added pop of fun!*

June

God Knows

There can be times in our lives where everything seems to be in disarray, one thing after another things seem to be hitting the fan, God's promises seem to be far off, and it appears the enemy is winning. But remember who God is! If we are committed to yielding to God's will and way, with confidence we can believe that He is in control, He has everything handled, and He will work them together. Emphasis on "if we are committed to yielding to God's will and way" because we can't expect God to move as swiftly and least problematically if He is continually cleaning up the messes we keep intentionally making (warning: that's a dangerous place to live, so I urge you to submit yourself to God and stop wilding out in disobedience; God's mercies are new each day, but our actions still have consequences). Obeying and surrendering to God is vital to our success in life and puts Him in a position to fully be in control as we give Him the wheel. And when the Creator of the heavens and the earth is in the driver seat and has the freedom to move and operate in our lives, there's no telling where we'll end up but it'll certainly exceed our expectations and no one and nothing can thwart the plans of God(Isaiah 14:24). Let God be in control, do you trust Him? Did you know that He has a plan for your life? Will you let Him be in control so that it can come to pass? Per usual, let's take a look at God in action in someone else's life in the Bible. Take note of how the enemy tried to cancel the plans of God and what God did as a result.

Read Genesis 37:5-11

1. What were some things Joseph's dreams revealed would happen?

....
....
....

Read Genesis 37:1-4, 11-20

2. Look at the root of Joseph's brother's actions. Why did they want to kill him? What sparked this desire?

....
....
....

Read Genesis 37:21-36

3. How do you think Joseph felt while at the bottom of the cistern and then being sold?

....

4. Upon being sold into slavery, who was Joseph sold to?

Read Genesis 39:1-6

5. Although his brothers abandoned him, did God ever leave Joseph's side? What does God do for Joseph?

6. Joseph started as a slave. What did he end up becoming?

7. How does this relate to the dreams Joseph had in chapter 37? How do you see God still working in Joseph's life?

Read Genesis 39:7-23

8. How did Joseph respond to Potiphar's wife?

9. What did Potiphar's wife say about the encounter? What happened as a result of Potiphar's wife lying? Were these actions of God or Satan?

Selah Moment:

Refer back to Genesis 39:19-23

Put yourself in Joseph's shoes. How would you feel after being abandoned twice by significant people in your life?

....
....
....
....
....

Have you ever been wrongly accused? How did you handle it?

....
....
....
....

10. Although Joseph was seemingly back to square one, where was God in the midst of this storm?

....
....
....

11. In all that you've read, did God ever give word that the plans for Joseph's life changed from those original dreams he shared with his family?

....

12. How does what happened relate to the dreams Joseph had in chapter 37? How do you see that God was working in the midst of it all and was in control?

....
....
....
....

> *Selah Moment:*
>
> *If you were Joseph, how do you think you would respond at this point? Would you still trust that what God told you would come to pass, or would these circumstances make you feel that God had forgotten about you and cause you to give up?*
>
> ....
>
> ....
>
> ....
>
> ....

Read Genesis 40

13. *Who did Joseph meet while in prison? Who did they directly work for?*

....

....

14. *What did God gift[2] Joseph with the ability to do?*

....

15. *How did Joseph use his time while in jail? Did he serve? Did he sulk? etc.*

....

....

....

16. *How does what happened relate to the dreams Joseph had in chapter 37? How do you see that God was working in the midst of it all and was in control?*

....

....

....

---

2   The word "gift" is often overcomplicated, but notice that Joseph says "God interprets," thus Joseph was aware that he was just a willing and available vessel being used by God. His "gifting" was God simply flowing through him to accomplish the task. I believe this spiritual gifting was a result of his intimacy and submission to the Lord. Are you desiring a certain gift/ability from God? With a pure heart, ask Him for it and to reveal the gifts of His spirit that He's placed inside of you, seek Him sincerely, and see what He does.

Read Genesis 41

17. What did Joseph first say to Pharoah in regards to his dreams being interpreted?

....

....

18. Briefly explain what happened.

....

....

....

....

....

....

....

....

19. How does what happened relate to the dreams Joseph had in chapter 37? How do you see that God was working in the midst of it all and was in control?

....

....

....

....

Read Genesis 42:1-9, Genesis 46:1-7, 28-34, and Genesis 47:12

20. How do you see Joseph's dreams he had in chapter 37 finally come to pass?
(Take note of how old Joseph was in chapter 37 vs chapter 41)

....

....

....

....

....

21. Although it wasn't as Joseph probably expected, did God's word (via the dreams) return void, or did they manifest (occur, come to pass)?

> Selah Moment: Did Joseph make the dreams God gave him come to pass? What was Joseph's part in seeing it all come to pass?

22. Based on what you've read, although trials came, how often was God ultimately in control? Circle one and explain.

(Not at all)   (Sometimes)   (Most of the time)   (The entire time)

> Selah Moment:
>
> **Read Genesis 50:19-20**
>
> How do these words and Joseph's life impact you? What thoughts or emotions are evoked?

Read Numbers 23:8, 19-21

23. What principles and attributes of God are highlighted in these verses?

24. *How do you see these principles and attributes of God in Joseph's life?*

....

....

....

....

....

To further get the point across, take a look at one more Biblical account. For the sake of the lesson, Adonijah represents the enemy, King David represents God, and Solomon represents the plans God has for your life.

Read 1 Kings 1

25. *Although Adonijah had his plans, what occurred in the end?*

....

....

....

....

26. *How do you see God being in control?*

....

....

....

Read 1 Timothy 1:18-19

27. *Why is it important to take note of the prophetic (when God reveals things to you about what's to come) moments God gives you about your life?*

....

....

....

Let's make it personal

As a follower of Christ and child of God, what promises have God made to you? Do you trust that He'll see them through? If you feel like God hasn't made you any personal promises, use these scriptures to help: Jeremiah 29:11, John 14:1-3 and Romans 8:28. Also pray and ask God to speak to you prophetically through His Holy Spirit! Then wait for an answer, you may see an image or hear a phrase immediately, but also pay attention to your dreams, God could use a person to tell you, He could highlight scriptures, or you could even see a vision. So, be vigilant!

....
....
....
....
....
....
....
....

What have you been waiting for or been wanting to happen in your life? How have you been waiting? Be sure to be honest with yourself and God here. Have you been preparing for what you desire? Have you prayed? Have you acted like Adonijah and tried to take things into your own hands? Explain and take time to repent(Revelation 2:4-5) and/or pray accordingly, if you're willing.

....
....
....
....
....
....
....
....

Remember, Joseph waited 13 years for the dreams God gave him to come to pass, waiting is a part of the process and how you wait makes a difference.

Above all else, in 1 Peter 2:9 and Revelation 3:11, God speaks to believers as being royalty. Thus, God has called you higher in terms of attaining the Kingdom of God (Heaven) in the quickly approaching future as Jesus is coming back. How are you living until then? How are you waiting on the Lord? (ie have you felt discouraged in the "delay" or are you waiting patiently, contently, and intentionally) Does your life look like someone who is of royal descent? Does your life look set apart from the world or do you blend in?

If you've grown tired of waiting and are feeling discouraged, what truths from the Biblical accounts of Joseph and King Solomon can you now hold onto to be encouraged?

Never forget that God is in control. He cannot lie, and He keeps His promises! Although you may feel like Joseph (before the fulfillment of the promise) at times in the process of becoming more like Christ or going through life, know that God will do exactly what He said. So, keep your eyes on Him, keep your priorities in check (Matthew 6:33), and process what you're going through with trusted friends and in prayer. Doing so, everything else will fall into place as God sees fit (Luke 22:42) and in His perfect timing.

In closing, take the advice of Jesus, and pray like this:

> *"...Our Father in heaven, may your name be kept holy. May your Kingdom come soon. May your will be done on earth as it is in Heaven. Give us today the food we need, and forgive us our sins, as we have forgiven those who sin against us. And don't let us yield to temptation, but rescue us from the evil one." Matthew 6:9-13, NLT (read it in other versions if you'd like).*

Worship playlist: *"Lord You Are Good" by Todd Galberth*
"Wait On You" by Maverick City Music

"May the God of hope fill you with all joy and peace as you trust in Him, so that you may overflow with hope by the power of the Holy Spirit."

Romans 15:13 (NIV)

Overflow

Another week, another scripture dissection! Yay for going deep into scripture. In today's study, you will pick apart Romans 15:13. When completing a scripture dissection, I like to first read the scripture a few times before doing anything. I then annotate various parts of the scripture to help highlight key things and make them pop out. I've done the dissection part for you on today's coloring sheet, but for you to get involved, you'll be tracing them to get a feel for the concept and of course, answering questions to go deeper. Be sure to read the scripture a few times before getting started! Lastly, the Holy Spirit may show you something I missed, so feel free to add to the annotation and take note of what He points out.

Read Romans 15:13 (NIV) - see coloring activity

After reading it a few times, assign colors to each part of speech below, and then trace them in the coloring activity.

Color	Part of Speech
	Nouns/Pronouns (words that are circled in the activity)
	Verbs (words that are boxed in the activity)
	Adjectives/Nouns that are describing (underlined words in the activity)

Use the three different colors you chose to trace the boxes, circles, and lines in the activity. As you do so, reflect on each portion. What stands out? What revelation has God given you as you read? Read the verse at least three times.

Now let's dive deeper...

1. What does this verse say about God? *(focus on on the annotated things associated with God)*

    a. What is He the God of?

    ....

    b. What can He give you?

    ....

    ....

June

2. What does this verse say about you? (focus on the verbs associated with "you")

    a.   What is required of you?

        ....

        ....

    b.   What do you think this looks like practically? (research scriptures on this topic; this is considered "cross-referencing")

        ....

        ....

        ....

        ....

3. What's the end goal? (focus on the words after "so that")

    a.   Per this prayer, what was Paul's desire for the Romans to have?

        ....

        ....

    b.   Who would God use to fulfill this desire in them(Romans/believers)?

        ....

Now let's cross-reference and find out more about a portion of this scripture.

Read John 16:4-16

Try out dissecting(annotating) verses 7-8 and 13-14 by yourself

4. Describe the Holy Spirit.

    a.   What does He do? (focus on the verbs)

        ....

        ....

    b.   What's another name for Him? (focus on the nouns associated with Him)

        ....

        ....

5. Based on your dissected responses and cross-reference, what does Romans 15:13 suggest and mean for you as a believer?

....
....
....
....
....
....
....

Let's make it personal

Re-read and meditate on Romans 15:13 again. What emotions do you feel, and what call to actions are you inspired to take on?

....
....
....
....
....
....

> *To further immerse yourself in the text, pray the scripture over yourself changing the pronouns "you" to "me" or "I" and speak directly to God changing "Him" to "You" as you pray*

How do you see God differently? What new knowledge or connections did God show you in His word? What do you desire to know more about?

....
....
....
....
....
....
....
....

Scripture dissection is a great way to pick apart the scriptures and study them. As you get more comfortable with the concept, you'll be dissecting chapters of scripture in no time! Carry the joy, peace, and hope of the Lord with you as you embark on your journey this week!

Resist

Any sports player has probably sat through a film review in which the entire team watched game footage of the upcoming opponents. During this meeting, the coach would be pausing and pointing out key things that the team does well or where they lack. Why? What's the purpose of these team meetings? The aim would be to get to know the opponent(enemy) and what the team would be up against to prepare strategically for the upcoming game!

Today, you will do the same! You're going to get to know the ways of your opponent(enemy), Satan. Why? For the same reason sports teams watch the films of their opponent, to know what you're up against as a follower of Christ. This film review will also allow you to prepare strategically for the battles(spiritual warfare) to come. Are you ready? God, your coach, has a plan of action for you to fight and win on a daily basis.

Read Isaiah 14:12-17 & Luke 10:18

1. What caused Satan to be cast out of Heaven? What did he think in his heart and desire?

....
....
....

Read Genesis 3:1-5

2. What tactic did Satan use to tempt Eve?

....
....
....

Read Matthew 4:1-11

3. What tactic did Satan use to tempt Jesus?

....
....
....

Read Genesis 3:1, 1 Peter 5:8, John 10:10, and Revelation 12:9-12

4. What characteristics of Satan do you notice?

....

....

....

C.S Lewis once said, "Humanity falls into two equal and opposite errors concerning the devil. Either they take him altogether too seriously, or they do not take him seriously enough."

Now that you've reviewed some of the enemy's film, let's take a look at the plan of action to fight. Spoiler alert: the game is fixed and your team(Disciples of Christ) WINS!

Read James 4:7-8

5. What does this scripture tell you to do? What is promised to occur as a result of your obedience?

....

....

....

6. Define "resist."

....

....

Read 1 Peter 5:8-10, Psalm 119:9, and Ephesians 6:10-13

7. How does God tell you to resist?

....

....

....

....

....

Read Ephesians 6:14-17

8. What defensive tools has God given you to stand against and resist Satan and his demons?

....

Read Ephesians 6:17-18, Luke 9:1, Luke 10:17-20, and Romans 8:26

9. What offensive tool has God given you to stand against and resist Satan and his demons?

Now that you're aware of the schemes of Satan and the tools you have to fight against him, relook at the Biblical accounts of Eve and Jesus.

Reread Genesis 3:1-7 and Matthew 4:1-11

10. Compare & contrast Jesus & Eve's responses to Satan. What tool did they both use to respond to Satan?

11. Where did Eve go wrong?

12. What did Jesus do differently than Eve? How did he use the offensive tool God has given us?

Read 1 Corinthians 10:13

13. What does God promise?

....

....

....

Let's make it personal

How does 1 Corinthians 10:13 impact to you? Are you encouraged, reassured, have questions, etc?

....

....

....

What temptations does Satan dangle in front of you most often? How have you seen him attack you most? (ie identity issues? lack of self-worth? struggling in your relationship with God? pride? other sin issues?)

....

....

....

....

....

How often do you give in to those temptations? Circle one.

Never   *Sometimes*   *Often*   *Always*

Next time you are tempted, be intentional about praying, speaking the word of God, and looking for God's way out so that you do not give in!

What are three things you're taking away from today's film review (devotional)? What has your Coach (God) shown you, and what tools has He given you today from the playbook (the Bible) to fight against your opponent, Satan?

1.

....

June

2.

3.

So, are you ready to fight? Every day brings a new battle, but just as every good coach always has a motivational pregame speech, take a look at your coach's; it's pretty dynamic: "In this world, you will have trials, but take heart, I have overcome the world! I have given you authority to tread on serpents and scorpions, and overall the power of the enemy and nothing will injure you. Nevertheless, do not rejoice in this, that the spirits are subject to you, but rejoice that your name is recorded in Heaven." (John 16:33, Luke 10:19-20) -Coach Jesus

Remember, the game is fixed, so each day, you have the victory if you stay on the right team (Matthew 25:31-46)! So, stay in the gym (1 Timothy 4:7-8, 1 Corinthians 9:27), take action, and stick to the game plan. Resist the devil and he will flee.

Coloring activity: *As you read today, the darts thrown by Satan are "fiery," so color the arrowhead and tail in hues of red, yellow, and orange. That's a representation of what the arrow looks like spiritually, but as you can see in between it, you have the power to RESIST!*

Worship playlist: *"Never Be Defeated" by Rich Tolbert Jr.*
"Victory Belongs to Jesus" by Todd Dulaney
"Victory" by The Clark Sisters

"When God says, 'launch out into the deep,' LAUNCH. OUT. INTO. THE DEEP!"

—Dr. Mark Rutland

June

Choose this Day

One thing that is a given and assured fact is that God is sovereign. This means that God is in control of EVERYTHING! He has His plans for you, and His mighty hand is continuously at work moving (or trying/wanting to move) pieces of your life. However, God has also given you the free will to choose Him and His way or say no and go about your merry way figuring life out on your own. In Joshua 24:14-15, Joshua gave the Israelites the opportunity to choose God or to choose to serve the gods of those around them. At that moment, they all chose God and said, "we will serve the LORD." Jesus also offers you the same opportunity each day to choose Him and follow His instructions or to turn away and follow your own ambitions.

Jesus has afforded you the greatest gift of all: salvation and life abundantly with Him. Do you trust Him enough to say yes? Choose ye this day. Today you will focus on an account in the Bible where the choice to follow and obey God was presented during a time of great uncertainty. How did the people involved respond? What was the reward or consequence? Take a look.

Read Luke 5:1-11

1. What did Jesus tell Simon to do?

....

....

....

2. Think of the track record of Jesus. Has He ever said something that didn't have meaning, purpose, or didn't align with what God said? (John 8:26-30)

....

....

3. So, if Jesus says something, what do you think that means or confirms? What does that mean for Simon in this biblical account in Luke 5?

....

....

....

4. What was Simon's initial reply to Jesus?

Fun Fact: Did you know that fishermen would usually catch their fish in shallow water at night because it was easiest to catch fish while they were feeding themselves closer to the surface of the water? Notice, during this Biblical account in Luke 5, it was likely daytime, and they were in the deeper end of the ocean.

Let's make it personal: Part 1

Knowing this fun fact, how would you respond? To help you answer this question, imagine that you're an expert at what you do, and a seemingly inexperienced person tells you to do something outside of what you know works. Would you listen, question, or ignore the person? Explain.

5. How do you think this fishing fact impacted Simon's (professional fisherman) initial reply?

6. What was Simon's second reply?

Let's make it personal: Part 2

What vision has God shown you for the direction of your life?

How does what God instructed you to require faith for you to see that vision through? Like Simon's situation, it may not make sense.

(Author's example: God called me to a new line of work so I had to downsize because I'd be making less money. In order to pay for different fees, I planned to sell all of my relatively new apartment furniture since I was moving out. However, God told me to give it all away for FREE! It didn't make any sense and I was a bit scared in the moment, but I listened and obeyed and it all worked out in the end. I hope this encourages you to do the crazy thing that doesn't make sense if God said to do so)

Is there anything you've tried to accomplish time and time again that just isn't working out? List them if so.

How have you acted as Simon did in his first reply to his Master, Jesus?

In regards to things God has given you the vision for or instructed you to do, have you responded to Jesus in this same manner as Simon did in his second reply? How? If not, what will it take for you to?

7. Looking back at Luke 5, what was the outcome of Simon obeying Jesus' command? What was the difference between the fishing experience Simon first spoke of and the time with Jesus?

....

....

....

8. How did Simon respond to Jesus after they caught the fish? (Compare to Isaiah 6:1-5)

....

....

....

9. Based on the different ways Simon responded to Jesus, how did this miracle shift his perspective of Jesus?

....

....

....

....

10. Did Simon know what the results would be when he said yes to Jesus and casted his nets in the deep water? What did it require for Simon to obey Jesus?

....

....

....

11. After catching so many fish, what does Jesus say Simon will now be? What does that mean? (use Matthew 28:19 to help)

....

....

....

June

Let's make it personal: Part 3

Do you trust Jesus? Select one and explain why.

    (Absolutely)   (Sometimes)   (Working on it)

....
....
....

Have you surrendered the things God has given you vision for to Him? Asking Him what He wants from you? How He wants you to accomplish them? If not, do so now. Some ways to do this are by giving it to God in prayer, then allowing your mind to rest, no longer overthinking the matter, and if there are any actions you've been overly controlling, stop doing them.

....
....
....
....
....
....

Do you think God would call you to do something without equipping you? Explain why or why not.

....
....
....
....

Read Hebrews 13:20-21, Romans 12:2, Philippians 1:6, and Philippians 2:12-13

12. What does this scripture say God will do to make sure His will is carried out in your life?

....
....
....

Read John 16:28-29, Revelation 7:9-10, Psalm 150, Matthew 24:14 and 2 Peter 3:9

13. What is God's will for ALL people?

....
....
....
....

Read John 17, Revelation 21:3, Matthew 28:19, Romans 12:3-8, and Daniel 12:1-3

14. What's God's ultimate will and purpose for all believers (disciples of Chirst)?

....
....
....
....

Read 2 Timothy 3:16-17, Ephesians 4:11-12, Acts 2:42, John 14:15-17, and Acts 1:1-5

15. What resources has God given you to equip you for everything He's called you to?

....
....
....
....

Let's make it personal: Part 4

Now that you see God's ultimate will for each of our lives, how are you living up to that? Take this time to pray, asking God for direction, increased faith, boldness, etc. Whatever you need in order to live out His will for your life, especially knowing His love for you!

....
....
....
....
....

....

....

....

So, whether you've tried chasing after the vision God has shown you a thousand times or just once, or maybe you've been running from God's plans and aren't aligning with Him, or you just feel stuck and don't know where to turn, seek God, pray, and don't be afraid to launch out into the deep when God says so. Like Simon (Peter), God's instructions might feel out of the norm or simply don't make sense to you, but trust Him anyway and obey. If you haven't accepted Jesus to come into your boat (life), that's vital, and you must start there. As your time with God opened today, all it takes is a choice! You can accept Jesus right here and right now by just saying yes.

> *"Yes, Lord, I receive Jesus as Master and Savior. Yes, Lord, I am a sinner in need of saving because I fall short of your glorious, perfect, and good standard daily. But I know You defeated sin and death because you raised Jesus from the dead. I need you Lord. Come into my life. I accept your hand, Holy Spirit, and I want your heart. Lead me and guide me toward your good and perfect will so that I may dwell in the house of the Lord forever and lead others there as well. In Jesus' name, I pray, Amen".*

As you saw with Simon (Peter), you can strive continuously without Jesus and still fall short, but the moment you accept Jesus as Lord, He will begin to transform your mind, perspective, and whole life. He'll give you divine insight and instruction. If you've prayed that above prayer for salvation with sincerity in your heart, you are now in a growing relationship with God, Jesus Christ. Stay connected to His word, get connected in a true Bible-teaching church, get baptized, and pray often. This doesn't mean everything in your life will come easily now, but it will be fruitful, and your eyes will be opened. Just trust that with Jesus as Lord of your life, He has the best interest for you. You simply must obey as Simon (Peter) did. You never know what God's preparing you for. Remember, Simon (Peter) ended up becoming the person whom Jesus trusted to "build His church upon" (Matthew 16:15-18). God has given you the greatest playbook and instruction manual to equip you for every good work, the Holy Bible. Study it, believe it, live it out, and when He says launch out into the deep, no matter how strange it may seem, launch out into the deep. God bless.

Worship playlist: *"Whose Report Shall You Believe(Shout)" by Charity Gayle*

Peace in Chaos

When people think of a peaceful environment, many would probably envision an island paradise with clear skies, the sound of rhythmic waves crashing, and a nice breeze in the summer. Although this is a peaceful scenario, in reality, you can't run to such a place every time you're looking to escape from the chaos of everyday life. So, where is your hope? Where do you turn when your anger is rising, anxiety has trickled in, or nothing seems to be going right? Where is the "escape" button? Sheila Walsh once said, "peace is not the absence of trouble, it is the presence of Christ in the midst of that trouble." Today, you will see exactly how to harness the peace of God through Jesus.

Read 2 Peter 1:1-2

1. Based on Simon Peter's opening statement, what will allow believers to gain more peace?

....
....
....

Read Matthew 8:23-27

2. What were the disciples' reactions to the storm?

....
....
....

3. What was Jesus' reaction to the storm?

....
....

4. Based on what you read in 2 Peter 1:1-2, why do you think Jesus was able to respond in such a way?

....
....
....

5. How did Jesus react to the disciples?

6. Why should the disciples have had more faith in Jesus? What was His track record up until that point? (Read Matthew 8:1-16 for reference).

....
....
....

7. How could things have been different if the disciples trusted Jesus and had faith?

....
....
....

8. How did this encounter with Jesus change how the disciples saw Jesus? How did they respond to Jesus when He calmed the sea?

....
....
....

9. So, although the disciples failed at having faith, was the teachable moment still worthwhile for them? Explain. (Sidenote: As you can see, the disciples struggled with faith, and they were directly in front of Jesus, so if you ever find yourself struggling, don't beat yourself up, just keep turning to God).

....
....
....

Read John 16:31-33

10. What does Jesus warn His disciples about?

....
....

11. Why did Jesus warn them about this? (See John 14:27-30 and John 16:1-4 for further reference).

....

....

....

12. Where does Jesus say peace will come from? Will there be an absence of trials and warfare when this peace manifests?

....

....

....

....

....

Read Act 26:17 & Acts 27:24

13. What promises were made to Paul in each of these verses? (verse 17 & verse 24)

....

....

....

Read Acts 28:1-6

14. What did Paul do when the snake bit him?

....

....

....

15. Based on the two passages, Acts 26:17 and Acts 27:24, why do you think Paul so easily had peace even during such an occurrence of being shipwrecked and bitten by a poisonous snake?(See Acts 27:25 too)

....

....

July

16. *Based on these sections of scripture (there are many others), you have now seen that storms, trials, and even demons flee, and peace abounds at the presence and mention of Jesus coupled with great faith. Why should this be encouraging to every believer?*

Let's make it personal

Like Paul, has God promised anything specific to come to pass in your life? List them.

If not, and if you need more encouragement, read Jeremiah 29:11, Isaiah 43:15-21, and John 14:1-3.

What promises does God make to those who believe in Him and are saved?

Many people read those above scriptures and may instantly think God will bring about tangible means of prosperity, like a job promotion, a big house, or lots of money. Although God very well could do those things, that is not what your peace should be wrapped up in. Your peace should be in the fact that God is sovereign and has a plan for you, and He knows it from beginning to end. So, whether God has spoken a specific thing to you or not, trust that His word(scripture) does not return to Him void, and he will see them through, you must only have faith. Have peace knowing that God is sovereign and has your best interest at heart, and, until you've made it to that room in the Father's house in which Jesus has prepared for you, God's not done with you yet(Philippians 1:6). He's molding you, carrying you, caring for you, and equipping you for times to come. As you endure, learn of Him, and focus on Him, you will have a peace that surpasses all understanding even as storms rage. Keep getting to know Him, keep trusting Him, and find peace in any challenging situation you find yourself in because you know He is right there with you sleeping on the boat. Take time throughout the week to meditate on Matthew 10:28 and Psalm 91.

Worship playlist: *"No Weapon" by Fred Hammond*
"Shalom" by Laura Hackett Park
"No Weapon" by Scottie Wop

proverbs 3:5-7

Lean Not

Similar to toddlers who have just learned how to tie their shoes or who have learned how to put on their seatbelt and refuse assistance from that point on from their parents, I believe, as humans, we have this "I've got it! I don't need help" kind of mentality. That's cute for a toddler, but as teens, young adults, and full-grown adults, those tasks get more complex, yet we still can have that same "I've got it" mentality, when in actuality...we don't. There's a reason God told us to trust Him and not rely on our views or desired actions of things. However, we must be humble enough to accept that advice, relinquish control, and give in. If you're anything like me, this is hard to do, but thank God, He's given us His word and His Spirit to guide us hand-in-hand to that point.

Read Proverbs 3:5-8

1. Write down Proverbs 3:5-6.

....

....

....

> Selah Moment:
>
> Define "trust" and "acknowledge" (remember to look this up in Hebrew as you've learned)
>
> ....
>
> ....
>
> ....
>
> ....

2. What is the first command given in verse 5?

....

3. How do the remaining verses suggest that you follow that command?

....

....

....

Read Psalm 139:1-6 and Psalm 147:5

4. What attributes of God are mentioned?

5. Define "omniscient."

6. Between you or God, who is the omniscient one?

7. With such attributes of God, why is it important for you to follow the commands from Proverbs 3:5?

Read Proverbs 3:6 and Ephesians 3:14-20

8. If you follow through with the command of Proverbs 3:5-6a, what can you expect from God?

Read Proverbs 16:9

9. What does this piece of scripture mean? How does it relate to everything you've studied today?

To trust God is a great thing and can be tough to do as we can't physically see Him though people make idols to "display" Him. Although He is the invisible God, evidence of Him is seen and known through His actions, things working together, miracles, signs, wonders, a mother giving birth to a child, a caterpillar turning into a butterfly, so many things allow us to see this invisible God in whom we are to put our trust in. In addition to the things I've listed above, if we look at the character of God, we will also see Him and know why He's so trustworthy.

Let's make it personal: Part 1

Do you believe that God's heart towards you is good? That He desires good things for you and for you to prosper? Explain why or why not. (Use 1 Peter 5:7 and 2 Peter 3:9 to find some truth of God's character if you need it).

Fill-in-the-blank with what you think the outcome of these things would be:
God's heart for you + God's all-knowing and powerful nature + Your trust(submission) in Him =

Read Luke 11:9-13, Romans 5:6-11, and John 3:16

10. Describe the character of God. Why is He trustworthy?

To fully trust in the Lord, He must actually be Lord of your life. Have you made that decision yet? If not, did you know it's simply a decision followed by action?

Read Mark 1:15 and Romans 10:8-13

11. What's required to make Jesus Lord?

....

....

> Selah Moment:
>
> Have you done this? If not do you desire to?
>
> ....
>
> ....
>
> ....

If yes, I must warn you that choosing to follow Jesus does come with having to let go of things and embracing new things that may feel costly(Luke 14:25-33 & Mark 10:17-27), but I believe it is worth it in the end as no person or thing compares to the riches that are to come and the relationship with God you gain presently as well. Now, take this time to do just what Mark 1:15 and Romans 10:8-13 says, Repent of your sins, ask God for His Holy Spirit, and turn to God. Pray to confess to God that Jesus is Lord, giving Him full control of your life, and believe at the core of your being that God raised Him from the dead. Repent of your sins and turn to God. Want some more guidance and added depth to your prayer? Follow the model of Jesus in Luke 11:1-4.

If no(or not right now), I pray that the Lord would continue to reveal Himself to you and your will would align with His. In Jesus' name. Amen.

Let's make it personal: Part 2

What areas of your life are you holding onto and struggling with trusting God in?

....

....

....

....

Why do you have these trust issues in regards to God? (If you don't know, take the time to pray about it and wait for God to reveal it).

As people say, "write your ideas down in pencil." It's great for you to think ahead and make plans and want to do various things but leave room for God to move. If everything you just read in the scriptures is true (which it is), God knows everything, and He wants to see you succeed. You can rest assured that if you follow God, He will NOT lead you astray.

If Jesus is Lord over your life, you have given Him full permission to make changes and dictate your decisions. If He was an evil or selfish Lord this would not be a good thing, but that is not the character of God, thus that is not the character of the Lord of your life. Although it comes with sacrifices of your own, being under the Lordship of Jesus is the best and safest place you can be, so congratulations if you've declared Him as such! Remember, God gives good gifts (Matthew 7:9-14), He sent His Son to die for you, and He cares for you deeply. So, lean not on your own understanding, but lean on God, allow Him the room to change things (although it may hurt), and know that it's all for your good. Be encouraged.

Coloring activity: *Write an open and honest letter to God telling Him all of the things you are struggling to trust Him with. Be sure to pray for God to loosen your grip on those things and to reveal the things you're holding onto if you don't already know. If you're doing well with trusting God, write a letter of thanks to God for being so trustworthy and any other characteristic of His that you want to thank Him for.*

Worship playlist: *"Lean on You" by: Chandler Moore*
"Hope" by Bryan Terrell ft. Franchesca
"At The Altar" by ELEVATION RHYTHM, Tiffany Hudson, & Abbie Gamboa

Get Up!

In his great prophetic nature, Jesus warned us long ago that in this world, we would have trials! It's inevitable. Things happen, like getting laid off, a business deal falling through, depression, wounds from your childhood surfacing because someone mishandled you, experiencing death in the family, car accidents, having to deal with mean people, temptation to fall back into old sin issues, lacking confidence because people have said hurtful things or simply due to self-doubt, debilitating health ailments, or getting through the common cold or flu. The list could go on and on! However, the beauty of God is that He doesn't allow us to go through those things for us to stay down because of them. God does not have a vendetta against us when He allows us to go through. In fact, it's the opposite. It's in those trials that you can learn and grow. It's in those trials that you MUST lean on God and grow closer to Him. It's in those trials that we are faced with the choice: do I stay in this place or do I choose to get up? It's in those trials that Jesus has encouraged you to take heart, for He has overcome the world and thus invites you into victory over that trial if you'd choose to rely on Him and get up!

Today, you will peek into the lives of three people who were going through trials and were seemingly down and out. Pay attention to their problems, state of mind, and how God intervened. May you find hope and solace in how God inevitably (spoiler alert) helped them GET UP!

July

Read the following scriptures and answer the questions in the table about each one.

	Mark 10:46-52	John 5:1-15	Mark 5:21-24, 35-43
What was needed?			
What hindrances were present? (ie. negative people, thought patterns, circumstances, or obstacles)			
How did the person respond to the hindrances?			
What did Jesus say/do?			
How did the person respond to Jesus?			
What was the outcome?			

Let's make it personal

Which Biblical account above do you feel most connected to? Which one stands out most? Explain.

....
....
....
....

How can you apply what you learned from that account to your own life?

....
....
....
....

What are you in need of?

....
....
....
....

What hindrances are there in you receiving that need? What's hindering you from bringing this need before God?

....
....
....
....

What does God say about your situation? (Pray and look up scripture about your need and/or share what God has already revealed to you).

....
....
....

How have you been responding to what God says? Have you been retreating? Feel stuck? Have you gotten up yet?

What would it look like for you to get up? What will it require of you?

Like Bartimeus, the invalid, and Jarius, you have to get your eyes off of your ailment/struggle and hindrances, and instead, fix your eyes on Jesus and approach God boldly. To do that, you must block out the lies, the naysayers, and/or your lack of confidence, and ask in faith for what you need. So, get up, Jesus is calling and waiting on you. Use what you've got to get to Him.

Worship Playlist: *"Walk" by Darlene McCoy*
" He Has Time" by Common Hymnal ft. Jamie MacDonald

July

You be You, Let God be God

When you've given your life to Christ, He becomes both Lord and Savior. We often focus highly on the Savior portion of Jesus' role, you know...the fact that He's saved your soul from eternal death (Hell) and separation from God. However, we neglect to consistently recognize and submit to the fact that He is also Lord (Acts 2:36). In my home country, America, we don't have much experience with 'Lordship" because we are under a democratic political system. However, our neighbors across the pond in the United Kingdom (UK) would probably be better at understanding Lordship because they are still under a constitutional monarchy having kings and queens as rulers. For others who may not know or have experience with it either, lordship simply means supreme power or rule." Thus, if Jesus truly is Lord over your life, God can tell you what to do, when to do it, and how to do it, and no matter what "it" is, you have vowed to obey. Such submission and obedience are vital, but it seems foreign to many, and therefore, many run from it. However, it is through such submission that your life is made simpler as you allow God to be God, and you play your part by staying in your lane as son/daughter. What does that lane look like? Let's peek into God's word and find out.

Read and reflect on Psalm 139:1-10, Job 9:4-10, Matthew 6:26-30, and Ephesians 3:20

1. List the various characteristics of God you notice in the table below

	Isaiah 9:6	Psalm 139:1-10	Job 9:4-10	Matthew 6:26-30	Ephesians 3:20
Characteristics of God you notice					

Let's make it personal: Part 1

Based on the lists you created above, why is it a good thing for Jesus (God) to be Lord over your life?

....
....
....
....
....
....

As a human, especially in this day and age of go-getters, striving to climb corporate or status-driven ladders towards success or simply making things happen for yourself, it is easy to lose sight of God and turn to rely on yourself. In the event of this occurring, you not only lose sight of God, but you also inadvertently put yourself on the throne and become our own "god."

Whether in big ways or small, how have you tried to be your own god (not trusting God and going rogue, or not staying in your lane)?

....
....
....

Read and reflect on Proverbs 3:5-6, Matthew 6:31-34, Hebrews 11:6, Mark 12:28-34, and Philippians 4:6

2. *What does the word of God tell you about what you are to do to "stay in your lane"? (Hint: What commands are given?)*

	Proverbs 3:5-6	Matthew 6:31-34	Hebrews 11:6	Mark 12:28-31	Philippians 4:6
I will stay in my lane by...					

Let's make it personal: Part 2

Using your answers from above, practically, what can you do to stay in your lane as a follower of Christ?

....
....
....
....
....
....

In closing, read 1 Thessalonians 5:16-18 (NIV) and fill-in-the-blanks. Be encouraged that you serve a God who is near to you, loves you, and wants to provide for your every need! Let Him rule and you stay in your lane as you follow these instructions:

"............................ always, ... continually, ... thanks in all circumstances; for this is God's .... for you in Christ Jesus."

1 Thessalonians 5:16-18 (NIV)

Worship Playlist: *"Wait For U" by Bryan Terrell*
"Yes & No" by David Dunn

August

Order over Chaos

Fun fact: Did you know there's such a thing as your Circadian Rhythm? It's an internal clock that cycles every 24 hours, helping to tell your body when to sleep, wake up, eat, etc. When traveling from one country to the next, you change time zones, which often gives you jetlag. Some believe that "grounding" (walking on the ground/grassy areas of your new destination) will help combat said jetlag and help you adjust to your new environment and reset your Circadian Rhythm (Down to Earth, 2020). God created your body to operate in conjunction with time! It's as though He's a God of order or something!(;

Have you ever heard the saying, "time is money?" If not, this saying perfectly illustrates that time has great value! Once time has passed, you cannot get it back! This concept of time is crucial to life, and throughout the growth of humanity, it is one concept that has remained and evolved in its form of keeping track of it! From watching the sun's shadow to using thousand-dollar watches, time is a vital commodity to the structure of our lives. Just think about it, what would life be like if we couldn't tell time. Need help with that visual?

Think about the answer to these questions: Without being able to tell time, how would farmers know when to plant certain seeds? How would a working man/woman know when the next train was coming in New York? How would students know when their next class was? How would one be able to tell when to take the casserole out of the oven? You see, time keeps things in order.

If keeping up with the time is so important for daily activities, how much more important is it for you to keep up with the time you are in for your life, aka "seasons," as mentioned in 1 Chronicles 12:32. When we look at the scriptures, God Himself acknowledges the importance of time and is the best at using it wisely. Let's learn from the Master of time and order.

Read Genesis 1-2, Jeremiah 1:5, and Jeremiah 29:10-11

1. Describe God's orderliness. Does God do things haphazardly, poorly, or on a whim? Explain.

....

....

....

....

....

....

....

Being that Jesus is God in the flesh (Exodus 3:14 & John 8:58), one can expect that He would have these same characteristics of orderliness that God (the Father) in the Old Testament has.

Read John 2:1-4, John 12:23, John 14:28-29, and John 16:7-12

2. Based on Jesus' responses, how do you see that He is truly a God of order?

....
....
....
....
....
....

So, if God, your Creator, the one whom you are made in the image of, is a God of order and time, don't you think you should also value it and be able to utilize it properly? Your ability to tell time and use of it is vital to not only your life but the lives of those God has assigned to your life! I'm not just talking about the time on the clock, but the times of your life. In the scriptures, this is known as "seasons."

Read Ecclesiastes 3:1-8

3. Through the verses, how do you see God articulating the idea of time (seasons) and order?

....
....
....

Sidenote: If your life is currently on the tougher side of things, remember that trouble doesn't last always. If you're on the "better" side of things, hold onto it, treasure it, and store it up for encouragement when you do go through the opposite. For, as you can see, there is an appointed time for everything.

Read 1 Chronicles 12:32

4. What gift did the men of Issachar have?

....

> **Selah Moment**
>
> Why was this gift important for David's army?
>
> ....
>
> ....
>
> ....

Read Esther 3:8-13, Esther 4:6-14, and Esther 8:3-8

5. Why was it important for Esther to understand the times and what season she was in? (For example, Why was it essential for Esther to understand her purpose during that time in history?)

....

....

....

....

....

Read Hebrews 9:27-28, Matthew 24:36-44, Matthew 25:1-13, Luke 12:35-40, and 2 Peter 3:9

6. Similar to Esther, why is it important that you pay attention to the times?

....

....

....

Let's make it personal: Part 1

Do you see why it's vital to use your time wisely and discern the seasons?

Have you repented and accepted Jesus into your life? If not, do you want to? OR Do you know a friend that hasn't? The decision to repent and follow Jesus is simply a matter of deciding to leave your old life behind and trade it for a new one with Jesus at the center as Lord and Savior. This does not mean that in this new life, everything will be dandy and sweet. However, it does mean that you'll have a confidant in the Holy Spirit (who is the greatest Helper of all time) readily available and accessible for guidance, discipline, and support. How can you gain such access? With sincerity in your heart, admitting you're a sinner in need of saving, believing that Jesus was sent into this world to die for your sins, rose from the dead after three days of being buried, and confessing with your lips that Jesus is Lord(rules supreme over your life), by this you shall be saved! There are no particular words to pray that prayer; it truly is based on the sincerity of your heart towards God. But if you'd like an example prayer, pray the following:

> *Father God, you said to remain watchful and I can see that I have done what is evil in your sight, but today I choose to give over all of those things to you. I repent and give you _____ (insert the various things you're repenting of). I no longer want those things because they are filthy and fall short of your standard of me. Thank you, God, for sending me Jesus and for loving me enough to allow Him to suffer on my behalf for my sins on the cross. I believe that not only was Jesus sacrificed for me, but He rose from the dead so that I may be able to defeat sin and death too. Father God, I confess that I need you as Lord over my life. I welcome your Holy Spirit into my life, and I need you to lead and guide me towards your truth. I need you to bring ultimate order and peace into my life. In Jesus' name, I pray, Amen!!!*

If you prayed that prayer (and/or added in your own words to God, according to the scriptures), you are SAVED!! Hallelujah! This is only the beginning, there's so much to come; a new understanding of God, yourself, others, and the world at large. So much is in store for you as you live out the purposes of God. Please also know your new-found (or reinvigorated) faith must be accompanied by actions that follow! No worries, you won't be alone, the Holy Spirit, the word of God, and the community of people God will put you around, will help you along the way. Feel free to send this section of today's devotional to a friend who needs to hear the gospel or needs another opportunity to hear and believe. Remember, our lives are short. In the next section of this week's devotional, you'll see exactly why sharing this portion of the devotional is so vital.

Read Matthew 28:19-20

7. Like Esther, how can you help to save people?

....

....

....

Read Matthew 25:41, 46, and Luke 16:19-31

8. What are you helping save people from by making disciples?

....

Read Acts 1:6-8, John 16:12-15, Matthew 24:1-14, and Luke 16:29-31

9. Although you cannot know the exact hour of the happenings of God, what gift has God given you to help you discern and tell time?

....

....

....

Read James 4:7-8, Philippians 4:6-9, and Psalm 119:9

10. How can you assure that your life has order? What are things you can do to cultivate God-given order in your life?

....

....

Read 1 Corinthians 14:33

11. What are ways you can identify if a decision you're making is in order and aligns with God?

....

Let's make it personal: Part 2

Why is it essential for your life to be in order with God? How can this impact others?

....

....

....

....

....

....

August

In your personal life, do you know what time it is? Do you know what season of life you're in? If not, take time to ask God to reveal and refer back to Ecclesiates 3:1-8. Explain.

(Note: If you don't have an answer right now, we are always in a season of waiting for the Lord's return, so you can start there).

....
....
....
....
....

Why is it important that you know this?

....
....
....

Knowing the season you're in, what areas of your life do you need more order in?

....
....
....
....
....
....

If you're ever tempted to take things into your own hands because things are moving slowly or you feel like you can do it all by yourself, don't. Keep trusting God and waiting patiently; there's a time/season for everything! Let God bring order to your life by seeking Him and allowing Him to align you with His will. Feel like your world is chaotic, stressful, and in disarray? Stop and pray! May no anxious thought consume you, in Jesus' name! Remember, God is a God of order, thus chaos cannot be of nor from Him.

Being that God does things in good and proper order, if you're waiting on something, ask Him to bring to remembrance if He's already given you instruction that you haven't followed. Upon remembrance, do the last thing He told you and wait for the next steps. For if you have not done step one and two, how can a God of order give you step three? He can't and won't.

Can't think of the last thing God told you to do? Feel like God doesn't speak to you? First off, that's not true, although He is silent sometimes for various reasons, God does speak to you. Ask Him for ears to hear, eyes to see, and for distractions to be removed. In the meantime, we can all fix our minds on fulfilling the two greatest commandments and the last command of Jesus to His disciples:

"But when the Pharisees heard that he had silenced the Sadducees with his reply, they met together to question him again. One of them, an expert in religious law, tried to trap him with this question: "Teacher, which is the most important commandment in the law of Moses?" Jesus replied, "'You must love the Lord your God with all your heart, all your soul, and all your mind.' This is the first and greatest commandment. A second is equally important: 'Love your neighbor as yourself.' The entire law and all the demands of the prophets are based on these two commandments." Matthew 22:34-40

"Therefore, go and make disciples of all the nations, baptizing them in the name of the Father and the Son and the Holy Spirit. Teach these new disciples to obey all the commands I have given you. And be sure of this: I am with you always, even to the end of the age." Matthew 28:19-20

So all in all, time and order are very important, especially knowing that Jesus is coming back! Prepare accordingly and help others too.

Worship playlist: *"Order My Steps" by The Brooklyn Tabernacle Choir*

ANYBODY CAN START, IT TAKES TENACITY TO FINISH

—Philip A. Mitchell

Run the Race

It's a given; Christians do not mesh with the world we live in! As Paul says in 1 Peter 2:11, we (Christians) are just sojourners in this world; we are merely passing through and thus we should not live like those of this world. This world is not our home, and in fact, it is only a pit stop on our journey to our true home, and we should not get comfortable here. Our true home is in Heaven with our Heavenly Father in one of His many mansions in which Jesus has preceded us and prepared a place for us (John 14:2) to reside. Being that God chose to snatch us out of our old ways of living, we must hold fast to this gift we have gained in Christ, for we all once were living in this world as though this was our home. In order to stay set apart, we must seek God wholeheartedly as we journey down this narrow path of righteousness. Will it be easy? Absolutely not, but let's look into the word of God for some hope to help us endure.

1. Define "tenacity."

....

....

2. What do you think it takes to be tenacious?

....

....

....

Read 1 Corinthians 9:22-27, 1 Peter 5:10, and Hebrews 9:28

3. What race is Paul talking about?

....

....

....

Read Revelation 12:12, John 16:33, 1 Peter 5:8-9, Matthew 7:13-14, Matthew 26:41

4. Why do you think it would take tenacity to finish the race? Why isn't it easy?

....

....

....

Read Romans 10:12, John 2:4-5, Matthew 7:21-23, and John 3:1-15

5. In 1 Corinthians 9:24, Paul mentions runners winning a prize. Will there only be one winner in this race? Will everyone in the world "win"?

....
....
....

Read Revelation 3:10-12, Romans 6:23 and 1 Corinthians 15:51-58

6. In 1 Corinthians 9:25, Paul mentions a reward being up for grabs. What is that reward?

....
....
....

Refer to other passages from this week and Read Matthew 26:40-41, Psalm 51:1-4, Hebrews 12:1-6, James 1:21-25, and John 13:34-35

7. How can you make sure you are running with purpose and don't miss the mark?

....
....
....
....

Read 2 Corinthians 10:5, Romans 12:1-3, Psalm 139:23-24, and John 4:23-24.

8. Lastly, how can you make sure you are not only physically doing the works of God(like those mentioned in Matthew 7:21-23) but that you are mentally and spiritually set on Him as well?

....
....
....
....
....

Read Philippians 1:6, Matthew 28:20, 2 Corinthians 12:9, Acts 1:8, and Isaiah 41:10

9. Who's always with you? Who can you rely on when you're feeling weak and like you can't go on?

....

Read and write Galatians 6:9-10

10. ....

....

If you're running this race with Jesus (no matter how long it's been), let me be the first to tell you I AM SO PROUD OF YOU and I know God is too! It's not easy to go against the grain of society & Satan. At times it's very hard to endure. Yet, by God's grace, I know you will make it through and win in the end. If you're tired of running, pause here and pray. Tell God everything you're feeling and going through. Ask Him for the strength you need to endure. Also share these things with a trustworthy and believing friend (Galatians 6:1-2) as you can't do this life alone. Use the LMIP section below to help you process your thoughts.

Let's make it personal:

What is the hardest part of running the race(following Jesus) for you in this season of your life? (i.e., praying, repenting, reading your Bible, being in community, not giving into temptation, loving others well, evangelizing, etc.) Explain.

....
....
....
....
....
....

What community (other people who are followers of Christ) do you have around you to run with? If you don't have any, pray for God to send you some and to point you in the direction of a church to be a part of. These people are important, see Galatians 6:1-10 again and Acts 2!.

....
....
....

What assignments has God given you that you need to complete? How well have you been doing at getting those things accomplished?

....
....
....
....
....
....

God is working on your behalf (Philippians 1:6), but you have to keep your hand to the plow and not look back (Luke 9:62). Remember, you're not running this race alone, you have other brothers and sisters going through the same struggles of living a holy and set apart life in the midst of darkness and temptations(1 Peter 5:9). By keeping your eyes on the prize and running alongside your other brothers and sisters in Christ, you will make it! Endure! Be tenacious in your pursuit of Jesus! And as you run, know that God is keeping your faith, giving you hope in Him, and noting your obedience and love for Him (Hebrews 3:6). I leave you with this: THEREFORE BRETHEREN BE STEADFAST, IMMOVABLE, ALWAYS ABOUNDING IN THE WORK OF THE LORD, KNOWING THAT YOUR LABOR IS NOT IN VAIN IN THE LORD."
-1 Corinthians 15:58

Worship playlist: *"My Revival" by: Lauren Daigle*
"I Will Be Undignified" by Rend Collective

The Love of God

No fancy intro today, as the scripture speaks for itself. God's love is unmatched when you look at how big His love is and yet how small our faithfulness to Him can be. I've noticed that it's been in the times of me messing up big time that I've seen the kindness and love of God most as He helps me out of the mess graciously or simply does something kind towards me afterwards(Romans 5:20-6:1). When you're able to know His love amongst chaos and surrender to Him in response, that's success(Romans 2:4). God's love is life-changing. Before you get started with today's journal entry, pray and reflect on Jeremiah 31:1-6. Get interactive with God's word via scripture dissection.

Using three different colors, trace the boxes, circles, and squiggly lines (assign one color for each shape).

Color	Part of Speech
	Nouns/Pronouns (words that are circled in the activity)
	Verbs (words that are boxed in the activity)
	Adjectives/Nouns that are describing (squiggly underlined words in the activity)

As you do so, reflect on each portion. What stands out? What revelation has God given you as you read?

....
....
....
....
....
....

Let's dig deeper into this verse.

Read Jeremiah 31:1-14

1. Who is speaking? Who is "I?"

....

....

2. Who is the audience of the text? (focus on verse 1)

....

....

Selah Moment:

Read Deuteronomy 7:6-11 (focus on verse 6)

What verb is used to describe what God did for the people of Israel?

....

Read Matthew 22:13-14 and 1 Peter 2:9

What verb is used to describe people who follow Jesus, God's elect?

....

Take a moment to think and reflect on those verses, what was Israel chosen for? What are you chosen for? What's the point in being chosen?

....

....

Due to your faith in Christ, God has reappointed you as a son/daughter(Galatians 3:29), able to receive the promises of God like that of Israel. Therefore, when you read in the Old Testament about what God promises, felt, or did for the Israelites, know that those sentiments and words can be mirrored in your life as He calls you the same name, "chosen." So, re-read Jeremiah 31:3, but this time, read it knowing that those very words apply to you as one of God's chosen ones. Lastly, I do want to be clear, our(the Church) state of being chosen doesn't replace the Jews, they will still inherit the promises of God upon their surrender to Jesus, but it does mean we have been "grafted" into the family. For more evidence of this, read Romans 3:29, Romans 10:12, and especially Romans 11:1-31.

3. "Love" in this verse is "ahabah" in Hebrew. Define "ahabah."

....

....

4. Define "everlasting" in English and "olam" in Hebrew.

....

....

If God's love is everlasting, nothing can change God's love for you. Therefore, which word below best describes this kind of love? Circle one.

CONDITIONAL   OR   UNCONDITIONAL

5. Define "drawn" in context of the scripture.

....

6. Why has God drawn His people? What is/was God's motivation for drawing in His people?

....

....

....

Selah moment:

Read Romans 5:8

How has God shown his love for believers and unbelievers?

....

....

....

---

7. Define "lovingkindness."

....

....

Read Jeremiah 31:3 and compare it to all of Jeremiah 31:1-14

8. Why does God promise for verses 4-14 to happen? (Focus on verse 3)

....
....
....
....
....
....

Let's make it personal

What character traits of God did you see in today's reading? Do you struggle with believing/seeing those traits played out in your own life?

....
....
....
....
....
....

In your own words, what does Jeremiah 31:3 say about the relationship between God and His chosen people? Are you included in the group mentioned?

....
....
....
....
....

Are you feeling unloveable? Do you feel like you've let God down recently or that something you've done is unredeemable? Read Jeremiah 3:12-14 for encouragement. Remember, there's no condemnation for those that love the Lord, so even when you make mistakes, recall to memory that God, the Creator of the heavens and the earth, cares deeply about you and has affection towards you. He is also rich in mercy and will draw you in with his lovingkindness. Hopefully, you are encouraged by today's section of scripture! Be sure to utilize "scripture dissection" in your future study time!

Coloring activity: *Add your notes from #3, 4, 5, and 7, to the dissection sheet underneath the proper word.*

Worship Playlist: *"Reckless Love" by Cory Asbury ft. Tori Kelly*
"Out of Hiding" by Steffany Gretzinger

Crafty with Purpose

Have you ever thought about how certain things were invented, like wifi, the lightbulb, apps, music, or a doorknob? Whether you've given it conscious thought or not, when you interact with any of these things, you are experiencing the results of creativity turning into craftsmanship.

In 2020, the world went through a crazy time period of being quarantined and socially distanced due to the rapid spread of a disease called COVID-19, causing life as everyone knew it to be shifted as places couldn't have more than 10-50 people gathered at once, schools were closed down, and when near people, you'd have to stand 6 feet apart. It was crazy! Rather than crumble, parents, teachers, leaders, business owners, and pastors had to get very creative to keep things flowing. Through putting that creative ability to use and having great discipline during that season of life, many were able to walk out of that season of quarantine with new and improved ways of doing things to enhance business and life in general. This is an excellent example of craftsmanship. That's also the story of how one of the first major online streaming platforms for churches began at Life Church (the creators of the popular Bible app) in years past. So, as Beth Moore said, "creativity turns into craftsmanship through discipline." Let's see how this relates to God and you.

1. Define "creativity."

....
....
....

2. Define "craftsmanship."

....
....
....

3. Define "discipline."

....
....

Read 1 Samuel 13:11-14, 1 Samuel 16:10-23 and 1 Samuel 18:1-16.

4. Who is David? Describe him.

....
....
....

Read 1 Samuel 17:4-16

5. Who is Goliath? Describe him. Was he described as a champion or loser?

....
....
....

6. What does Goliath say to the Israelites?

....
....
....

7. What were Goliath and the Philistine's scare tactics?

....
....
....

This was an unconventional encounter, so it would require some unconventional methods: creativity.

8. Did the Philistines' scare tactics/crafty scheme work on the Israelites? How long did Goliath wait for the Israelites to send someone who would fight him? How often did he parade in front of them, taunting them? (verse 16)

....

Read 1 Samuel 17:12-15

9. Although described as a warrior in chapter 16, was David a part of Saul's army? What was his role?

....

Read 1 Samuel 17: 26-58

10. What was David's attitude towards Goliath? Did he feel the same way the other Israelites did?

....

....

....

11. Despite his brother's prideful comment, what did David decide to do?

....

....

....

12. Why was David confident that he could beat Goliath?

....

....

....

13. As David was going up against Goliath, did he do anything different than what he knew? What was the result of the fight?

....

....

14. How do you see David's creativity? What tools did he use?

....

....

....

15. How do you see David's discipline?

....
....
....
....
....

16. What type of craftmanship was developed and used in David's life? (Also see 1 Samuel 13:14 and 1 Samuel 16:14-23)

....
....
....

17. If David hadn't been disciplined in the skills and ways God was growing him in, how might the ending of the biblical accounts with Saul's torment and Goliath being defeated be different? What would have happened if David wasn't skilled (having craftsmanship) in the areas you mentioned above?

....
....
....
....
....

18. Finally, based on David's words, who did he give the glory to? Was it himself and all of his hard work, stature, or abilities?

....
....
....

For David to kill bears, lions, and beasts of nature, he had to get creative with his tools. His shepherd's staff wasn't enough. So, he used stones and a slingshot. Through consistently using this creative invention, it was no longer just a nifty gadget or doohickey, it was a tool of superb craftsmanship which, when coupled with the craftsmanship of David's faith and intimacy developed over time, was all perfected so much that he was able to use it with great precision and confidence in God to slay Goliath. God is a genius, be sure to ask Him what He wants to cultivate through you (spoiler alert: one thing He wants for all of us is a heart that longs for Him, trusts, and obeys Him as David did).

Let's make it personal

How is your faith in God and your overall relationship with Him? Are you like David or Saul's soldiers in the face of trouble? Explain and then pray accordingly.

....
....
....
....

What gift (ability, whether spiritual [Romans 12:4-8 and 1 Corinthians 12:4-11] or physical [things you're naturally good at or have an eye for]) has God given you?

....
....
....
....
....

How disciplined have you been at perfecting it? If you haven't been disciplined in using and perfecting this gift, what are some changes you need to make in your life to be more disciplined?

....
....
....
....
....

Are others able to benefit from the gift God has given you? Has it developed into a skill that is used? How can/does God get the glory from you utilizing the gift?

....
....
....

Is sharing the gospel a skill/craft of yours, or is it still in the baby stages of being creatively intertwined into your life? How can you use your gift to share the gospel?

....
....
....
....
....
....

Using the gifts God has given you to push forward the gospel and defeat our enemy (Satan) is vital, and it takes discipline and practice. Through discipline, practice, and intimacy with God, you can get from one end of the spectrum to the other of creativity to craftsmanship. At this moment, pray for increased faith, awarenessof the gifts God has given you and the presence of God. Ask God to be your shepherd directing you to the places, people, and mindsets you need as you grow. Ask Him for His Spirit and the discipline, strength, courage, tenacity, and grit to persevere beyond the limitations and intimidations the enemy would use and try to set against you. God will be faithful to give those things to you, just as He did for David. In Jesus' name! As you die to your flesh(sinful and human desires) and allow the Lord to consume you with His Spirit, you will see God move dynamically as He did for David and thus Israel as a whole in the end.

If you desire to grow in the area of developing the craftmanship of sharing the gospel, see Appendix E at the back of this book for tips and practical application. I'd also like to recommend the following other books to help in this area as well:

"Just Walk Across the Room" by Bill Hybels
"How to Tell the Truth: The Story of How God Saved Me to Win Hearts--Not Just Arguments" by Preston Perry

Worship Playlist: *"Good Shepherd" by Esmeralda Violeta*
"Go Tell It On The Mountain" by Annatoria

Time of Reflection: Part 2

*R*eflect on the past four months of life, then honestly and vulnerably answer the following questions. If you need more lines, use the "additional pages" in the back of this journal!

What are some memorable or important things that have happened in the past 4 months (these can be good or bad, happy, sad, or anyhwere in between)?

....
....
....
....
....
....
....
....
....
....

What have you been doing well? What do you want to celebrate? What has brought you joy?

....
....
....
....
....
....
....
....
....
....

As you reflect, what main emotions have you felt in the past four months?

....
....
....
....
....

What have you not been doing so well? What are you struggling with? Do you have any fears? Has anything been painful to endure? How do you need help?

....
....
....
....
....
....
....
....
....
....

How is your relationship with God? Use the questions below to help you explain.

- *How have you been seeking after Him? Do you think you've "found Him"?(Jeremiah 29:13) How so or not?*
- *Have you felt connected to Him? How so or not?*
- *Are you disappointed or angry with Him? Are you feeling grateful for Him? Do you believe you can trust Him? etc. Take this time to celebrate with Him in the areas you have felt grateful in. Be sure to slow down as you answer these questions and ask the Lord to ease your heart and help you work through any tough areas. Ask Him for His perspective of situations you've experienced and ask Him to show you how He sees you as you've endured. Wait to hear His reply.*

    If you need to process some tough emotions or moments, here's a grief cycle model I've followed, you can shorten or change it as you need(timeframe: 1-7 days, depends on you): cry(express emotion) > pray vulnerably (verbally and/or written) > cry > hear God (be still to listen) > share (tell a trusted and prayerful friend what you're going through) > hear God (be still to listen) > cry > accept what God said > pray (release the situation) > cry > sing praises & thank God as you move on (Psalm 30:1-5)

What deep desires do you have in life right now? How have you seen inklings or ways of them being fulfilled? Do you think they haven't been fulfilled at all? Explain.

(Note: Only God can satisfy our deepest longings, so be sure to take note of how He's bringing fulfillment even if you don't see the physical manifestation of your desires as you imagined. If you don't see Him doing so, take this time to pray vulnerably expressing that, ask Him to open your eyes to see all He is doing, and surrender your desires to Him.)

What goals do you have? How are you taking responsibility to reach them?

....
....
....
....
....
....
....
....
....

How do you feel best supported and cared for by friends and family? On a rate of 1-10, how supported and cared for have you felt by them? Explain.

....
....
....
....
....
....
....
....
....
....
....
....

What God-approved things do you enjoy doing? How often have you been participating in them? How have those moments been for you?

> *Note: "God-approved" does not just mean going to church or to church events. It means things that are not against His commands. God also values rest and enjoying life while maintaining our righteousness in Christ, see Ecclesiastes 8, so be sure to take time to just enjoy life with Him.*

....
....
....
....

If you could change one thing about your life right now, what would it be? Why?

> *Suggestion: Pray and ask God about this thing. Ask Him for the revelation of why you want it, ask if it's a pure desire to have, and the provision if it's in God's will. Ask God to search your heart and show you the root of your desire.*

What areas of growth do you want to see happen within yourself over the course of the next four months?

Now, take a look at your first time of reflection from April and take mental note of the changes you see, the trends you notice, and how you are motivated to press on and forward in these next few months.

September

Plans, Plans, Plans!

For some people, making plans brings about a sense of security. From to-do lists to full-blown minute by minute schedules, planning things out brings about a sense of order for many. Today, you will begin to look at how God sees planning and what He values most that should be on your calendar. Let's take a look!

Read Ecclesiastes 1:1-2 and Ecclesiastes 12:13-14 (AMP)

1a. Compare and contrast the words of King Solomon in both of the passages. What does he say is meaningless? What does he say is meaningful? (Suggestion: Take a month to Study the book of Ecclesiastes)

....
....
....

1b. What is the end resolve? What should we be watchful of in life?

....
....

Read James 4:13-17

2. What does James say about your life? What does he mean by it?

....
....
....

3. What does James offer as the proper way to make plans?

....
....
....

4. What do you think both King Solomon and James would agree on?

....

Read 2 Corinthians 4:16-18

5. How do Paul's words bring the topics mentioned by King Solomon and James together? What's the main idea?

....

....

....

Read 1 Corinthians 3:10-15, Matthew 6, Matthew 22:36-40, Matthew 25:31-40, Luke 10:38-42, and John 13:3-17

6. What actions do Jesus warn against?

....

....

....

7. What type of actions matter and are considered eternal and will last?

....

....

....

Read Proverbs 3:5-6, Proverbs 16:3, Psalm 37:5, 1 Corinthians 3:10-15, and James 4:13-17

8. What's a guaranteed way to know your plans will be successful?

....

....

....

Selah Moment:

Pause here and pray a prayer of surrender, committing all of your ways and plans to Jesus. These plans could be anything from your travel plans, choosing a college, starting a business, marriage, or any other big or small life decisions; it all matters and God wants to be included in it, so it's best to give it over to Him. If you're anything like me, be sure to repent for any ways you've pridefully taken your life into your own hands and made plans without God. Feel free to write your prayer below or simply say it to the Lord.

....
....
....
....
....
....

Read this portion of "Only One Life, Twill Soon Be Past" by C.T. Studd, a global missionary.

> "Only one life, 'twill soon be past,
> Only what's done for Christ will last.
> And when I am dying, how happy I'll be,
> If the lamp of my life has been burned out for Thee."
> — C.T. Studd

9. Based on the above scriptures and the poem above by C.T. Studd, why is it best that you follow God's plans for your life? What is God most focused on regarding how you live?

....
....
....
....
....

Read 1 Chronicles 28:2-7, 1 Kings 8:12-21, and Psalm 127:1-2

10. Why is it always important to have an intimate relationship with God and talk to Him about all plans you have?

....

September

....

....

Let's make it personal:

Although you may already know, with these next two activities, you will be able to get a glimpse of whether you have an eternal mindset or temporal mindset. Be completely honest with yourself when answering the various questions; this is YOUR journal; no need to put up a facade.

Activity #1-

List the important things you've done in the past, plans you have presently, and what you do regularly:

	PAST	DAILY (Present)	PLANS/DESIRES (Future)
List various things you've done/accomplished/learned and desire for the future.			
#1: How much of the things you listed above can rot, be stolen, or come to an end?			
#2: How has God gotten (or will get) the glory from the things you listed? How is He on display?			
#3: Who/what was/is the purpose and motivation to accomplish it?			
#4: Who benefits from the success of the things you listed?			
#5: Did you talk to God about the things you listed?			

Activity #2-

Be completely honest with yourself and complete the following questionnaire by circling one answer per row that best sounds most like you.

Mainly focused on what's in front of you and feels good	Focused on the future and what's right
Prefer physical blessings from God	Prefer intimacy with God
Majority of your daily activities focus on God and the gospel in some way	Majority of your daily activities focus on worldly things
Working on things you want to do with no regard of others or God	Working on things God has called you to even if it's not what you prefer
Focus more on appearance and possessions	Focus more on someone's soul and heart
Use your gifts to benefit others	Use your gifts to benefit you
Rarely ever help those in need	Intentional about helping those in need

Comparing your answers to the key in the back of your journal, how many eternally (Heavenly) focused answers (outlined statements in the key) do you have circled versus the temporal (Earthly) focused statements (non-outlined statements in the key)?

_____eternal   _____temporal

*Note: Temporal things are NOT bad (doing makeup, chilling, making money, etc.)! The danger is when there are significantly more things you're doing that are temporal and have no eternal value than what does, especially if it's sin. Also, note that going to church and praying all day isn't all that is eternal. Spending quality time with family, being in community, and doing a service project have an eternal reward as well. As a good rule of thumb, check your purpose(motive and intention at the deepest and most honest level) of doing _____ (insert action), as that's one way you can tell if it has eternal or temporal value.

Take inventory of your answers in both activities: If most of your answers are centered around you and leave no room for God or others, nine times out of ten, you have a temporal mindset in accomplishing the "purpose" for your life.

- *What adjustments do you notice you need to make in order to have an eternal mindset and motives behind what you do? How can you get Jesus at the center? If you're doing well with having an eternal mindset, what have you been doing that you should continue?*

Do you see a need for a new balance? What things need to change for you to have more of an eternal mindset?

Based on your responses, take this time to pray to ask God to make you more sensitive to His Holy Spirit and increase your eternal/Kingdom-mindedness today. If you live a life with eternity in mind, ask God to draw you nearer to Himself and to lead and to guide you towards the plans He has for you. May you live a life of great meaning, a life on a mission of eternal meaning. If most of your life is centered around things that will pass away, you're living a meaningless life. Remember to ask yourself, "why am I doing this?" if the answer doesn't have eternal value, if it doesn't have Jesus at the foundation, if it's daily functions go against God, or if you haven't consulted God about it, stop, pray, and rethink the decision. Ask the Lord how He wants you to do things, how you can get it to have eternal value, and ask if He wants you to do it at all. Life is so short, and days go by quickly. For greatest impact on earth and the best eternal rewards in Heaven(1 Corinthians 3:10-15), make eternity-minded decisions.

Worship Playlist: *"Lace Up Your Boots" by Circuit Rider Music, Eniola Abioye, & Black Voices*
"We Make Space - Live" by Melissa Helser
"Follow?" by Chinonso Ude ft. Amarachi Ude

Broken Jars

Humans are ever-changing, on the go, and ambitious beings formed in the image of God. However, one thing about humans that many of us would hate to admit is that we are fragile. Our minds can't carry the weight of too many burdens, we are needy, and our emotions fluctuate depending on the circumstance; it's how we were wired. No matter where you are on the spectrum of those things, nine times out of ten, you can relate somehow. If you can't, you can definitely relate to this one: humans are innately sinful! It's a fact, we were born into it, and there's no getting around it. If you are a human, sin runs in your veins (Romans 3:23).

However, despite all of these flaws, shortcomings, and our fragility, God chose long ago to use humans to carry one of the most precious gifts and use us in His grand plan of restoring us and the world to the immaculate beauty it once was in the Garden. Why in the world would He do that? What in the world is that gift? If we're so "fragile," is there a way for us humans to be "fixed?"

Let's find out.

1. Define "mend."

....

Read Psalm 147:2-5

2. What do you notice about the human condition of the Israelites in these verses?

....

....

....

3. What do you notice about God's abilities?

....

....

....

Selah Moment:

At a deep and most honest level, do you believe this about God?

Based on how you live/behave will expose the truth of this answer(ie if you really believe God knows everything, you will live a life of trusting Him more easily). Pause here to ask God to open your eyes to see Him rightly.

....
....
....
....
....
....

Read Isaiah 61:1-7

4. After reading, find at least four examples of brokenness and how God promises to mend it.

	Brokenness	**Mended**
Isaiah 61:1	People were captives	They would have freedom

As you can see, God has immense power to redeem and restore. He mends and turns what was into what is and should be.

Brokenness is not a limitation or impossible obstacle for God. Let's look at some other people who were broken and see how God responded.

Read 2 Corinthians 12:6-10

5. What's a thorn?

6. Why did God allow Satan to give Paul a "thorn in his flesh?" Why didn't God just take it away?

7. Why does God allow you to have weaknesses even though you are saved?

8. Based on Paul's example, rather than beating ourselves up about our weaknesses, imperfections, and brokenness, what should we do instead?

Read Matthew 21:28-32

9. Who does Jesus say will enter the kingdom of heaven? Why?

10. Read the scriptures mentioned and fill in the table

	Describe the person before he/she encountered God.	How did God intervene/respond?	Describe the person after he/she encountered God.
Mary Magdalene: Read Luke 8:1-3 and Mark 16:9-11			
Zaccheus: Read Luke 19:1-10			
People of Nineveh: Read Jonah 1:1-2 and Jonah 3 Note: Nineveh is in modern-day Iraq			

Wow! As I read about the transformation of these people after encountering the living God, I am moved to tears. God is so merciful, loving, kind, and able. And although He is grieved by it, He is unoffended by our weakness, sin, and brokenness. Of course, He doesn't like the sin they or we get caught in, but these scriptures make it evident that He desires to save us from those sins by any means necessary(even to the point of death on a cross). Sit for a second to reflect on the transformation and mending God provided and is still able to provide. Ask Him to transform and mend you in the areas that are not like Him. Also, pray for Him to make you more like Him so that you will deal with people's brokenness with grace like He does.

Read 2 Corinthians 4:1-15 AMP

11. What has to happen for you to carry light in this dark world ruled by Satan?

....

....

12. *What is the "precious treasure"? (See Colossians 1:24-29 for more support)*

....

....

....

13. *What do you think it means for us to be like "fragile jars of clay"? (Put yourself in the shoes of the original audience of the ancient days)*

....

....

....

....

14. *Why did God decide to use people who are so "fragile" to share this treasure with those of all nations? (See 1 Corinthians 1:27-29 for additional support)*

....

....

....

....

....

....

Read Matthew 26:41

15. *What does Jesus say is the remedy to our weakness?*

....

....

PSA: God uses weak and broken people because He mends us, making us whole and strong in Him!!!

Let's make it personal:

What areas of your life do you truly see your brokenness? What sin(s) do you struggle with? What internal or external battles do you need help with? (Note: these answers can include matters of your character, how you treat people, your thoughts, etc.)

....
....
....
....
....
....

Whatever those things are, take this time to release and surrender them to God in prayer and repentance. Ask Him for His help in those areas, crying out for His saving grace to free you, pull you through, and help you endure. Remember you are not. Remember, you are not alone in your brokenness, and God still desires to be with you. The need for repentance is natural and necessary (See Romans 2:3-5 and 2 Corinthians 7:9). You can either write down your prayer below or just speak it outwardly to God.

....
....
....
....
....
....
....
....
....
....
....
....

Have you given your life to Christ? He's the ultimate healer of that brokenness caused by sin. If you haven't, I urge you to keep reading.

By giving your life to Christ, you simply choose to enter into a relationship with God so that you're walking with Him every step of the way, readily allowing and welcoming Him to mend your brokenness and put you back together again. So, don't worry, when you fall, He will help you get back up and mend the broken pieces. He'll even mend the pieces that were broken prior to you coming into a relationship with Him. Want to be mended, healed, and whole? Pray this prayer with the sincerity of your heart, feel free to add to this, and speak freely to God, laying every broken piece at His feet.

> *Father God, you are the author and finisher. You know everything about me, and you've seen all that has happened to me and all I have done. God, I am broken and need your healing touch. I've sinned and fallen short of your glorious and holy standard. I repent of _____ and any other unknown sins. I leave it all here at your feet. Heal my soul God, heal my mind, my will, and my emotions. Heal any broken areas of my heart and mind. Lord, I forgive _____ for mishandling me and causing wounds. Thank you, Father for the precious blood of Jesus. Thank you for sending Him to the cross on my behalf and allowing Him to die in my place so that I could be made whole. Thank you, God, for your mighty power that raised Jesus from the dead, giving me victory over sin! I will no longer be conquered by sin, for I accept Jesus as Lord over my life. I don't want to do life on my own, nor do I want to do it my way. I just want You, God. I want your will to be done in and through my life. I want your ways to be my ways. I want your thoughts to be my thoughts. Lord, I surrender. Take this broken vessel that I am and make me whole; put the pieces back together again. Transform the ugly areas of my life into something beautiful and new. Heal me, God, from the inside out. Fill me with your Holy Spirit. Lead and guide me as I grow closer to You and read Your word. I just want to be close to You, God, and I'm so grateful for the blood of Jesus that made that possible. Hear my cries, Father. Change my heart, Lord Jesus. And draw nearer to me than ever before, Holy Spirit. In Jesus' name, I pray, Amen.*

Did you decide to give your life to Christ with sincerity? (sidenote: you don't have to cry to show that you're sincere; it's a matter of your heart. Is your heart in it? If it is, your actions will follow). If so: Yayyy! Hallelujah, all of Heaven rejoices!

As you saw today, God uses weak and broken people to carry a message that will bring a gift of wholeness because He loves to make all things new. Jesus gets all of the glory from our victory as He mends us in the process of surrendering to Him. Sounds contradictory, right? Or, maybe it just sounds like it requires a miracle! Well, good thing our God, Yahweh, Jesus, El Shaddai, the God of Abraham, Isaac, and Jacob specializes in miracles! Be confident that God knew what He was doing when He entrusted you to carry and share His message in that fragile jar of clay of yours: your flesh. When you feel that your jar has broken to pieces because you've messed up, remember who saved you and that His blood has the power to mend (Romans 5:12-21 & Matthew 26:27-29), so repent and keep moving forward.

In closing, If people have mishandled you, know that God did not want that to happen, but can redeem and transform those soul hurts and can still work things together for your good (Genesis 50:20). Finally, remember that trouble doesn't last always because soon, Jesus will return, and we can expect complete restoration and wholeness upon that day (Joel 2:25-26 and Galatians 6:9). Be encouraged.

Coloring Activity: *The picture for this week was inspired by 2 Corinthians 4:5 and an ancient Japanese art called "Kintsugi," which means "golden repair." When pottery breaks, the potter puts the pottery back together with a special lacquer and then dusts it with powdered gold, platinum, or silver, making a beautiful masterpiece out of something that was once broken! Sounds like what Jesus does with our fragmented and broken souls, right?*

So, in today's picture, color the jar with your choice of color, but color the cracks that have been filled in with red to represent what the blood of Jesus does for us broken vessels; it mends them.

Worship Playlist: *"Revival's in the Air" by Bethel Music & Melissa Helser*
"I Need You" by Chris Tomlin
"You Are Welcome" by Psalmist Raine
"Carry this Weight" by SON.

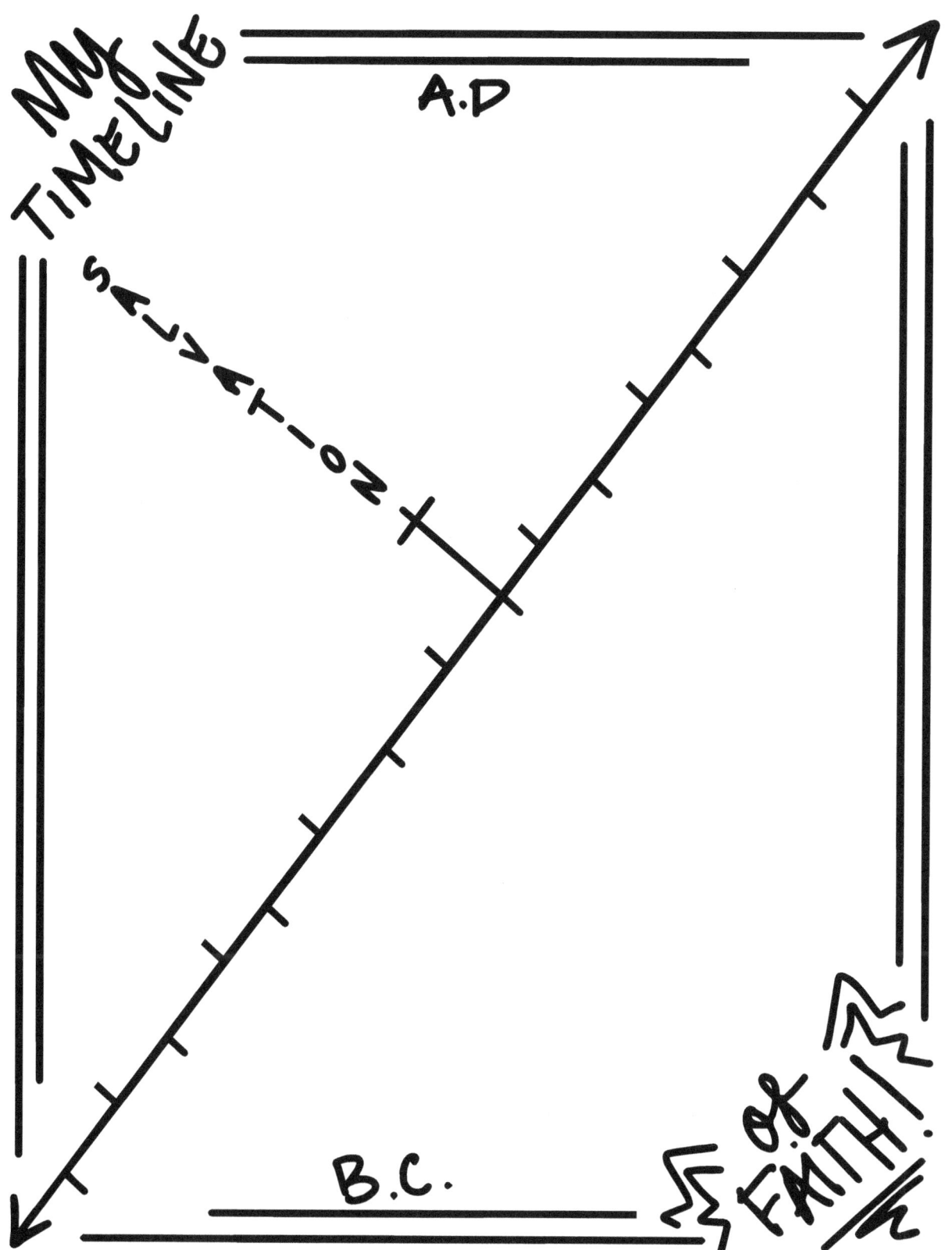

Tell Your Story

The summer I was saved, people would always talk about their testimony. However, for the longest time during said summer, I was convinced that I didn't have one because nothing traumatic had happened to me, and my salvation story was simple (God tugged on my heart during worship one day). I was looking for grand things to have happened to be able to qualify as "testimony worthy." But, in actuality, every moment up to my point of salvation and even afterward were worthy of writing on my timeline of journeying with God and seeing His goodness, aka my testimony.

Today is all about reflecting on the mighty work God has done in your life chronologically. Having your testimony written and memorized is like a business owner having an elevator pitch ready at any time in case he/she encounters an investor and needs to talk about his/her business on the spot. Similarly, having your testimony ready is for those random (or planned) interactions with a stranger, friends, or family member who needs to hear about the goodness of God. It's for those who are lost and in need of the Savior you have found in Jesus. Your testimony is a first-hand account of the existence of God. Your testimony has great power; it has more power than you probably know! Let's take a look.

Read 1 Corinthians 13:8-13

1. Despite the ability for people to prophesy(to tell of future events according to God), will we ever see the full picture and know all of the details presently? Explain how you know.

....

....

....

2. When will you be able to see everything in full?

....

....

Read Revelation 12:9-12

3. What two things does God say defeated Satan?

....

4. Define "testimony" (Remember the best way to define Biblical words)

Therefore, it was through the sacrifice of Jesus and their faith and knowledge of Him (which they witnessed in Heaven) that gave them the authority, assurance, and boldness to fight until the end, defeating Satan. Imagine the immense victory that could be possible as you plant seeds by sharing your testimony! Only God knows the number of people who would be saved because of your testimony. Don't be silent.

Read John 4:16-42 and Mark 5:1-18

5. How do you see the power of Jesus(the lamb) and the testimony of those who encountered Him?

Read 1 Peter 3:13-17

6. How does knowing your testimony help with living out these verses?

Let's make it personal:

Before you start, pray that God would bring to your memory and reveal the various things that led to your salvation. Pray also that He would give you the words you're supposed to say in your testimony.

While writing your testimony, use these four questions to get the framework of your testimony on paper (be sure to add snippets of it to the coloring activity):

What things did you struggle with before giving your life to Christ? What was your life like before you accepted Jesus as Lord and Savior?

....
....
....
....
....
....
....

When did God spark a desire for you to know Him? Explain. Who or what did God use to draw you closer to Him?

....
....
....
....
....
....
....
....
....

When did you surrender your life to Christ? Explain. Why did you give your life to Christ?

....
....
....
....
....
....
....

....
....

What is life like now, after giving your life to Christ? What events, after you were saved, helped you to grow in your faith? What areas do you struggle with still? How do you handle them differently now that you're saved? How do you carry yourself now?

....
....
....
....
....
....
....
....
....

TIP: When sharing your testimony with people, you may have to adjust it depending on who you are speaking to (1 Corinthians 9:20-22). This doesn't mean you lie or make things up. What I mean is you change the vocabulary you use to make it simpler or you may focus on a particular portion of your testimony rather than sharing the whole thing from start to finish. Your testimony likely has different parts to it, different areas of your life that were transformed that the listener would relate to. For instance, my testimony includes growing up in the church but not fully surrendering my life to the Lord until college, it also includes sexual immorality and how God protected me in that and opened my eyes to the purpose of purity, it includes a bad relationship, God closing doors, a shift in my attitude, encountering God during worship, and so many other things. Sometimes I am able to share my full testimony with people, but other times God may highlight a portion of it for me to go into more deeply so I'll only share that part of how God changed my life. Thus, my tip is, feel the freedom to just share what you're sensing God highlighting in your story of redemption based on who He's led you to share with, it all has great power.

Coloring Activity: *In this week's activity, you will create a snapshot of the main events on the timeline of your walk with Jesus. On the left side of the cross, mention significant dates (if you know them) and occurrences that shaped your life before Christ (B.C.*

These may not have been the best moments, but they were a part of your journey. Remember, it doesn't have to be traumatic or grand events). As you get closer to the cross in the middle of the timeline, begin talking about people and occurrences that led to you eventually giving your life to Christ. Underneath the cross and "salvation" in the middle, briefly share about the moment you gave your life to Christ. To the right of the cross, share significant moments that have helped to mature you in your faith. If you had any significant setbacks, you should share those as well, as we know we aren't completely free of sin just because we give our lives to Christ, we just have a way out (which is sometimes hard to take and we succumb).

Bonus: *Share your timeline with someone! You never know how your unique walk (testimony) with Jesus could help or encourage another.*

Worship Playlist: *"Transparent" by Edot (Mister Clark, EC)*
"Memories" by Franchesca
"Higher" by Madison Ryann Ward
"All Around Me" by Flyleaf
"Slum Sinner" by J. Monty

Set a fire down in my soul

Ablaze

*O*ften when we are first saved (give our lives to Christ), we are high on life with a great amount of zeal, passion, and fire for God and all things related to Him. From sharing who He is with family, friends, and strangers to simply being excited about church, many can attest that at the beginning (or at some point during their walk with Jesus), living out one's faith was lit! However, we are human and may go through tough or dry seasons where we feel unmotivated, stale, and lacking said zeal and fire like the coals of a grill after the cookout is over. What are we to do in these moments? Do we let the fire burn out and get cold, or do we salvage it?

I thoroughly suggest the latter option, but how can you do that? How can you reignite the flames? How can you keep burning for Jesus? Of course, God's word has the answer!

1. Write down 2 Timothy 1:6-7 (NLT).

....

....

....

....

2. Read this scripture in the NKJV and MSG version, what does it mean to "fan into flames?"

....

3. What gift is Paul talking about in 2 Timothy 1:6? (See Acts 8:14-17 for additional support)

....

Read Revelation 4:5

4. What is the Spirit of God described as?

....

....

....

....

September

Read 2 Timothy 1:7, Galatians 5:22-23, 1 Corinthians 12:1-11, Isaiah 11:2, and Luke 12:11-12

5. What does this gift give you the ability to do or have?

....

....

....

6. Read the following scriptures and state how you can practically fan the flames and set yourself up to go deeper with God in your everyday life.

Hebrews 10:24-25	Jude 1:20-21	1 Samuel 30:6-8	Romans 12:6-8	Psalm 42:5-6	John 4:31-34	Joshua 1:8 and Psalm 48:9

Let's make it personal:

There's a song that says, "set a fire down in my soul, that I can't contain, that I can't control, I want more of you God, I want more of you God."

What do you think it looks like to have more of God in your life?

....

....

> **Remember:** *God doesn't restrict how much we experience Him, but we do. God says to draw nearer to Him, and He will draw nearer to you (James 4:8).*

Are you restricting how much of God you experience? Think about how you spend your time. How much room have you made in your life for Him? How many areas of your life have you surrendered(let go of) to Him? Explain.

God loves you more than any person in this world ever could and He desires a deep and intimate connection with you, not just surface-level works or actions(Matthew 7:22-23). More than your sacrifices or works, He wants your heart. If you have given your life to Jesus and have accepted His Holy Spirit, you literally are carrying God within you. Don't forget that! So when you're feeling stale, lacking zeal, or like the coals mentioned in the opening statement, rather than choosing to sulk and sit in it, reignite that fire by fanning into flames that great and mighty gift you have been given. Stir up the Holy Spirit! God wants to use you in His great plan of reconciliation (leading people back to Him). Don't sit on the sidelines. Get in the game and operate in the authority He has given you to lead people into a relationship with Him(Matthew 28:16-20) starting with yourself. NO FEAR! NO TIMIDITY! ONLY POWER, LOVE, AND SELF-DISCIPLINE/SOUND MIND!

In the words of a viral tiktok: *"Holy Spirit, activate, activate!" lol.*

Worship Playlist: *"Set a Fire" by Jesus Culture*
"Vessel" by Ryan Ofei
"Love Note" by Abbie Gamboa
"Just to Worship" by Kristin Taylor

October

October

Vision

Throughout the book of Exodus, God gives Moses instructions and foreknowledge before the information is needed to be put into action. He gave Moses visions of what was to come for the Israelites. Why would God do this? Was it to prepare him for what was to come? Or maybe it was to give Moses hope as he was reluctant to give God his yes to lead the Israelites in the first place. Either way, with God coming to his aid in this way, all Moses had to do was relay the message and obey God when the time would come. Not only would God give Moses vision, but He would also give him and the Israelites provision (provide their needs) to see the vision through.

Similarly, God is ready and willing to do such things for you too! He may have already given you a glimpse of something He has planned for you in your future as you walk with Him. If you feel like God hasn't given you a vision for something, it's ok! Just ask Him and trust that God has you in His hands and as you walk with Him, He will show you things you wouldn't have imagined. Let's see how else God gives vision in His word.

Read Habakkuk 2:2

Have you heard this scripture before? If you have, in what context did you hear it?

....

....

....

Many people have used this when inspiring others to write down their visions and goals, which very well could be a physical way to apply this scripture to your life. But how often has the actual purpose of this text been spoken about? Today you will do just that, but trust, you'll still walk away with a grand scope of vision directly from God.

Read Habakkuk 1:6-17 (AMP) and Daniel 1:1-4

1. In verse 6, what people group is being discussed in this chapter? Describe them.

....

....

....

2. Knowing that, why was Habakkuk complaining to God?

....

Read Habakkuk 2 (AMP)

3. In context of Habakkuk 1, why was it important for Habakkuk to write down what God was telling him and "make it plain?"

....
....
....

4. Summarize the vision God gave the prophet Habakkuk that would happen at an appointed time. Would the Chaldeans(Babylonians) prevail in the end? What would happen to them? What positive thing was also prophesied to happen?)

> Note: "Woe" is an expression of grief and judgment.

....
....
....
....
....
....
....
....

It is said that when God gives vision, He often echoes. Meaning, He will repeat Himself no matter who the messenger is. For example, one of the first times I was told a prophecy for my life, I was told that God was training me up to speak and that I needed to use my voice. Following that moment, time after time, other men and women of God in different places would tell me the same thing. God was "echoing". In the same way, the vision God gave Habakkuk is echoed throughout the Bible and plays into an even bigger plan. Not only would the Chaldeans be destroyed at an appointed time, but others would be too. Take a look at how God echoed and what this vision was unto.

Read Daniel 2:31-45

5. What was prophesied to happen to Babylon and other powerful kingdoms?

....
....
....

6. What kingdom will reign victoriously in the end? (Compare to Habakkuk 2:14 & 20 and Luke 1:31-33)

....

Read Daniel 4:28-33 and Daniel 5

7. What happened to Babylon and it's kings?

....
....
....
....
....

Quick History Lesson:

The Book of Habakkuk was written between 610 B.C & 605 B.C The Book of Daniel was written between 540 B.C & 530 B.C

If you're like me and History class is/was not your strong suit in school it is important to know that in telling time with regards to "B.C" years, time descends. Thus, although we'd think 540 B.C happened before 610 B.C, and although the book of Daniel comes before the book of Habakkuk in the Bible, in both regards, it is actually reversed. Thus, everything written in the book of Daniel happened AFTER God showed these things to Habakkuk in the vision of Babylon.

Why does this matter? This emphasizes the fact that everything God says and gives vision for will undoubtedly come to pass! Remember in Daniel 2, God spoke of a Kingdom that was coming that will be eternal. In Habakkuk 2, God also spoke of His glory filling the earth. With other portions of the vision already taking place, we can be assured the remaining portions of the vision will take place too. These things will come to pass, nations will fall, sin will be judged, and those who are on God's team will be saved.

Let's read about another vision God gave to a disciple of Jesus named John, it hasn't come to pass yet and applies to you and everyone else in the world directly, so pay attention!.

Read Revelation 20:7-17 and Revelation 21:8 (Refer to Matthew 7:21-33, Matthew 11:20-24, and Matthew 23:1-36 as well)

8. Like the fate of Babylon, what is also soon to come?

....

....

....

Read Matthew 25:41

9. Who was Hell and eternal separation from God intended for?

....

Read 2 Peter 3:9-15 and Revelation 22:14-18

10. What does God desire?

....

....

Wow! Pause here and reflect on what God said. Thankfully, just as this week's coloring activity suggests, God not only gives vision, He also gives provision to accomplish it. After you've taken a moment to meditate on what you read above, continue for good news!.

Read John 3:16, John 4:10-14, John 14, and 2 Corinthians 5:20-21

11. How has God provided for us to accomplish His vision(desire) as mentioned in 2 Peter 3? How should we respond?

....

....

As you can see, God provides for the visions He gives. Please fight to know and believe that whatever God has spoken to you personally will come to pass and as you obey Him, you will see every resource you need be given. Know that this will still require participation on your part, but as you walk in obedience to God, your needs are guaranteed to be met. Need further convincing?

12. Read the following scriptures and complete the chart to see how God showed up.

	What was the vision?	How was the provision made?
Exodus 35:4-35 and Exodus 36:1-7		
Nehemiah 1:1-11 and Nehemiah 2:1-8		
2 Samuel 7:1-13, 1 Kings 3:3-14, 1 Kings 5:2-18, and 1 Kings 6:14 & 38		

There you have it. The beautiful flow of God giving vision and Him giving the provision necessary for it to be accomplished. Ultimately, please know that God didn't give three people (and many others) visions of Jesus' return for no reason. It is a FACT that Jesus is coming soon. Before the time comes mentioned in the books of Habakkuk, Daniel, and Revelation, it is crucial that you are prepared ahead of time. Maybe you feel as though you've gone astray or that you've never been on the right path. It's simple to get back to God! Will you choose the only way to Him today? As you've learned this week, God didn't only give vision of what was to come, He provided a way too, will you take it?

"Jesus answered, "I am the way and the truth and the life. No one comes to the Father except through me." John 14:6

Let's make it personal:

How has this week's journal entry impacted you? What do you desire to do as a result?

....
....
....
....
....

With such a heavy message like this week's, I'd like to suggest three action steps as we prepare for Jesus' soon arrival:

#1: Accept God's Gift of Salvation and/or Repentance

As Jesus says in John 10:30, "The Father and I are one." So loving Jesus is loving God. Knowing Jesus is knowing God. Believing in Jesus makes you right with God as you were separated from Him because of your sins (anything unpleasant to God's sight or that falls short of God's standard). However, if you repent of your sins and confess with your mouth and believe in your heart that Jesus Christ is your Lord and Savior (meaning He died to be our Savior and rose showing His authority as Lord), you will be saved. So, talk to God and do just that. If you'd like a little help, you can say this prayer and feel free to add to it and share your heart with God.

> Lord I know that I am a sinner and have messed up many times (Romans 3:23). I repent of _____. My sin has separated you and me from each other, but today, I want to place my faith in you and accept your free gift of life and salvation (Romans 6:23). I confess that Jesus is Lord and supreme ruler. I believe that He was sacrificed on my behalf but was raised three days later (Romans 6:4-5). Thank you, God, for His victory! Thank you, God, for washing me clean because of the blood of Jesus. Lord, welcome me into your arms as I surrender and place my life in your hands. In Jesus' name, I pray, Amen!

*All of Heaven rejoices!

If you have the opportunity, get baptized as a public declaration of what you've decided on this day! Date:

#2: Hold fast to the salvation you have gained (Revelation 3:11 and Matthew 24:13)

How?

Prayer*   (1 Thessalonians 5:16-18, Acts 3:19)

Community   (Hebrews 10:24, Acts 2:42 & 44)

Reading God's Word   (Psalm 1:2, Acts 2:42, Psalm 119:9-16)

#3: Make disciples (Matthew 28:18-20)

May the vision and provision of God prepare you, keep you, sustain you, and spur you to acts of righteousness until Christ's return. Amen.

*= Some ways you can pray daily is to pray the revelations God has been speaking to you via dreams, visions, His word, Holy Spirit, etc. I also suggest you sit and ask the Holy Spirit to show you what's on God's heart and pray what you sense Him reply. If you don't think God speaks to you, ask Him to and be sure to write down His response and pray it.

Obey

The picture says it all. Let's dive into scripture to see the effects of obedience to God and the lack thereof. Yep, it's that simple.

Read 1 Samuel 15

1. What were God's instructions?

....
....
....

2. What did King Saul do instead?

....
....
....

3. What was King Saul's reason for disobeying God?

....
....
....

4. King Saul blamed his disobedience on the troops he was supposed to be leading. Who was punished, the people or King Saul? What does this show about leadership?

....
....
....

5. Based on the scriptures, what is more pleasing to God - obedience or sacrifice?

....

6. Samuel mentions various sins in verse 23. Is one sin greater than another? Explain

....

....

....

7. What did King Saul lose as a result of his disobedience?

....

....

Sheesh! That was sobering! You good?

Read Colossians 3:1-7 (NKJV)

8. What does Paul say will happen to those who live a life of sin?

....

....

9. What does Paul call the people who live such lives?

....

> Selah Moment:
> Based on what you've read so far, does God hold obedience with HIGH or LOW value? How do you know?
> ....
> ....
> ....

Now, take a look at some people who did obey God.

> Selah Moment:
> Before you go on, to encourage scripture memory, refresh your memory about someone you read about in past journal entries:
> Read Numbers 13:25-31 and Numbers 14:20-24

> *What set Caleb apart? What was the outcome for him?*
>
> ....
> ....

Read 2 Kings 4:8-37

10. *When the Shunammite woman's son died, what did the mother choose to do to try and save her son's life despite the customs of the day?*

....

....

....

11. *What did Elisha instruct Gehazi to do to try and save the boy's life?*

....

12. *Did Gehazi obey although it may have seemed like an odd instruction?*

....

13. *Were Gehazi's efforts successful?*

....

Although the boy's mother and Gehazi were both obedient to either their unction or instructions given, it did not save the boy's life. However, without their steps of obedience, there is no guarantee that what happens next would've been possible. So, remember, whether the outcome is what you expected/desired or not, your obedience is what matters! You give God the room to move on your behalf in whatever way He sees fit when you are obedient despite what customs say or how weird the instructions may seem.

14. *What did Elisha do when he arrived at the Shunammite woman's home? What was the result?*

....

....

....

Background: *Elisha was the successor of a prophet named Elijah! Everywhere Elijah went, Elisha was not far behind. Elisha learned and gleaned from him. Upon Elijah's ascension into Heaven, Elisha followed in his footsteps and continued the work of the Lord.*

Read 1 Kings 17:17-24

15. *What did Elijah do to raise a boy from the dead?*

16. *What conclusion can you draw about Elisha's actions? Did he make up his methods on his own, or did he obey the instruction/example set by his mentor, Elijah?*

Similarly, God has given us an example in Jesus Christ Himself. Take heed to the life of Jesus and pray that God would make you more like Him as you obey and follow His example.

Read 2 Kings 5:1-15 (See Leviticus 13 for more details)

17. *What was the issue with Naaman? Do a little research on the issue and describe it.*

18. *Who did Naaman have to go to?*

19. *What did Elisha tell Naaman to do? What would be the result if he obeyed?*

20. *How did Naaman respond? Why?*

21. Did Naaman obey immediately? Why or why not?

22. Who spurred Naaman on to obey?

23. Although Naaman did not want to follow the instructions of Elisha, what happened when he did?

Read Luke 11:27-28

24. What does Jesus have to say about obedience?

In these various accounts, you've seen some results of obedience and disobedience. You've seen how people have had to overcome various obstacles to obey, from religious customs and odd instructions to instructions that one disagreed with. Reviewing these accounts, now take the time to analyze your level of obedience and obstacles you face.

Let's make it personal:

Based on these various accounts, what have you learned about obedience and how God values it?

Do you love Jesus? If your answer is yes, read John 14:15. How can you show your love for Him?.

....

Assess your own life, how often and readily do you obey God immediately? Circle one and explain.

(Never)   (Rarely)   (Sometimes)   (Frequently)   (Always)

....
....
....
....

What obstacles cause you to disobey God's word(written in the Bible or spoken to you directly through the Holy Spirit)?

....
....
....
....
....

Lastly, read and reflect on Matthew 21:28-32.

What did God show you? What conviction did these verses bring?

....
....
....
....
....

In closing, if you have chosen to give your life to Christ, know that God has provided you with everything you need to live this life of godliness in His word (2 Peter 1:3). All you must do now is obey. Read and reflect on Psalm 119:57-64. Are these words the desire of your heart? Lastly, take note that Jesus instructed us(believers) to make disciples and TEACH THEM TO OBEY(Matthew 28:19-20). How can you teach others to obey and be qualified in the end if you yourself are not obedient to God? Submit yourself to God afresh today and pray asking Him to shift your mind and spirit to a place of surrender and obedience unto Him despite the trials and obstacles you may face.

Amen.

Worship Playlist: *"On the Altar" by Upperroom & Elyssa Smith*
"Obedience" by Lindy Cofer & Circuit Rider Music
"Follow" by Essence Natay

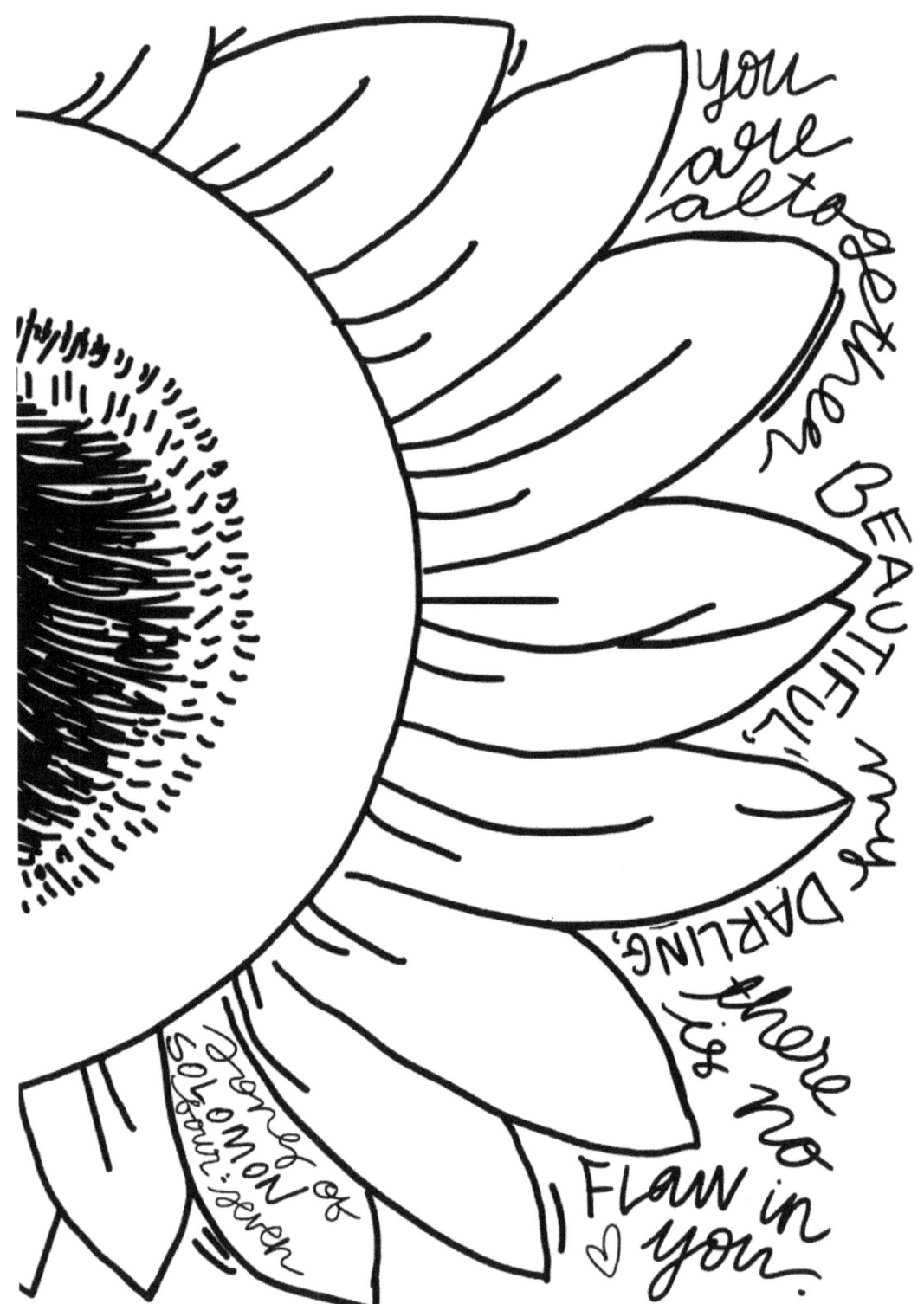

Altogether Beautiful

Before you read, biblical scholars point to two purposes for the Book, Song of Solomon (aka Song of Songs). One aim is to express the tangible love and expression of marriage as the dialogue is between a married couple. The other proposed purpose is that it simultaneously represents how Jesus, the bridegroom, loves, views, and relates to His bride, the Church(all believers). Yes, gentlemen reading this, if you didn't know, you are a part of the bride of Christ. This can be rather mind-boggling but don't overthink it. This kind of symbolism is also present for us ladies as "sonship" is the term used to describe both the sons' and daughters' relationship with God as a Father. To be clear, God is not confused about who you are as an individual, he knows the gender He assigned to you and the part you'd play in His plan. With that clarification, let's see what God has to say about us and our identity in His eyes and what our best response could be if we so choose.

Read and write Song of Solomon 4:7

1. ....
....
....

2. How does Solomon view His wife?
....
....
....

3. How does this show us how Jesus (the bridegroom) sees the Church (you, if you are saved, the bride)? (See Ephesians 5:25-27 and 1 Peter 2:9 for additional support).
....
....
....

Putting Song of Solomon 4:7 and Ephesians 5:25-27 side by side, we can see that in our decision to surrender to Christ and become His bride, we enter into a transforming and purifying relationship, one that ends in complete beauty and flawlessness. This, however, doesn't happen for everyone on the earth, who is being described in each of those scriptures?

_____(write the answer). Thus it takes entering into a marriage with Jesus Christ, the bridegroom, for such flawlessness to be made manifest in you.

In Romans 4:17 it says that God is "the God who gives life to the dead and calls into being things that were not." He identifies us, calls us, and based on our response, we can become who He says we are! Let's look more into this.

Just because God sees perfection, it doesn't mean we in our flesh are perfect because, in actuality, we aren't (hence why we needed Jesus to be our Lord and Savior). God, rich in grace and mercy, provided us a way to be altogether beautiful in His sight and in communion with Him. Although we still struggle here on Earth, God's love is so deep that His mercies are new each morning. These mercies are not to be abused with reckless living and living with no regard to God; His mercies are meant to spur us to repentance daily. Let's take a look at a few prominent people that were imperfect but whom God still used.

4. Fill in the table below:

	Read Genesis 17:1-19 Person: Abram & Sarai	Read Matthew 16:16-19 Person: Simon	Read Isaiah 62 People: Israel
How did God identify the person? What did God call this person? (Hint: Pay attention to the meaning of their names)			
When did God give the person this name, before or after they became it?			
BELIEVING God and having FAITH was/is required of each of the people you've read about in order for them to BECOME who God called them to be! James says that As James and the writer of Hebrews shows us, FAITH IS FOLLOWED BY ACTION. So...			
What act of faith was/is required of the person/people to live up to the name?	Read Romans 4:18-21	Read Luke 22:31-32. Acts 2:38-41 Acts 10:9-29	Read isaiah 59:20-21 and Acts 2:36-39

Read John 1:12-13, Romans 4:16-17

5. What does God say you can become?

....

Read John 3:3-5, Acts 2:37-40, Acts 10:43-48, and Romans 3:22-31

6. What's required for you to achieve the new identity mentioned above?

....

....

....

God calls you by a name that the world could not, He calls you His son/daughter and He won't relent in molding and shaping you until you are restored to this full identity(Philippians 1:6). Will you have the faith to see it through? Will you lay down every other identity that the enemy and world would like you to believe you are? If you're reading this, you still have time to BECOME what God says you are. If you've never decided to have faith in Christ, this word is for you. If you have given your life to Christ, but have been struggling with your identity, this word is also for you: You're not too far gone and you haven't done or been in any situation too dark that God can't bring light to. Turn back to God today and let Him mold you into the altogether beautiful one He sees. If you aren't struggling with your identity, keep looking at Jesus you radiant one.

Let's make it personal:

List different names you've been called or identified as that do not align with God. List any lifestyles you've taken on that do not align with God as well.

(TIP: List any identity or way of living that doesn't align with God's way, desires, or character that you entertain in any way)

....

....

....

Present these names and lifestyles to God and ask Him to give you a new name and show you a new life. Ask Him to show you the way He sees you. Write down any pictures He shows you, words you hear, or scriptures He shows you. (TIP: Slow down here and wait on the Lord. Ask the Holy Spirit to show you how God sees you, etc. This may take only a second or it could take minutes, hours, or days. He will answer you. Keep your eyes and ears open)

....
....
....
....
....
....

Now, like Abraham, Peter, and Israel, you must have faith in Christ and walk with Him to become this new creation from the inside out! Are you married to Christ? If not, that's the first step to seeing the new you unfold. To become who God sees you as and not the one the world has claimed you as. Accept Jesus and choose to forgive those who have played a part in you not seeing yourself as God does. Here and now, I apologize on behalf of any person who has ever called you or treated you as anything other than your true identity which is a child of God, beloved, adored, holy, altogether beautiful, and pure. May God heal every broken place and uproot every lie you've believed. I speak freedom over you in the mighty name of Jesus.

Use this space to write your thoughts, a prayer, and/or anything coming to mind at this time. Please also seek after wise godly counsel if this topic is hitting you deeply; you don't have to endure this alone

....
....
....
....
....
....

As you've seen this week, God loves you and desires for you to be His! Just like His relationship with Israel, God's love and fight for you to become who He says you are is relentless. He desires you to be with Him so much that He came down from His throne and place of perfection(Heaven) to live on this sin-filled earth in human flesh via Jesus, just to repair your relationship with Him. You read that correctly...God came all the way from Heaven to physically be on this earth to save you. He was willing to go the distance then to meet you right where you are here and now.

The Lord is not afraid of your past or present imperfections and sins. He desires to meet you where you are so that you can be saved and transformed into the altogether beautiful one He's made you to be. This transformation isn't for nothing, it's unto you being able to live freely now and dwell with Him eternally at the end of this life. You don't have to and you can't "clean yourself up" before turning to Jesus and you can't earn or win His attention or forgiveness. He sees you right where you are whether you're like Zaccheus in a tree or the invalid on the ground with no hope, He sees you and desires you!

Your willingness to surrender your life to Him in faith and repentance is all that's required; this is what Jesus died for you to be able to do. God will continually bring about the cleaning and maturing you need as you walk with Him and choose His way.

Choosing God's way may not always be easy as temptations will come, but remember there's always a way of escape. Lastly, depending on your past and your family history, a process called deliverance maybe necessary due to entertaining other gods, dark ways, and spirits, but even this is done with and because of God not before, see Appendix D for more info on this.

Will you partner with God in becoming the flawless one He sees? All that is required of you is surrender and acceptance of Him.

Worship Playlist: *"Slow Me Down" by Charles Weems*
"Beautiful" by Wind & Color
"Beautiful" by Mali Music

The Great Escape

We live in a perverse world filled with temptation and the plague of sin. How do we keep from falling to these ways? Is there any escape? Where is the light at the end of the tunnel? Today, you will explore this idea of a great escape from the sins that so easily entangle us and discover how it is possible to live in this world, but not of it.

Read Psalm 1:1-6

1. Who is blessed based on these scriptures?

....

....

Read 1 Peter 1:13-19, Leviticus 11:44-45, 1 Peter 2:9, and 2 Corinthians 5:21

2. Who is righteous and holy? How can you become righteous and holy?

....

....

....

....

Read Psalm 119:9-16, Romans 1:16, and Hebrews 4:14-16

3. How can you be sure to intentionally live a pure lifestyle?

....

....

....

Read 2 Peter 1:3-11

4. What causes the corruption of the world?

....

5. How can you escape the corruption of this world? (See 2 Peter 2:19-20 and Romans 1:16-18 for additional support).

....

6. What qualities should you be growing in as a result of escaping the corruption of the world? List the attributes in order Peter stated.

7. Why is it important to grow in these areas?

Read 1 Peter 2:10-12, 2 Peter 1:12-15, and 2 Peter 3:8-18

8. List practical strategies Peter gives for growing spiritually(See Matthew 25 and Romans 12:2 for aiddtional support):

Read Acts 2:36-47

9. How did the early believers escape corruption and thrive?

....
....
....
....
....
....

10. Write and meditate on 1 Corinthians 10:12-13(NASB 1995)

....
....
....

> Selah Moment:
>
> Acts 2:37 says, "Now when they heard this they were cut to the heart, and said to Peter and the rest of the apostles, 'Brothers, what shall we do?'", do you allow the word of God to go beyond your mind and let it impact your heart? Allowing it to expose your desires, letting it trigger emotions, or causing you to repent, etc. Explain.
>
> ....
> ....
> ....
> ....

Let's make it personal:

What are your normal ways of "escaping" struggle, anxiety, stress, and other uncomfortable things? Who or what do you turn to for relief and comfort most often? Be honest with yourself.

....
....

Today you made two lists that have practical ways to grow in your relationship with Jesus. How do you measure up with that list? Are you putting any of them into practice currently? If so, how? If not, why?

....

....

....

....

....

....

....

....

....

....

I want to challenge you to intentionally put at least two of the strategies above to practice each day next week. Write down how it goes on a note sheet at the back of the journal. Remember, with all things dealing with Jesus, He doesn't want your relationship with Him to just be like a checklist, as that leads to legalism (just following rules with no heart). However, He does want your heart, willing obedience, sacrifice, and submission as that's the 100% sure way of showing your love for Him and to stay pure as you walk in the light.

God is so patient(2 Peter 3:9) and has provided our way out of the bondage of sin, but you must be willing to accept Him and walk down that narrow path daily! Our God is such a good God that He's provided everything you need to make it through! Remember, what you learned last week in 1 Corinthians 10:13, God promises to provide a way out when you are tempted to fall back into the corrupt ways of this world. So, in the face of temptation, will you choose to press escape or will you stay? The choice is always yours.

Worship Playlist: *"Familiar" by Madison Ryann Ward*

November

November

Deeply Rooted

Close your eyes and imagine that you have a yard full of weeds, whether pretty dandelions or heinous vine types of weeds that are an eyesore; the choice is yours as weeds are weeds. Have the visual in your mind? Now imagine you hire a landscaper to come to clean the yard up. Would you rather that landscaper simply mow the lawn and cut the weeds off the surface of your yard, or would you rather him/her to take the time to spray weed killer and pull the weeds from their roots to get rid of them? You see, the former option would definitely be quicker and get your yard to look nice, but the downside is, those weeds would be back faster than you knew it. However, although the latter option would take more time, your yard is better off because pulling the weeds from the root assures that sin...I meant those weeds, would no longer have a hold on your heart... whoops, I did it again, I meant your yard. Pulling the weeds from their roots would assure that they would not grow back overnight or the next few weeks and beyond. If you commit to this process of getting and pulling up the roots of what don't belong would leave your yard healthy underground and appealing to the eye on the surface. The sin issues we see on the surface of our lives are a lot like the weeds we see in yards as it all starts from somewhere, a seed, but then it grows and takes root. The question is, are you willing to take the time to do some digging to get to it and remove it? Let's see what scripture has to say about finding the roots and landscaping our hearts from the weeds of sin and the consequences if we don't deal with them.

Read Genesis 4:1-12

1. Compare the lifestyles of Cain and Abel below.

	What was his job?	What offering did he bring to God?	How did God respond to his offering?
Cain			
Abel			

Sidenote: God may not have responded well to Cain's offering because it says he simply "brought some of the fruits of the soil as an offering to the Lord." Whereas, we see in scripture that God wanted the first fruits of their crops (Proverbs 3:9) that were harvested. God wanted His first and best.

2. How did Cain feel when God responded to Abel's offering to God versus his offering?

....
....
....

3. What did Cain do as a result of how he felt? What outer sin was committed?

....
....
....

The sin mentioned above is like the weeds in the yard. Weeds don't just come from nowhere, they start as a seed, then grow deeply rooted over time.

4. What sparked Cain's outward sin? Why did he do it? (What was at the root of Cain's sin against his brother? (See 1 John 3:12 for additional support).

....
....
....

Read Genesis 4:10-24

5. What consequence(s) came about because of Cain's sin? How'd Cain's sin affect his lineage?

....
....
....
....

Let's make it personal:

Someone once said, "Salvation is immediate and free, but deliverance costs(requires greater sacrifice) and can take time," and I agree! Although some things God does deliver us from upon salvation or during other moments of deliverance, there are other things we need to be delivered from that require inner healing(for more info on deliverance and inner healing, see Appendix D at the back of this journal). One way to seek inner healing is to get to the root of things and pull them out. Thus, I invite you to fast and pray this week for God to reveal the roots of sin issues, unhealthy actions, and faulty thought patterns you mayt have. I pray even now that the Holy Spirit will reveal what you didn't even know existed, that He'd search you and reveal every anxious thought, and what's behind it so that you may be free to live life and life abundantly. This week's study is shorter than normal because it's important for you to sit with God and pursue freedom. I invite you to take 3 consecutive days this week to fast and pray, meditating on Psalm 139:23-24, and using the method below to uproot the "weeds" of your heart and mind. For more info on fasting, see Appendix F at the back of this journal.

As you seek God and pursue freedom this week, use the chart below to expose the roots of weeds in your life, uproot them, and plant the beautiful flowers of God's truth instead.

Here's how to use the chart:

Column #1: Write down any sin issues, unhealthy actions, and/or poor thoughts you struggle with (If you need help, Galatians 5:19-21 lists some examples)

Column #2: Pray and write what the Lord reveals to you is at the root of it (maybe He will remind you of a moment from your childhood, something spoken or believed by family, He may speak a single word to you or show you a picture, the Holy Spirit can speak in various ways write down what He reveals; you may also already know what's at the root but are ignoring it, write what you know too).

Column #3: Find scripture (the Truth) that opposes the root (the lies and things against God); i.e. if the root is anger, find scripture about peace or being slow to anger. (TIP: fruits of the Spirit are a great place to start, see Galatians 5:22-25)

Column #4: It's time to put in the work, pray! REPENT for the sin, RENOUNCE agreement with the root, and RECLAIM the ground by speaking the truth of God's word, coming into agreement with what His word says. It's important to embrace this newness in the days following by REMINDING yourself (and satan who will try to tempt you to go back to those old ways) of your new commitment. If those old ways sneak up, say out loud your new belief. (NOTE: This column isn't there physically because you need to speak it out loud, but also feel free to use the blank pages at the back of this journal to write it out too). "

Use this first example of Cain as a guide.

Outward Sin Issue(s) unhealthy actions, poor thoughts, etc (weeds)	What's at the root?	Scripture(s) to combat and pull the weeds out!
Cain murdered his brother, Abel	Anger, envy, and disobedience to God	1 John 3:11, Micah 6:8, Ephesians 4:26

In closing, know that God has you on a journey of getting back to Him; back to the beautiful garden He always wanted you to be a part of in fellowship with Him. Remember Adam and Eve before sin? They dwelled in the garden with God. He wants that for you again and the time is surely coming when the world will be restored to this original state, dwelling with Him forever. Before this time comes though, He wants you to be His garden. He wants you to be His DWELLING PLACE. He wants His Spirit to live in you (if your faith is in Jesus and you've been baptized by His Holy Spirit, He already does live in you) for you and Him to be ONE! Now, think about the perfection that God is and the garden Adam and Eve lived in, do you think that garden was full of weeds or the most beautiful and fragrant flowers and plants? Most definitely the latter, so guess what, God wants YOU (your heart, your mind, your body) to be full of this beauty too, free of the weeds of this world.

How? God the Father, sent His Son, Jesus, to die and be raised to offer you healing and make you whole! So, accepting His Son is step one to being made into God's perfect garden. Then, as you journey through life with the help of His Holy Spirit, the Word of God, community, and renewing your mind, you WILL be restored to God's good and perfect design, uprooting weeds and allowing beautiful flowers to blossom. This complete perfection won't come fully until the Lord's return, but you can and should be reaping the fruits of being in a relationship with God as His chosen, holy, and set apart one. Have you given your life to Jesus? If so, you can't expect God to leave you full of weeds and it be okay(aka you can't keep living in sin, having poor thoughts, etc). No, He is a great gardener and will point out the weeds that must go, will you submit and let them go? This week's journal entry is a lifelong process, so come back to it as you need.

Worship playlist: *"Cycles" by Jonathan McReynolds*

God is With You

As a believer, God has made you many promises in His word. However, one thing He never promised you was a trouble-free life. In fact, He told you ahead of time that troubles would come your way. At times, these troubles will be short-lived. Other times, these troubles may be extended into a "wilderness season" and require endurance. Where is God during these trials and trouble? How are you to act during these moments or seasons?

Would you believe me if I told you that you are "fit for the wild," able to endure and make it through even the most challenging things? But don't take my word for it; search the scriptures for yourself and find out below.

1. Define and describe a "wilderness."

....
....
....

Read Exodus 13:17-22

2. Do some quick research. Who are the Philistines? How are they described?

....
....
....

3. After being freed from Pharaoh's rule, what path did God choose to lead the Israelites?

....

4. Why did God choose to lead them along this path?

....
....
....

5. Did God leave it up to the Israelites to find their way through the wilderness alone? Explain.

....
....
....

Read Exodus 14:1-12

6. Why did God allow Pharaoh to pursue after the Israelites?

....
....
....

7. How did the Israelites respond to the trouble they saw with their eyes?

....
....
....

Read Exodus 14:13-18

8. What did Moses say in response to the Israelites?

....
....
....

9. In verses 15 and 16, God sternly spoke to Moses. What did God tell Moses?

....
....
....

10. Why do you think God spoke to Moses so abruptly?

....
....
....

11. What happened to the Israelites after Moses obeyed God's instructions?

....
....
....

12. Ultimately, did the Israelites survive this portion of their wilderness season? What did this do for them spiritually?

....
....
....

Read Exodus 15:1-21

13. How did the Israelites respond to God delivering them?

....
....
....

> Selah Moment:
>
> How does seeing God show up for the Israelites when they were struggling and without make you feel?
>
> ....
> ....
>
> Think of a time when God came through for you when things were tough. Pause here and thank Him. Feel free to write it down for remembrance later.
>
> ....
> ....

14. *Read the following passages of scripture and answer the questions.*

	Where were the Israelites?	What was needed?	What did the Israelites do?	What did Moses do?	What did God do?
Exodus 15:22-27					
Exodus 16:1-18					
Exodus 17:1-6					

15. *Analyze what you have written about each occurrence. What conclusions can you draw about God's ability to provide even through the wilderness? What is the best response in the waiting?*

....
....
....
....
....

<u>Read Psalm 119:65-72, Romans 5:1-5, 2 Corinthians 1:3-7, 2 Corinthians 4:16-18, and John 16:33</u>

16. *If you endure suffering/wilderness seasons/hard times presented to you in life, what can be produced from it?*

....
....
....
....
....

17. What hope do you have to make it through those hard times that will be presented?

....
....
....
....

Read Proverbs 27:12 (KJV, AMP, ESV, NLT)

18. If God knows a form of suffering is best for you, He will allow it. What does this verse encourage you to do and warn you against doing?

....
....

Let's make it personal

Describe a time in the past or present when you went through a wilderness season(i.e. you've faced many trials, felt you were stuck or alone, a time of great discomfort, and/or were in a foreign place with many unknowns)

....
....
....
....
....
....
....
....
....

How did you respond? (If it's presently, how are you responding?) What did God show you during it?"

....
....
....
....
....
....

Has God given you instructions during your current trials? If not, pray that He does and ask Him to shift your perspective to see all that He's doing around you. If so, what are those instructions?

....
....
....
....
....
....
....

What tool(s) did/has God already given you for you to move forward successfully?

....
....
....
....
....
....
....

After reflecting on the verses and questions today, how do you see yourself in the Israelites?

....
....
....
....
....
....
....

In the future, how would you like to respond when you face troubles in the WILDerness seasons to come?

....
....
....
....
....
....
....

Just as you saw in these Biblical accounts, God provides and is always with you, even in the (wild)erness. Like Moses, Jesus intercedes on our behalf to God. All we must do is cry out to Him in prayer and faith. So, if God brings you to a wilderness point in your life, know that He will be with you, and He plans to take you through it, side by side, hand in hand. So, stay close, trust, obey, and wait on Him. At all costs, resist all urges to turn around and go back to what is familiar for fear of not making it through. Although it may not be easy, remember, you're fit for the wild because God's got your back.

Worship playlist: *"Come Away" by: Jesus Culture*
"Not Alone" by: Sstedi

Don't Tap Out!

When you're on the edge of giving up, what leads you up to that point? Typically it's hardship in some form or fashion. You've tried and tried again, but things don't seem to be going the way you wanted nor planned, people have said demeaning things, you lose desire (and/or resources), your thoughts are against you, and the list goes on and on. However, if Jesus promised that those who endured until the end would be saved, there must be a recipe of not tapping out in this walk with God and then not tapping out in the natural realm of things as well. As always, let's see what recipe God has for enduring in His word.

Warning: This week's journal entry is lengthier, so I suggest you divide it up throughout your week in order to get the fullness. Don't rush or cram.

1. Read the following verses and then answer the question.

	What actions describe our enemy, Satan?
Luke 22:31-32	
John 8:44	
1 Peter 5:8	

Go back to Luke 22:32

2. What does Jesus pray for Peter to withstand against the devil?

3. Therefore, what is Jesus showing you about Satan and his tactics? What does Satan ultimately want when trials, temptation, and trouble come your way?

> *Selah Moment:*
>
> **Read James 1:2-4 and 12**
>
> *How does James say you should respond to trials?*
>
> ....
>
> *In verse 3, what does James relate "trials of many kind" to?*
>
> ....
>
> *Why did James say that you should have joy during trials? What do trials cause to happen/be produced?*
>
> ....
>
> ....

James said, "facing trials of many kind" and "testing of your faith" are parallel to each other; they're one and the same. These heavenly tests God presents to you are meant to make you firm in faith so that you will endure until the end. So, once again, we see how faith is involved with trials. Thus, based on Luke 22:32 and James 1:2-4, there are two results that going through trials can bring: either the enemy will steal your faith OR God will strengthen your faith and take you deeper in your relationship with Him. Which will you allow? Will you tap out or endure? Pray like Jesus did for Peter, that your faith would not fail.

Go back to 1 Peter 5:8-9

4. What does Peter tell you to do to protect yourself from the enemy's schemes?

....

....

At this point, you've seen three times that maintaining your faith is important in order to not tap out or give up when things get hard! How do we actively do this? How do we lean into our faith rather than abandoning it? What is our faith to be in? Let's learn from God Himself on this.

Read Matthew 4:1-11

5. How many times was Jesus tempted?

....

6. Pay attention to how Jesus started each response to Satan. While being tempted by Satan, how did Jesus respond each time?

....

7. Therefore, what was Jesus' weapon for fighting back against Satan?

....

8. Using His weapon of choice, how many times did Jesus lose and fall into the temptations of Satan? Did Jesus' weapon work?

....

> Selah Moment:
>
> On a scale of 1-10, rate yourself, how well do you know God's word to be able to quote it while you're in trouble?
>
> ....
>
> Do you believe God's word is true?
>
> ....
>
> As you've just read, Jesus knew and believed the word of God so much that He was able to use it as the sword it is(Hebrews 4:12 and Ephesians 6:17), to fight back against Satan and pass the test!

9. In verse 1, it says that Jesus was led to the wilderness to be tempted. Therefore, this encounter with Satan was ordained and allowed by God. Why do you think Jesus had to go into the wilderness to be tempted and tested by Satan?

....

....

....

Let's make it personal:

Referring back to your answer from the Selah moment, do you believe God's word written in the Bible is true? If yes, keep moving to the next question. If not, write your questions and ask God to answer them (Author transparency moment: I had an intense time of shaking where scripture didn't seem trustworthy and I was very afraid that my faith in Jesus was done because of it. In this time I cried (literally), asked for prayer from my community, and prayed for God to answer my questions...guess what, He did days later! Don't be afraid to ask and share with the community of believers God's placed you with).

....
....
....

What sin are you easily or often tempted to do? And/or what sin are you currently comfortable with? (Disclaimer: sin is anything that is against God's character, ways, or design) Bonus question: What lies are you believing about God, yourself, or others?

....
....
....

Find one or two scriptures that speak the truth of what God says about the sin(s)/lies you mentioned above that Satan tries to get you to enter into or believe.

....
....
....

Next time you're tempted, recite those verses out loud with confidence to flip Satan's trap back on himself. Also, just as Satan tried Jesus, likely, the temptations and areas of struggle you notice in your life are connected to the very areas in which God has planned for you to do great things. For example, Satan questioned and tempted Jesus in the area of His identity as the Son of God!

As for us, this could look like someone who is called to be a teacher may struggle with taming his/her tongue or fear of speaking; someone called to be a prophet may struggle with fear of man, and someone called to be a mother or father may struggle with his/her identity and self-worth, each resulting in outward sins of various kinds. So pro-tip, in addition to knowing and believing the scriptures, get to know yourself according to God's eyes and will, this will help you see the traps a mile away and help in resisting the devil too! As you resist, HE WILL FLEE!

For Jesus to make it through the wilderness and time of temptation, He had to have faith in what His Father's word said. Have faith! Sometimes it can be hard to relate to Jesus or feel like you can live like Him or live up to His standards because although He is fully man, He is also fully God. If you struggle with this perspective, try to see Jesus from the perspective of Isaiah 53:3 and Philippians 2:6, we serve a God that understands first-hand the things we go through in everyday life. However, to show you that it's possible not to give in and tap out when life gets hard, let's read about some ordinary people, like you, that allowed their faith to remain strong and didn't tap out.

10. Read the following scriptures and answer the questions for each.

	Describe the problem the person had.	What reason did he/she have to tap out and give up?	Instead of tapping out, what did he/she do instead?	What was the outcome?
Matthew 15:21-28				
Mark 10:46-52				
Luke 8:42-48 and Mark 5:24-34				

Read 2 Thessalonians 2:3 (AMP)

11. What is going to happen before Jesus returns?

....

....

12. Although the people you have read about thus far did not tap out on their faith, there will indeed come a time when a lot of people will tap out and give up! How can you be sure you're not a part of that group? What can you do to remain steadfast? (Re-read James 1:2-4 and 12 with 2 Thessalonians 2:3 in mind)

....

....

....

> Selah Moment:
>
> How does James 1:2-4 & 12 hit you differently knowing many won't remain in the faith? Does it change your perspective of trials and suffering? Explain.
>
> ....
>
> ....
>
> ....

To keep yourself from being a part of this group of people, let's see how you can protect yourself and stay in perfect peace with God.

Read Ephesians 6:10-18.

13. What does God instruct us to put on?

....

14. Why are we instructed to put it on? What will it do?

....

....

15. List the name of each piece of armor. (Challenge: do extra biblical research to learn more about each piece)

....

....

....

....

Read Galatians 6:9, Jude 1:20-21, 1 Peter 5:4, Zechariah 9:16-17, and James 1:12.

16. What is awaiting you if you do not give up and tap out on your faith?

....

....

....

Read John 16:33 and 1 John 4:4.

17. Write them, memorize them, and say them out loud whenever you face trials.

....

....

....

....

....

Read Matthew 26:36-56 and Matthew 16:15-19.

18. Why didn't Jesus tap out despite the suffering He endured? What did He do? What did Jesus tell Peter?

....

....

....

....

Let's make it personal

Which piece of armor do you struggle with most and need to be better about wearing? Explain.

....

What things have you gone through that have made you want to tap out or give up?

    a. *in your relationship/walk with God:*

    b. *in your everyday life:*

Using the life of Jesus and many others via scriptures from today, what can you do to make sure you don't tap out?

    a. *in your relationship/walk with God:*

b. *in your everyday life:*

It's a given that trials will come, matters of life will get hard, people may speak down about you and your abilities, and things may simply not go your way, especially if you're striving after matters of God. However, do not be dismayed. Lean in a little bit closer to God and wear your full armor. Remind yourself that God has not given you a spirit of fear nor timidity, but of power, love, and a sound mind. Remember the authority you carry over the devil(1 John 4:4, Luke 10:19), stay fully covered in the armor of God, and fight back! We do not wrestle with flesh and blood, so even the enemies you may have face-to-face in this world are not the real enemy; the enemy is always the devil, so fight with the spiritual armor God has provided for you(especially praying and using the word of God) and stand firm as times get darker and the day of the Lord gets closer! Selah.

Worship Playlist: *"Can't Give Up Now" by Mary Mary*
"Always on Time (ft. Mid November)" by Imrsqd & Moflo Music
"Firm Foundation" by Maverick City
"You're Gonna Be Ok" by Rave Jesus & SON.

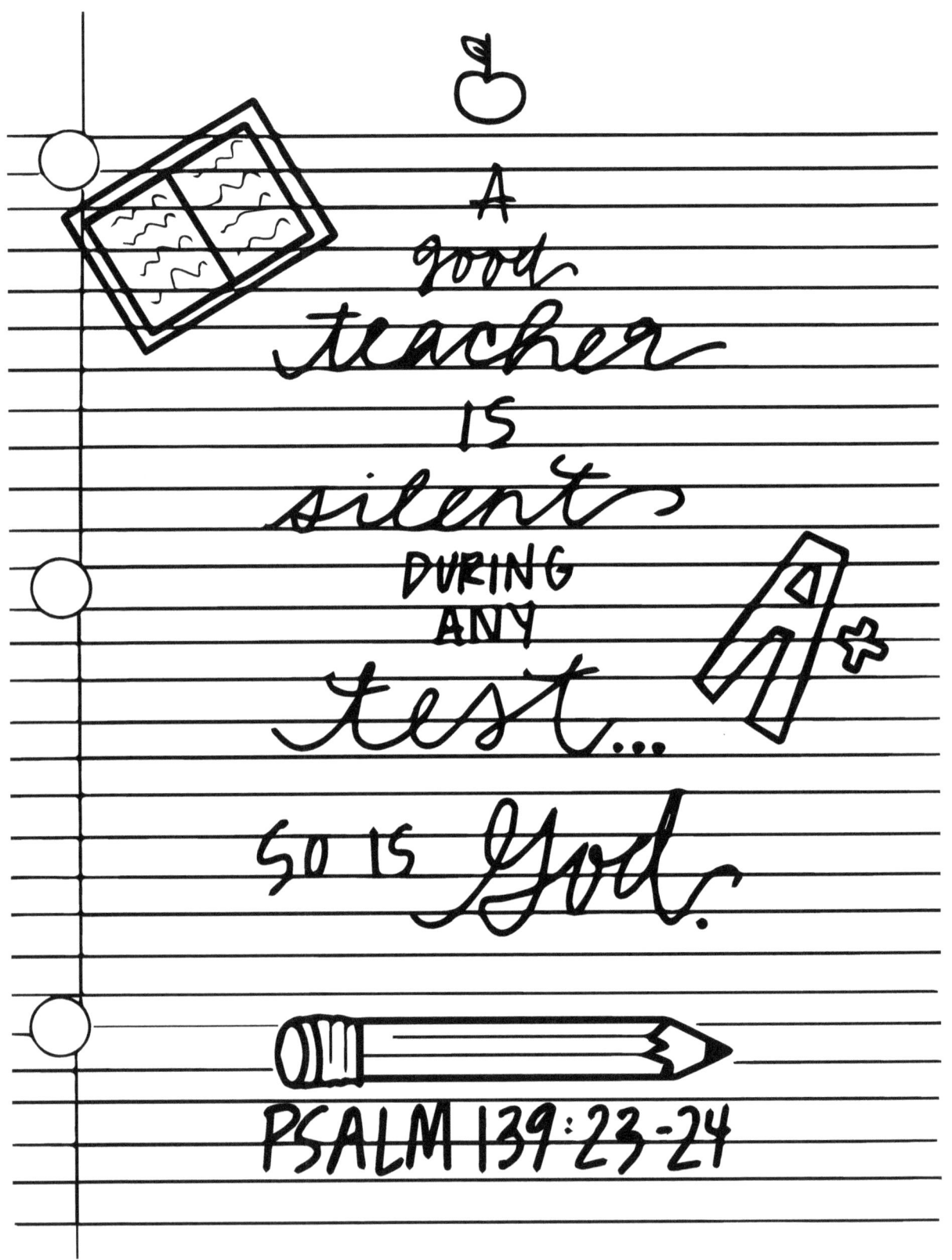

Unreliable Faith

Psalm 139:23-24 says, "Search me, O God, and know my heart; try me and know my anxious thoughts; and see if there be any hurtful way in me, and lead me in the everlasting way." If you've ever prayed a prayer like this, one where you ask for God to reveal what's inside of you or even for God to give you more of something like patience or grace, you may have found that you were not given those things easily, but were tested and tried allowing you to grow in that area! If you've never prayed a prayer like this, let me be the one to tell you, God will gladly give you these desires of your heart, but sometimes it comes unexpectedly and likely not how you'd plan it yourself.

One thing is for certain, if you ask, you shall receive if what you ask for is of pure motives and aligns with God's will. God wants us to be strengthened, pruned, and to grow in His spiritual giftings, fruit, and all matters of Him, especially in the areas of faith and love! Sometimes God may ease you into these things and give you what you asked for without much effort. However, other times, God may be abrupt and place you in situations and tests that require you to lean on Him to make it through and get what you asked for. Why does God do this? Why doesn't He just give us everything we need/ask for with ease and comfort? I've come to find that especially in the area of faith(confidence in God), if it's untested, it's unreliable. Do you really trust God the way you think? Do you really have the faith you say you do? Storms expose the answers to those questions. During said tests, Jesus, like any good teacher, may be silent while the test is commencing. Is this cruel or is this allowing room for growth? Let's take a look at how someone first-hand went through a test that would rattle anyone.

Read Matthew 14:22-33

1. What did Jesus say to Peter in verse 29?

....

2. How did Peter respond?

....

....

....

3. Once Peter stepped outside of the boat, did Jesus give him any further instructions or guidance?

....

4. Focus on verse 30. What happened to Peter in the midst of this test of faith?

....

....

5. Why do you think this outcome occurred?

....

....

....

6. How did Jesus respond as a result of Peter's actions?

....

....

....

7. What did Jesus say was the reason Peter sank?

....

8. Although Jesus was silent, what does Jesus' response say about His character and His proximity to Peter (and you) during this test & trial?

....

....

....

....

> *Special note: Did you realize that Jesus said, "You of little faith...." He did not say, "You of no faith...," showing that Peter did have faith and was still in good standing with God (Hebrews 11:6), but he needed a bit more to fully complete the mission. Maybe Peter specifically had faith in Jesus and His ability to walk on water, but he didn't have enough faith in the authority Jesus gave him to walk on the water and remain there amongst strong winds too. Jesus thus gave Peter real, raw, and constructive criticism for Peter's betterment. Isn't Jesus truly the best "Rabboni" (teacher) ever?*

November

9. *Take a look at four other well known people who were tested. After reading about their experience, answer the questions.*

	How was the person tested?	How did the person respond?	What did this test expose about the person?	Did the person pass or fail the test?	Where was God during it all?
Read Genesis 3 Adam & Eve					
Read Genesis 22 Abraham					
Read Mark 4:35-41 Jesus' Disciples					
Read Acts 2:12-41 Peter					

Selah Moment:

If they failed, what could the person have done differently? Where did he/she mess up?

....
....
....
....

> *If they passed the test, what did the person do well? What strategy can you takeaway from their experience?*
>
> ....
> ....
> ....
> ....

Read Isaiah 41:10-13

10. Although God may be silent at times, what does this scripture say about His proximity to His children? Is He near or far? Explain how you know.

....
....
....

Read James 1:12 and 1 Corinthians 9:24-25 (KJV)

11. When you press through and endure the various tests/trials in this life, what is promised?

....
....
....

Read Luke 12:8-12

12. How did Jesus say the disciples would pass the upcoming test they would be faced with? Who would help them?

....
....

*Like a note sheet is to a student,
so the Holy Spirit is to a believer.*

Let's make it personal

How does knowing that God is with you/close to you make you feel? How does God's response to Peter in Matthew 14 make you feel?

....
....
....
....
....
....

What tests or trials have you faced recently? Do you feel like you passed or failed? Did you feel like God was near or far? Explain.

....
....
....
....
....
....
....
....
....

If you feel like you failed, what should you be praying for to be better equipped next time? Did you cry out to God as Peter did when he began to sink? If not, cry out right now and talk to your Heavenly Father about it all.

....
....
....
....
....

....
....
....
....

Although you may fall short at times, failing the test presented, know that God will never leave you or forsake you. Although He does discipline and corrects His children, He won't beat you or yell harsh words at you for your mistakes, He is a God of mercy and love who disciplines with a compassionate heart; pay attention to His voice of correction. Keep your faith and keep your eyes fixed on Jesus to pass the tests that come your way, learn from your failures(repent when necessary), and keep going.

Worship Playlist: *"Another In The Fire" by Hillsong UNITED & TAYA*
"One More Day" by Sons of Sunday

December

December

Pressed

Whether anticipated or unexpected, when trials hit, it can hurt physically, mentally, emotionally, spiritually, or a mixture of all of them. As times get darker, Jesus has warned us through the scriptures that pressure and tension will increase and the fight to stand in faith will become more difficult for His disciples. Will you overcome? Will you endure until the end? I pray you will. Have you ever felt the tension of standing in faith and denying your flesh or what the world says is right? Jesus told Peter, "the spirit is willing but the flesh weak", this proves that there is a battle within us to choose Christ over everything else. Where is our hope? How can we stand the pressure tests when they come? Take notes as you read this week because now, more than ever in history, we are closer to times of great tribulation and must be able to stand the pressures to come.

Read 2 Corinthians 4:8-12

1. Write out verses 8-9 below.

....
....
....

2. Summarize the above verses in your own words.

....
....
....
....

Read Romans 6:5-6, Matthew 16:24-26, 2 Corinthians 1:5, and Romans 12:1

3. Now, focusing on 2 Corinthians 4:10-11 again, explain what Paul meant in these two verses.

....
....
....
....

4. Based on 2 Corinthians 4:12, why are the above verses necessary and worthwhile? (See 2 Corinthians 5:20, 2 Corinthians 13:9, Matthew 28:19, and Acts 2:38 for additional support).

....
....
....
....

Read 2 Corinthians 4:13-18, 1 John 4:4, and Romans 8:28-31.

5. Is there any consolation(comfort/relief) for Christians despite the many trials and moments we/they are hard pressed? What is it?

....
....
....
....
....

Do some research:

6. What is required for a diamond to be created on Earth?

....
....
....
....
....

7. How was olive oil traditionally created?

....
....
....
....
....

Both of these items go through similar hardships and immense pressure when being created, but they both have great value and beauty upon completion. Presently, the most valuable diamond is worth about $400 million. As for olive oil, if you go to any grocery store today, you can find an array of options at various prices. But in B.C. days, olive oil was a delicacy, and you can infer the value based on the account of the Widow and Elisha in 2 Kings 4:1-7. So, know that the crushing and pressing you feel as a believer is worthwhile! For just as the diamonds and olives, great value and beauty comes when one endures and "presses" through.

Read Mark 13:9, 23, 33-37, Mark 14:32-38, and 2 John 1:8

8. What verbs are repeated and meant to help you overcome times of great pressure? What did Jesus do to endure His time of greatest pressure?

....

....

9. Define "stay on guard", "watch", and "pray". Remember to define these based on the greek definition.

....

....

....

....

Read Mark 14:43-47, 66-72, and John 18:10-11

10. How could Peter's responses have been different if He had stayed on guard, watched, and prayed as Jesus told him in the garden?

....

....

....

....

Let's make it personal

How has your prayer life and intimacy with God been? Are you alert and awake? (Hint: one way to test how alert you are, what signs of the end times have you noticed, see Mark 13:3-13 and 2 Timothy 3:1-5) Explain.

....
....
....
....
....
....

Do you freely and readily share the gospel with people? If so, what motivates you to do so? If not, what hinders you?

....
....
....
....
....
....
....

Who do you know that is not saved? Make a list.

....
....
....
....
....
....

Take this time to pray for them and be intentional about sharing the gospel with at least 2 or 3 of them this week. One valuable way to share with others is by expressing what you've given up in order to obey God and be in a relationship with Him AND what you've gained and look forward to because of this sacrifice. Also, it's important to note that having a relationship with the person you're sharing with can also be more effective, so listen to and get to know those you desire to share with and ask God to speak directly to them through you.

When you're ready, here are some great scriptures for sharing the gospel and leading someone into salvation: Romans 6:23, Romans 10:9, and John 1:9-13. See Appendix E at the back of the book for more tips.

> *Note: the person you share the gospel with may not give his/her life to Christ in that moment, but be confident in this, that what you shared with him/her was a seed planted or a seed watered. God will bring the increase in time (1 Corinthians 3:6-9).*

Although you will go through many trials living in this world and not of it, remember that your righteousness in Christ and your choice to live for Him is not in vain. You are aiding in the salvation of others, thus snatching them from the pits of Hell by living righteously even in the midst of trials and adversity. There is an eternal reward for those in Christ, and if there is any consolation, remember you are not alone in this crushing and pressing, for your other brothers and sisters in the faith are enduring the same trials around the world (1 Peter 5:9).

Worship playlist: *"New Wine (Live)" by Hillsong Worship*

December

Blank Canvas, Clean Slate

Better than any new year's resolution that comes once a year, God's mercies are new each day of the year! That's 365 new mercies each morning (Lamentation 3:22-23)! Although this grace, mercy, and a clean slate is available, have you ever struggled with accepting all of it from God because you were too focused on the fact that you failed so badly? That's called condemnation, and guess what? God has provided a way for you to turn that failure into the opportunity to begin again and be better with no strings attached. Don't believe it? Let's look at God's word for the receipts.

Read Genesis 6:1-17

1. What displeased God?

....
....
....

2. How do we know God was displeased? How did God react to the way humans were acting?

....
....
....

3. Why did God flood the earth?

....
....
....

Read Genesis 8:20-21 and Genesis 9:8-16

4. After the flood and Noah's sacrifice, what does God promise never to do again? What symbol of this covenant did He instill?

....
....
....

Read Leviticus 4:1-3, 27-28

5. What did God require people to do to be reconciled to Him?

....

....

....

Read 2 Corinthians 5:14-21 and John 12:47-50

6. What was Jesus' purpose in coming into the world?

    (**Hint:** *Pay attention to how Jesus is similar to the animals God required scriptures above*)

....

....

....

7. Did Jesus judge and condemn the world for its heinous actions of sin and not obeying His word?

....

8. However, when will judgment happen?

....

....

....

Read Romans 6:23 and Romans 7:24-25

9. What do you need to be saved from?

....

....

....

Read Romans 8:1-6

10. Who is there "no condemnation" for?

....

....

11. Based on your answer to #10, what is first required of you so that you're not condemned when Jesus returns?

....

> Selah Moment:
>
> Knowing the above things, why is it important to not condemn yourself for falling short? (Also see Appendix A in the back of the journal for more insight)
>
> ....
>
> ....
>
> ....
>
> ....

Not convinced that God doesn't require you to condemn yourself? God, in all of His goodness, gave you an example of how much He loves you and readily is waiting to offer you a clean slate and a blank canvas. Take a look.

Read Luke 15:11-24

Marred with sin, defeat, mistakes, and awful mess-ups, if the prodigal son's life was a painting, how would you describe it after he left home? Circle one

Beautiful, a true Picasso piece of art   OR   *Hideous, filled with mistakes, poor color choice*

12. What caused the prodigal son to decide to return home?

....

....

13. Define "repentance." (Merriam-Webster's definition is great)

....
....
....

14. What part of the prodigal son's journey showed repentance?

....
....
....

15. How did his father receive him? Was he worried about his mistakes and failures?

....
....
....

16. Based on the father's response, what was the only thing required for the prodigal son to gain a clean slate? A new canvas? A fresh start with his father?

....
....
....

> Selah (Pause and Reflect) moment:
>
> — If the prodigal son would've seen returning home as a means of highlighting that he failed rather than the opportunity to begin again, do you think he would've gone home?
>
> — If the prodigal son would've kept his same way of shameful thinking (condemnation, worried about having to face his family, continuing to work with the pigs, etc.), how would his life have turned out differently?

Read Isaiah 1:18-20

17. Compare the prodigal son's father to God, our Heavenly Father. What similarities do you see?

....

....

....

Just as the Prodigal son realized, don't be so consumed in the fact that you have sinned, fallen short, and gotten in a bad place/situation. You're never too far from God. Simply repent and see God's forgiveness (a blank canvas) as an opportunity to begin again rather than a sign of you being a failure. God loves you and welcomes you back with open arms; just make your way down the road home. Remember, there is no condemnation for those who are in Christ Jesus and God desires nothing more than to embrace you even while you're covered in dirt, but He doesn't want to leave you in that condition. He wants to clean you up and offer you salvation through accepting His Son as Lord and Savior.

Have you made that decision? If so, skip ahead to the "let's make it personal" section. If not, do you want to? According to Romans 10:9-13, all that is required is for you to confess with your mouth that Jesus is Lord and believe in your heart that God raised Him from the dead. Although it requires simple steps, this is a very big decision and shouldn't be taken lightly. If you desire to put your full trust in God, take a moment to pray. Need help? Pray this and add whatever else you feel you want to say to Him:

> Father God, thank you for offering me the special gift of eternal life so that I can escape death and have a chance to be made new daily. Father God, I desire to be made new. I repent of every sin I've committed known and unknown and admit I need a Savior. I believe in my heart that you raised Jesus from the dead and I confess that Jesus is Lord and He reigns supreme. I put my life in Your hands. Please lead me, guide me, and direct me as I embark on this new journey with you. I need you daily, baptize me with your Holy Spirit and bring conviction so that I may strive to not sin against you. In Jesus' name, Amen.

If you prayed that prayer sincerely, today is a new beginning! And I'm so happy for you! Life is better in community, so ask God to lead you to a good Bible-teaching church or small group and continue to seek the Lord daily. He loves you so much.

Let's make it personal

After salvation, sin isn't completely eradicated overnight and thus daily repentance is necessary. What mistakes have you made lately? What sin have you entered into, and, rather than repenting and trading in your faulty canvas for a new one, you're holding onto it?

....
....
....
....
....
....

Do you desire to let go of those sins and run back to God now? Are you ready to exchange your filthy canvas for a blank one?

Circle one: YES   *or*   NO

If your answer is yes, simply stop right now and confess it all to God. If you need help with repenting, read Psalm 51 to see how David repented to God after committing adultery!

After you have repented, what do you desire to do with your blank canvas/clean slate now? What are some boundaries you should put in place so that you don't keep falling into those same sins?

....
....
....
....
....
....

God has paved the way for us to run back to Him every time we sin and fall short. Learn from the messed up paint strokes, repent, and trade in your faulty canvas for a blank one every time.

God's grace is sufficient. So, although needing a fresh start signifies that you messed up, be thankful that Jesus paved the way for you to have new mercies each morning. Just as God could see Adam and Eve hiding, He can see you, He loves you, and He's ready to embrace you with open arms and with a blank canvas to begin again. Let go of your pride and turn back to God. He's waiting for you, just as the prodigal son's father was waiting for him.

Worship Playlist: *"To You" by Maverick City*

December

Worth the Wait

*E*ver wanted something so badly that you just couldn't wait to get it, achieve it, or just look at it!? If there is a delay in between the desire and the fruition of those moments, it is often tough to trust God's timing and wait on Him to provide in giving you the open door or giving you His "yes." Rather than allowing your thoughts to run wild, grow discouraged, worry, or speak negatively, God offers another solution; to wait on Him, the Lord! Let's peek into God's word and see precisely what waiting on Him looks like and what it looks like if we choose to move ahead of Him.

Read Psalm 27:14

1. Define "wait."

....
....

2. Define "Lord."

....
....

3. Therefore, what does it mean to "wait on the Lord?"

....
....

Read Genesis 12:1-7, Genesis 13:14-18, Genesis 15:4-5.

4. What were the two consistent promises that God gave to Abram?

....
....
....

5. How old was Abram when God gave him this promise?

....

Read Genesis 11:29-30.

6. During the time of the promise God gave to Abram, did he and his wife have any children?

....

> Selah Moment:
>
> How do you think Abram felt hearing these promises from God despite his current state? How would you feel or react if God made a promise to you while your circumstances didn't look favorable for said outcome to come to be?
>
> ....
> ....
> ....

Revisit Genesis 12:4-8 and Genesis 13:1-4,17-18

7. How did Abram respond to the instructions of the Lord? How did he wait on the Lord to fulfill His promises?

....
....
....
....

> Selah Moment:
>
> What are some practical tips you can take away from Abram's waiting? How can you apply Abram's tactics to your life while you wait on the Lord?"
>
> ....
> ....
> ....
> ....
> ....

Read Genesis 15

8. After some time of not seeing God's provisions as He'd promise, what do you notice Abram began to do?

....
....
....

9. How does God respond to Abram's worry (fear) and doubt?

....
....
....

If you are waiting for something and are worried or doubting, be encouraged that God is ready to listen to your cries, don't give up or lose your faith in Him. Instead, pause here to talk to Him about how you're feeling and where you're at.

Selah Moment:

Ask God to restate His promises to you again. If you wrote them down, take time to go back and read what He said then write it down below.

....
....

Reflect on the character of God and remind yourself of who He is. Read Numbers 23:19, Titus 1:2, Hebrews 6:18 and Matthew 7:11, what do you notice about God? How can you use this to encourage yourself to wait on Him?

....
....
....
....

How do you feel knowing the above character of God and seeing how He responded to Abram when he was struggling to wait and believe?

....
....
....
....

Read Genesis 16

10. Had Sarai been able to have children yet?

11. How long had Abram and Sarai lived in Canaan? (this is about how long they'd been waiting for God's promise of offspring to come to pass too).

12. After time went by, what was Sarai's solution for their circumstance?

13. What was the result of Abram and Sarai's impatience, unbelief, and not waiting on the Lord?

14. How old was Abram when he received his first son outside of the promise/will of God?

Read Genesis 17

15. How old was Abraham?

16. What is God's only stipulation to Abraham for himself and his descendants to partake in the promise?

17. What does God reiterate about Sarah?

....

....

....

18. Why was Abraham in disbelief and humored by God's promise?

....

....

....

Note: God got more specific with Abraham as he got closer to the promise coming to pass.

19. What was Abraham to name his son?

....

20. Although in disbelief and skepticism, how does Abraham respond to God's orders as he awaited the covenant (promise) coming to pass?

....

....

....

Read Genesis 21:1-5 and Hebrews 6:13-15

21. What happened?

....

....

....

22. How old was Abraham?

....

23. *Using Abraham's current age in Genesis 21, subtract it from his age in Genesis 12 when God initially told Abraham (Abram) the promise. How long did Abraham and Sarah have to wait on the Lord?*

....

Sit with this reality for a second: Abraham and Sarah waited that many years for a piece of God's promise to come to pass. Although it was long awaited(in their and our eyes), God's word did not return void. He did not lie to 75 years old Abram all those years ago.

Read 2 Peter 3:8-9

24. *What promise is the world currently waiting on to come to pass?*

....
....
....
....

25. *What does this scripture also suggest that we, as a people group, are waiting for? Why hasn't it come to pass? (See Ezekiel 18:23 & 31-32 for additional support)*

....
....
....
....

26. *What is unique about how God tells time?*

....
....
....
....

Read Matthew 25:1-13

27. *What did the wise bridesmaids do while they waited for the bridegroom (Jesus)?*

....
....

28. What happened to the bridesmaids that were not prepared and did not wait on the bridegroom well?

....

....

....

Read Matthew 6:33-34, 2 Peter 3:11-13 and 1 Corinthians 15:56-58

29. Write Matthew 6:33-34 in the translation you connect with most.

....

....

30. In order to effectively wait on the Lord, you should "remain in readiness." So, while you wait, what should you be doing spiritually?

....

....

....

....

....

Let's make it personal

On a scale of 1-10, how much do you trust God(especially in times of delay)?

....

What moments in life (childhood, conversations, scriptures you've read, etc) have helped you to trust God? If applicable, what moments in life have caused you to struggle with trusting Him, especially in times of delay?

....

....

....

....

This week, you saw that God is a trustworthy Father who keeps His promises and doesn't lie. Take some time to thank God for who He is and ask Him to soften your heart and help you to believe these truths, to heal the wounds of life that have made this reality hard to accept. Write your prayer below or any revelation God gives you.

....
....
....
....

Ultimately, we are all waiting for Christ's return. Are you waiting well? How so? How not?

....
....
....
....
....
....

Think back to the Selah moments and what you learned earlier in this journal entry about how to practically wait on the Lord. Pick at least two things you're going to intentionally apply to your life to "remain in readiness" and prepare for what you're waiting for.

....
....
....
....
....
....

Whether you desire to own your own home or business, desire a boyfriend/girlfriend/spouse or an enhanced relationship, desire a pet or a baby, or desire to see equality in this world; whether you desire your patience to be stronger or your heart to be softer, wait on the Lord. During the waiting process, ask God to check your heart behind the desire, ask Him to perfect you and make you better during the process, and ask Him how you are to prepare yourself if that desire is in His will for you. It's also very important to know who God is (His character, what He's done, His many names per the scriptures) in order to trust Him in the face of waiting and adversity. So, as you continue to read the Holy scriptures, take note of God's character and hold onto it. For starters, remember, if God made you a promise, as He did to Abram and Sarai, He will NOT allow it to return to Him void, meaning He will not let that promise fall short. So, decree, declare, and believe that it WILL come to pass! Seek God and seek Him wholeheartedly for direction and comfort as you wait on Him... it will be worth the wait in the end.

Worship playlist: *"Wait on You" by: Elevation Worship & Maverick City*
"The Father's Song (Live)" by UPPERROOM & Elyssa Smith
"dad song" by Abbie Gamboa & UPPERROOM
"Wait For U" by Bryan Terrell

Chosen by the King!

Remember when we were in school and teams had to be picked for a game or activity? Team captains were chosen, and everyone else stood waiting to find out whose team they'd be drafted for. In these amateur drafts, no one wanted to be the last pick for fear of feeling left out, not good enough, or simply not cared about. Talk about stress! To top it off, these team drafts were often based on popularity, with a bit of talent needed on the side. Nonetheless, we were likely so anxious to be picked for a team that would last all of 10 minutes.

Although we'd love to say this mentality of wanting to be chosen first or third (but definitely not last) was buried and left behind in those school days, it probably wasn't. Whether you're up for a new job, working toward a promotion, wanting to start dating, or simply entering a raffle, the desire to be picked in some form or fashion is still there; the team captains and who you're up against have just changed. In a way, being chosen for the greatest team of all requires a draft too. The team captain is God Himself and everyone in the world are in the running. Let's see how God chooses His team.

Read Deuteronomy 7:1-11

1. *What group of people is God speaking to in this text? (See Exodus 1:8-14 and Exodus 3:7-10 for additional support).*

....

....

....

2. *How does Moses describe God's people whom he's speaking to in this text?*

....

....

....

....

3. *Being that God deemed them as a holy people, what did He command that they do/not do? (See Genesis 17:9-14 for additional support)*

....

....

4. Why did God choose this group of people to be His chosen ones? (See Genesis 12:1-9, Genesis 15:12-14, Genesis 17:15-22 for additional support)

....

....

....

> Selah Moment:
> So in those days, what was required for you to be chosen for God's team?
>
> ....
>
> ....

Read Acts 10:9-48

5. What did Peter battle with when God first gave him the vision?

....

....

....

6. What was God's response to Peter's denial of what he heard and saw in the vision?

....

....

....

7. What did Peter tell Cornelius was unlawful? Why did Peter go against the law?

....

....

....

8. After Peter engaged with Cornelius and saw what God did, what did he and the other Jews with him come to realize? (See Romans 3:28-30 and Galatians 3:28-29 for additional support)

....

....

....

Read Matthew 22:1-14

9. Why did the king open up the wedding to all people?

....

....

....

10. Based on the parable, who is invited into the Kingdom of Heaven?

....

....

....

11. Why was a man kicked out of the wedding?

....

....

....

12. Therefore, who can stay in the kingdom of Heaven? What's the dress code? What must you have on? (Very Important: Read Isaiah 61:10, Job 29:14, Romans 3:20-24, and Revelation 19:6-8)

....

....

....

....

Read Romans 11:1-19

13. *Why were Gentiles (non-Jews) allowed to partake in being God's chosen?*

....

....

....

14. *How does this relate to the parable you read in Matthew 22:1-14?*

....

....

....

Read John 15:10-17 and Romans 5:8-9

15. *As a believer, did you choose God first or did He choose you first? Explain.*

....

....

....

....

16. *Although you must choose to give your life to Christ, how did Jesus (God) first choose you? (See Matthew 26:38-46, Matthew 27:45-54, John 6:44, and Galatians 3:13 for additional support).*

....

....

....

17. *In Jesus choosing you, what has He called you to do with this selection? (See Matthew 28:18-20 and John 14:12 for additional support).*

....

....

....

December

Read Exodus 3:13-14 & John 8:58

18. What does God say His name is?

....

....

Read 1 Peter 2:9, Deuteronomy 14:2, and Hebrews 10:10-14

19. What has the great "I Am" said about you as a believer?

....

....

....

20. WOW! So God, the creator of the universe and author of life calls YOU, CHOSEN for His team. How will you respond? (See Psalm 71:15-16 and Psalm 107:1-2 for some tips)

> *Sidenote: if you haven't accepted Jesus as your Lord and Savior, you are invited to the team, will you say yes? You too can be called chosen, you are welcome and wanted!*

....

....

....

Read Galatians 3:23-29, Galatians 11:1-24, and 1 Timothy 2:1-7

21. At the beginning of this week's journal entry, you read that the descendants of Abraham, Isaac, and Jacob(Israel) were the chosen ones, why are you now able to be called "chosen" too? Did God change his mind about Abraham's descendants?

....

....

....

Say this loudly and believe it: I AM CHOSEN BY GOD, THE GREAT I AM! THE CREATOR OF THE HEAVENS AND THE EARTH HAS HAND-PICKED ME AND DRAFTED ME ONTO HIS TEAM! HALLELUJAH! I AM CHOSEN!

Let's make it personal

Before the foundation of the world, God, the creator of the universe and everyone and everything in it, had you in mind and planned to deny Himself of His riches and status and instead fight for you because He desired and longed to have you as part of His family! God came all the way from heaven to earth in the flesh of Jesus, to choose you for His team! How does this make you feel?

....
....
....
....
....
....

Choose this day, how will you now live knowing what God says about you? Knowing that you have been chosen (or invited) for the greatest team/family of all?

....
....
....
....
....
....
....

If you're struggling with feeling rejected and left out by your earthly friends, family, or peers, take this time to share that hurt with your loving heavenly father. Express every pain and cry out to Him. Then ask Him to heal and fill those wounds in your heart so that you can thrive in Him.

Well, there you have it, be encouraged that you've been drafted as a first-round pick onto the greatest team of all time, God's team. Know that He cares for you deeply, has great plans for you, and has called you higher! Whether you accept that calling is up to you. What will you choose?

Worship Playlist: *"Man of Your Word" by Maverick City Music*
"Last Days, Pt. 2" by Bryan Terell
"Most High" by Marcus Rogers ft. Live
"HI-C" by HOLY GIRLXHLYGRL, Porsha Love, & Wande (ft. Queen Lee & TK Lee)

December

Time of Reflection: Part 3

Reflect on the past four months of life, then honestly and vulnerably answer the following questions. If you need more lines, use the "additional pages" in the back of this journal!

What are some memorable or important things that have happened in the past 4 months (these can be good or bad, happy, sad, or anyhwere in between)?

....
....
....
....
....
....
....
....
....
....

What have you been doing well? What do you want to celebrate? What has brought you joy?

....
....
....
....
....
....
....
....
....
....
....
....

As you reflect, what main emotions have you felt in the past four months?

....
....
....
....
....

What have you not been doing so well? What are you struggling with? Do you have any fears? Has anything been painful to endure? How do you need help?

....
....
....
....
....
....
....
....
....
....
....
....

How is your relationship with God? Use the questions below to help you explain.

- *How have you been seeking after Him? Do you think you've "found Him"?(Jeremiah 29:13) How so or not?*
- *Have you felt connected to Him? How so or not?*
- *Are you disappointed or angry with Him? Are you feeling grateful for Him? Do you believe you can trust Him? etc. Take this time to celebrate with Him in the areas you have felt grateful in. Be sure to slow down as you answer these questions and ask the Lord to ease your heart and help you work through any tough areas. Ask Him for His perspective of situations you've experienced and ask Him to show you how He sees you as you've endured. Wait to hear His reply.*

    If you need to process some tough emotions or moments, here's a grief cycle model I've followed, you can shorten or change it as you need(timeframe: 1-7 days, depends on you): cry(express emotion) > pray vulnerably (verbally and/or written) > cry > hear God (be still to listen) > share (tell a trusted and prayerful friend what you're going through) > hear God (be still to listen) > cry > accept what God said > pray (release the situation) > cry > sing praises & thank God as you move on (Psalm 30:1-5)

....
....
....
....
....
....
....
....
....
....

What deep desires do you have in life right now? How have you seen inklings or ways of them being fulfilled? Do you think they haven't been fulfilled at all? Explain.

(Note: Only God can satisfy our deepest longings, so be sure to take note of how He's bringing fulfillment even if you don't see the physical manifestation of your desires as you imagined. If you don't see Him doing so, take this time to pray vulnerably expressing that, ask Him to open your eyes to see all He is doing, and surrender your desires to Him.)

....
....
....
....
....
....
....
....
....

What goals do you have? How are you taking responsibility to reach them?

How do you feel best supported and cared for by friends and family? On a rate of 1-10, how supported and cared for have you felt by them? Explain.

What God-approved things do you enjoy doing? How often have you been participating in them? How have those moments been for you?

> *Note: "God-approved" does not just mean going to church or to church events. It means things that are not against His commands. God also values rest and enjoying life while maintaining our righteousness in Christ, see Ecclesiastes 8, so be sure to take time to just enjoy life with Him.*

If you could change one thing about your life right now, what would it be? Why?

> *Suggestion: Pray and ask God about this thing. Ask Him for the revelation of why you want it, ask if it's a pure desire to have, and the provision if it's in God's will. Ask God to search your heart and show you the root of your desire.*

What areas of growth do you want to see happen within yourself over the course of the next four months?

Now, take a look at your first time of reflection from April and take mental note of the changes you see, the trends you notice, and how are you motivated to press on and forward in these next few months.

END OF JOURNAL MESSAGE

Wow, you've made it to the last page of your journal. Yay for seeking God beyond Sunday morning! Write yourself a note of encouragement and reflection on the past year.

....
....
....
....
....
....
....
....
....
....
....
....
....
....
....
....
....
....
....
....
....
....
....
....

GO IN PEACE, LOVE, AND FULLNESS OF JOY.

Additional Blank Pages

Use these pages to take any extra notes you'd like in your journal.

CBJ: A 52-Week Devotional

Date: _____

CBJ: A 52-Week Devotional

Date: _____

Date: _____

Date: _____

CBJ: A 52-Week Devotional

Date: _____

Answer Key

JANUARY 379
Is God's word really written in the Bible? 379
Be Still and Know 379
Beacon of Light 381
Primary Concern 382

FEBRUARY 382
The Path to Purity 382
Do you love Jesus? 383
Faith OVER Feelings 384
Seek God 385

MARCH 387
Mountains and Valleys 387
No Time for Negativity 387
Affirmation 388
Be a Good Steward 389
Shine On! 391

APRIL 392
Time with God 392
One Way 394
Finished Work 395
Deeply Loved 396

MAY 398
Pray Without Ceasing 398
Testimony 398
See God, Experience God 399
Snatched Thoughts 400

JUNE 400
God Knows 400
Overflow 403
Resist 403
Choose this Day 405

JULY 406
Peace in Chaos 406
Lean Not 407
Get Up! 408
You be You, Let God be God 410

AUGUST 412
- Order over Chaos 412
- Run the Race 413
- The Love of God 414
- Crafty with Purpose 415

SEPTEMBER 416
- Plans, Plans, Plans! 416
- Broken Jars 418
- Tell Your Story 420
- Ablaze 420

OCTOBER 421
- Vision 421
- Obey 422
- Altogether Beautiful 423
- The Great Escape 424

NOVEMBER 425
- Deeply Rooted 425
- God is With You 426
- Don't Tap Out! 428
- Unreliable Faith 430

DECEMBER 431
- Pressed 431
- Blank Canvas...Clean Slate 432
- Worth the Wait 433
- Chosen by the King! 435

Answer Key

JANUARY

Is God's word really written in the Bible?

1. Instruction (giving us direction), conviction (to unsettle us when we do what is wrong in God's sight), correction (to point out our errors and show us the right way), and training in righteousness (to show us the correct way of doing things and how to live rightly before God). Ultimately, it equips us to do all God has called us to do and give us hope presently, and for the future of being one with God for eternity!

2. God inspired or "breathed out" the scriptures. This means it was through the power of God, the inspiration of God, and God instructing, directing, and guiding the writers via His word and Holy Spirit that the Bible was written to record what was said and what occurred.

3. A prophecy is the communicated and enforced revelation of truth before it occurs, a prediction telling of future events.

4. Before Christ.

5. Anno Domini, which means "in the year of our Lord."

6. This shows that Jesus' life was so monumental that even unbelievers couldn't help but acknowledge the existence of Christ and the shift that resulted because of Him. Thus also validating the Bible's truth and ability to be a reliable source of not only God's word and instruction, but also world history in general, as the Bible tells the accounts of God and people before, during, and after Jesus walked the Earth.

7. You'd probably expect that sentence to be a jumbled mess and be completely different from the original message.

8. The only way for a wall of that caliber to collapse there would have to have been an earthquake. The city was burned, and the Israelites did not live in Jericho after it was destroyed per God's instructions. They were also instructed to not take any plunder, so that explains why there were so many remains left amongst the rubble.

Be Still and Know

1. Definitely not.

2. Noun: a supreme ruler, especially a monarch.

Adjective: possessing supreme or ultimate power.

3. SOVEREIGN

4. Protector, refuge, strength, helper, and all-powerful

5. I think of stillness as a peace that surpasses a personal state of being.

6. The opposite of stillness is chaos - a perception of busyness but not getting anything done.

7. It is protection from outside forces.

8. Knowing that God is your protector, help in the midst of trouble, and is all-powerful, you can rest assured that He will do exactly what He says and be exactly who He is now and forever (Hebrews 13:8).

9. God had to give Satan permission to test Job, and He gave him parameters as to how far he could go in those tests. In Ezekiel we see that for witches or sorcerers to have any power, God had to allow them to have it. Being so, He also had the power to take such power away.

10. God is all-powerful, and even Satan himself has to answer to Him.

11. Job was allowed to go through the hardships to test his faith.

12. God was still watching over Him. We know this because He brags about Job's response to Satan's tests.

13. He was visibly distraught, in pain, and complained, but he never stopped praising God, and he didn't blame God for what happened in his life, even though his own wife told him he should do otherwise.

14. Job understood that he came into this world with nothing, and when he died, it would be the same way. Job also understood that God has the sovereign power to give and take away. Understanding these things helped him stay as unattached as possible to the temporary earthly things and, instead, still praise the eternal God he still had.

15. Job began to reflect on his past arrogantly, not remembering that God made those many provisions. Job focused heavily on his mistreatment, which led him to question why God "abandoned" him and had "done" this to him. Being more focused on the idea that he was a "good man," he also felt he had done nothing wrong and never sinned to deserve that treatment (Job 34:6), all of which caused him more turmoil.

16. Job is reminded of what very little power he has, as all of his answers to God's questions are no! We see that God is sovereign because he is all-powerful and all-knowing, and He has all of the answers to every question He asked of Job. We see this same trend in Isaiah; God is seen as incomparable, all-powerful, sees all and knows all. It is through God that we can find our strength in any circumstance.

17. Job was humbled as he reflected on all God said, which then led him to repentance.

18. God restored Job immeasurably and allowed him to live to see his grandchildren's children to the 4th generation!

Answer Key

Beacon of Light

1.

	The group of people mentioned	**God**
Isaiah 1	The people of Israel have turned away from God, but outwardly they were still offering sacrifices and participating in festivals and celebrations unto God. They enjoyed doing what they wanted Monday- Saturday, but on Sunday, they'd be "holy."	Meanwhile, God hated it all because His children, His chosen ones, had abandoned Him inwardly. This is like us choosing to live of the world and allowing our sin to take over rather than turning to God and being with Him. Yet, we still tithe, serve at church on Sunday and do religious acts while our hearts are far from God. God would rather our presence than our presents.
Isaiah 58-59	These chapters show Israel's desire for God to answer them and see their fasting as something meaningful to Him. Yet, their actions were only about them and had little to do God's desires or treating others well. They also engaged in further destruction and no one stepped up to save the people.	God acknowledged the Israelites' longings but told them that He didn't like how they fasted and told them His desires for what true fasting looks like. God also shared His plan to step in and save His people.

2. Descendants of Jacob, aka Israel

3. To call the people of Judah back to God because they'd wandered away.

4. To emerge, to get up or stand up.

5. For this to be commanded of them, they must have been in a seated or given up state; they weren't standing firm as they should and were likely defeated in some way.

6. Israel didn't value or honor God's commands as they should, they were guilty of much unrepentant sin, and yet wanted God to answer their prayers amongst fasting.

7. God pursued them

8. The glory of the Lord.

9. Jesus

10. God will cause all light to go out, thus darkness will cover the earth. Per the scriptures, this will all happen at the second coming of Jesus; aka Jesus' return.

11. God wants us all to be in a relationship with Him, celebrating and rejoicing with Him at the wedding. He also doesn't want any of us to perish the way satan and those who follow him will.

12. We must repent and become a part of His bride, being cleansed from our sins and being clothed afresh with his righteousness and holy lives.

Primary Concern

1. Worrying leads to you being ruled/enslaved to whatever you're worried about and the means you take to achieve comfort. It is a waste to live this way because God made you and allowed you to live for more than just the matters of everyday tangible things in life. (I don't know about you, but this changes my perspective on my need to acquire a multitude of things for myself, thus freeing up more financial resources to give to others).

2. God provides. We see that in Him providing food for the birds and "clothes" for the lilies, things in which they did not work tirelessly for, but it was out of God's love that He provided for them.

3. Little faith.

4. Unbelievers - because they do not know God, thus they do not currently have a Heavenly Father to be their provider.

5. God

6. Believers or those who make God's Kingdom their primary concern

7. God promises to supply your needs.

8. If you live for the Kingdom and make God your primary concern.

9. Heaven, where God dwells.

10. Of chief importance; principal; earliest in time or order.

11. Possible answers: It is something you think about most, it holds a lot of value in your life, and, in comparison to all other things, it is of utmost priority.

12. Possible answers: When faced with options, you choose God over worldly things and live righteously; you read your Bible, pray, live according to what God says (i.e., tithing, helping others, loving others, etc.).

FEBRUARY
The Path to Purity

1. By living according to the Word of God. Obeying God's word and storing it in your heart. To do this you must read and know the word of God.

2. Freedom from adulteration or contamination; freedom from immorality, especially of a sexual nature.

3. God is very specific about what sexual immorality is. Sexual immorality is when one has sex with anyone outside of marriage, of the same sex, of the same family, or a different species, another's spouse, and even lustful thoughts of another.

4. You are told to flee from, put to death, not awaken sexual desires before it's time, and put an end to the things causing you to fall into said sins (ie removing certain people from your life, cancelling subscriptions to

websites or channels you shouldn't be on, not watching certain movies, etc).

5. In order to honor God and the sacrifice He made. This also allows you to honor yourself by not "becoming one"(technically meaning to become married) with various people outside of your spouse and you honor the commitment you made to God when you gave your life to Christ.

6. Sex is permitted within the construct of marriage!

7. By choosing to stay pure, you choose to honor your marriage (whether you are married now or not). Sex also unites those who are having sex. If the person you have chosen to have sex with is not your spouse, you are tied to someone who isn't planning to be committed, welcoming many issues. As Paul said, sexual immorality is the only sin that you commit against yourself as the sin takes place inside of your body. It defiles those who partake in it, therefore bringing about God's judgment on those who choose to act in it continually. As a believer, your body is a temple for God, so it is best to keep it pure.

8. Your sins.

9. Jesus died for your sins to no longer have a hold over you.

10. Those who wash their robes.

11. Those who have cleansed themselves from sin/unrighteousness with the blood of Jesus by repenting and giving your life to Jesus.

12. Purity means free of contamination and when people "wash their robes", they are symbolically freeing themselves of the contamination and stain of sin.

13. By believing in Jesus, confessing and repenting of your sins, and then continuing to walk in the light by obeying His commands.

14. Those who choose to live a life of doing witchcraft, being sexually immoral, murder, worship idols, and live in falsehood and thus do not wash their robes and are not holy.

Do you love Jesus?

1. Peter, Andrew, James, and John. They were all fishermen.

2. They immediately left their fishing equipment and followed Jesus.

3. Peter proclaims that Jesus is the Messiah, the Son of the living God.

4. Peter vows that he would not fall away or betray Jesus. He even said he was willing to die for Him.

5. Jesus says Peter will deny Him three times.

6. Peter followed behind Jesus after His arrest, while sitting amongst strangers (likely unbelievers), Peter was questioned about his relation to Jesus. This led to him denying affiliation to Jesus. Ultimate betrayal.

7. He followed Jesus and wept at the revelation of his betrayal of Him. Please note I am not saying that just

because someone cries or weeps after messing up always means he/she loves the person he/she has hurt. However, in this case, the author mentioning Peter's state of being could point to this for him.

8. Jesus asked Peter if he loved Him.

9. To prefer, "actively doing what the Lord prefers", it's embracing the will of God, choosing His choices.

10. Peter responds by saying, "Yes, you know I love you."

11. Affectionate friendship

12. Phileó is affection, friendship, and passion. Whereas agapaó is rooted in action, obedience, and sacrifice.

13. We must keep His commands.

14. Agapaó

15. God will supply us with the Holy Spirit to help and we will be loved by God and He will be revealed to us and at home within us never leaving or forsaking us until the end.

16. No

17. Those who do the will of God, helping His people, and those clothed in righteousness (Colossians 3:12) will inherit the Kingdom of God. Those who simply do works for God with no affection, those clothed in iniquity (unrepentant sin), and those who do not obey His commands and don't serve others will not inherit the Kingdom of God.

18. Love God with all your heart, soul, and mind.

Let's make it personal

Possible answers; spend quality time with Him, get to know Him by reading about Him in God's word, talk to Him by praying, and be still and listen for His voice/pay attention to what He's saying to you. (God uses His word, people/animals, circumstances, and sometimes His own voice to speak to His people).

Faith OVER Feelings

1. God knows you and desires for you to be close to Him. God knows your unspoken words and the depth of your heart. Jesus is also holding all things together, including you. Lastly, if you feel He is delayed, pray and ask Him for His perspective on the situation as His delay could be purposeful just as it was for Mary, Martha, and Lazarus.

2. God knows exactly where you are in your life, and He has gone before you and has His hand on you. With Him being so close, all you have to do is talk to Him and ask Him for clarity or direction.

3. Although you can isolate and hide from friends/family, like Adam and Eve, you cannot hide from God. God

Answer Key

is with you, even in those dark places. He never leaves your side even if you feel otherwise.

4. God has made you wonderfully complex and intricate. Great thought and care were put into creating you. Every part of you was on purpose and planned!

5. When I feel surrounded, I can seek after God and exchange my thoughts for His. Asking Him for His perspective and His thoughts because His thoughts and ways are much better than mine; full of goodness and truth. I can trust God to have the solution because He is all-powerful, all-knowing, and has better character than me or any other.

6. Although God loves each of us immensely, if people do not surrender to His Son, His final judgment will have them be treated as enemies of God like like Satan. It's also very important for you to know yourself and what environments and people bring temptation that you are weak and vulnerable to. Pray for the salvation of your friends and for the Lord to bring you good company that will walk with you on this journey with Jesus.

7. Judgment day is coming quickly, and unbeknownst to use. Until then, God is withholding Himself from pronouncing judgment so that many more can be saved before that day

8. By remembering that the people who do not believe in God are watching your life and knowing that although you have free will, you choosing not to give in to the same sins as those around you and instead choosing to live according to God's word could be the reason a friend or family member chooses to get to know Jesus. When people see that a transformation is occurring in you, they take notice (especially if you've just given your life to Christ and the friends you used to run with are still living in the world). Be the reason they see Jesus in action; their soul could be saved. And staying submitted to God yourself so that you won't end up falling away.

9. Praying for God to search and examine your heart, welcoming God to test you, and pointing out flaws that offend Him will surely keep you in a state of humility and repentance.

10. As you live a life full of forgiving those who have wronged you, God promises to forgive you as well. So by forgiving others and repenting you can be made right with God afresh because of the righteousness of Jesus you have accepted. As quickly as you come to your senses and realize you are wrong is as quickly you can repent and turn back to the Father. Please note: If you have sinned against God this is no laughing matter and repentance is necessary, But due to the patience and loving kindness of Jesus there's also a promise of the Father still embracing you and calling you His; there's no condemnation when you're in Christ. Lift your head.

11. DO NOT FEAR! GOD IS ALWAYS WITH YOU! HE IS EMMANUEL!

Seek God

1. To be soft, flexible, able to be bent; to live or spend in enjoyment. So "delighting" in the Lord isn't about feeling good, but it's about our actions towards God.

Selah Moment(possible answer): To love Him deeply, enjoy His company, to think about Him daily, to be swooned. I imagine a baby cuddling up next to his/her parents.

2. This shows that God desires to be desired by you. He desires to be wanted by you and for you to enjoy Him.

3. They will accept and obey His commands.

4. By seeking God through reading and meditating daily on the Word of God. Being a student of God's word and declaring the scriptures.

5. To love the Lord, our God, with all of our heart, mind, soul, and strength.

6. Love your neighbor as yourself.

7. God is angered by it. He is a jealous God and thus wants our attention.

8. You will ultimately be disappointed as those things will fail you because they can perish. Idolizing things not of God means you're entertaining darkness and thus your whole being will become dark too. God also explicitly shows us that our loyalties will be divided and thus we will not be able to give Him the full attention and honor He is due.

9. God promises His presence(He will be found by them), provisions(provide all they need), and he/she will be blessed(favored by God).

10.

Isaiah 64:5, Joel 2:12-13, Ephesians 2:8-9, and Micah 6:6-8	Isaiah 29:13-14, Isaiah 64:6, and Matthew 7:21-22
-We are commanded to trust in the Lord, delight ourselves in Him, and commit ourselves to Him. -We are saved by grace through faith; works are not what saves us. -Act justly, walk humbly with God, and love mercy. -Joyful workers of righteousness	-People honored God with their words, but their hearts were not with God. -He/she follows rules. -Righteous acts are like filthy rags. -No true authentic relationship with God, but doing works instead.

11. Suggested answer: The left side. It is more focused on walking with God and being with Him before works are mentioned. On the right side, works are at the forefront, and the relationship with God is lacking. So, all in all, God wants us to be in a relationship with Him first, and through that faith move, we will then desire to do work for Him (James 4:18).

12. Sat at Jesus' feet and spent time with HIm.

13. Tried to fix and prepare things for Jesus. Jesus said she was distracted with MUCH serving, so it must have been excessive.

14. Mary. Jesus said she chose the better part as there's few things necessary to please Him and that's sitting with Him.

15. God desires your heart and attention. He desires a relationship with you.

MARCH

Mountains and Valleys

1. God is with you as you walk through it.

2. To protect and guide.

3. No, because God is with you, and you can be comforted knowing He is able to guide you and protect you through the valley with His rod and staff.

4. God will work things out for your good.

5. Those who love Him.

6. All things.

7. His Son, Jesus.

8. Suffering

9. His glory.

10. Although we can have victories in this present life, the ultimate time of sharing in the glory of Jesus Christ is when He comes back to get us to be with God in Heaven.

11. You will conquer it as you remain in God's love. Jesus has overcome the world, so you don't have to worry about being stuck in your suffering. Whether presently or when we get to Heaven, the suffering will be overcome and you will reap reward if you don't give up. You will be restored, confirmed, strengthened, and established.

12. While suffering, do not lose heart. Don't give up on your relationship with God (Galatians 6:9).

13. Light and momentary (temporary). Although the troubles you will go through may seem more than "light and momentary," the eternal glory you will experience outweighs each of them!

14. Don't focus so heavily on what you see in front of you (the troubles, the suffering, the hardships), but fix your eyes on what is unseen (God).

15. James says to be joyful when trials come your way because those trials have a purpose and will strengthen your character and mature you.

No Time for Negativity

1. The power that lies in your tongue.

2. God said He was giving the Israelites the land of Canaan.

3. The land was bountiful and "flowing with milk and honey," meaning it was prosperous. But the people

seemed powerful, and their towns were large.

4. Caleb believed that God would bring them safely through the land, and they could conquer it because God would be on their side as He promised.

5. They were afraid and didn't believe they could face the people of the land and win. They believed they were too weak, and the people of Canaan were too strong and fortified to go up against.

6. The other leaders.

7. The Israelites complained and made up their own ending of imminent death. They would rather go back to Egypt and be slaves than continue into Canaan.

8. Negatively. They thought they were too feeble.

9. They believed what people said.

10. God was angry because the Israelites didn't believe what He said, even though He'd done many miraculous things for them before.

11. They were not able to ever see the land God promised: Canaan, the land flowing with milk and honey. This happened to them because they allowed their eyes and thoughts to overshadow what God said. They also tested God in their unbelief

12. God promised that he and his family would still be able to enter into the land and receive all God promised. Caleb was granted this honor because he had a different spirit (courage, rational being, mind) than the other leaders and he obeyed and believed God fully.

13. You must take the negative thoughts that aren't like Christ captive(ackowledge the thought) and make it obedient to Him(replace it with the truth of who Jesus is).

14. We should think about things that are true, noble, right, pure, lovely, admirable, excellent, and praiseworthy. In a gist, we should think about good things according to God's standards.

Affirmation

1. The sword of the Spirit and prayer. To use these weapons effectively, you must read and know what the Bible says. You must then declare those words in prayer and petition.

2. "It is written," followed by scripture that is in the old testament.

3. Through spending time with God by reading and studying the Bible daily and applying it to your life.

4. Caleb believed what God said from the beginning and knew they'd be able to conquer the land God promised.

5. Caleb and his family would be able to enter the promised land of Canaan.

Answer Key

Scripture	Affirmations (What God says about you)
Ephesians 2:10 Ephesians 2:18-20 Ephesians 2:22	I am God's handiwork. He formed me in His image. I am special to God. He prepared for my arrival well in advance. God took time to create me. I was created to do good works through Christ. God has known me from the beginning and planned for me to do great things for Him. I am a friend of God (John 15:15). I am a member of God's family and household because God is my father. I am a temple for God and have access to Him through the Holy Spirit within me. I am held together by Jesus Christ. He is the cornerstone of my faith. Day by day, I am being sanctified and becoming a better temple for the Holy Spirit to reside. I am a work in progress. God is building me day by day.
1 Peter 2:9	I am chosen by God. I am a royal priesthood. I am holy. I am God's special possession.
Song of Solomon 4:7	I am beautiful and have no flaws physically because I am fearfully and wonderfully made in God's image. (Psalm 139:14, Genesis 1:26)
2 Timothy 1:7	God has not given me a spirit of fear. God has given me a spirit of power, love, and a sound mind. I have a spirit of power, love, and a sound mind.
Romans 8:37	Although troubles will come, I am more than a conqueror because of Jesus. I am more than a conqueror, and the schemes of Satan will never prevail against me because the same Spirit that raised Jesus from the dead lives in me (Romans 8:11, John 16:33). Jesus loved me enough to sacrifice Himself for me.
Isaiah 54:17	No weapon formed against me will prosper because God protects me. I have covered myself in the full armor of God, and I will block the fiery darts that Satan throws by holding up the shield of faith (Ephesians 6:10-18).

6. You will be satisfied and reap the consequences of your words. Whether good or bad, you will receive those fruits. So I, the author of this devo, urge you to speak life.

Be a Good Steward

1. The job of supervising or taking care of something.

2. A good steward would be someone who does an excellent job of taking care of something given to them.

3. The good stewards were the two servants who were able to multiply the amount of money that their master gave them. Based on the definition of stewardship, which means to take care of something, the servants knew the standard of care their master desired, and they met those standards. Their master was pleased, told them well done, and gave them more to steward.

4. The poor steward was the man who only returned with the same bag of money. Although he knew the character of his master being a "hard man" and a businessman who would expect more, out of fear of disappointment or failure, he mishandled what was given to him by not living up to his master's standards of excellence. According to his master's standards, merely returning what he gave him wasn't appropriate. The master was displeased and took his money and gave it to one of the good stewards.

5. The master praised and celebrated the good stewards and trusted them with more responsibilities. However, the master took away the poor steward's money, and he was reprimanded for being lazy and wicked in knowing his master's character but still choosing to go against it.

6. Each scripture states that your life on Earth is short and numbered and has an expiration date that can't be exceeded. Time on Earth is described as being a mist and no longer than the width of David's hand.

7. Life is short, and your days are numbered. Once that final day comes for you, that's it; it can't be changed.

8. Knowing God; Seeking the Kingdom of God (Heaven) and righteousness (being made right with God). (Matthew 28:19, John 14:6, Romans 3:22-26)

9. Jesus told His disciples to go and make more disciples and to baptize them and teach them to obey His commands. Jesus also promises to be with them until the end.

10. Seeking God and helping others seek God by telling them about Him and what He's done through Jesus and sharing the gospel (Romans 6:23). We are to also love God and (healthily) love ourselves, and others. The only way you can accomplish any of this is to be like Mary and sit at Jesus' feet and learn from Him.

11. Jesus is coming again, and He will take with Him those who are righteous (been made right by God via accepting Jesus as Lord and Savior). But, those who have not decided to be in a relationship with God by then will be sent to Hell. God's heart is for no one to perish, but this requires for people to come to the knowledge of Jesus so they have the opportunity to be saved.

12. You can love God well and seek after Him by obeying His commands, sitting with Him, meditating on scripture, praying, revering/honoring Him, living a surrendered life, singing His praises, and thanking Him. (Note: There are likely many more ways, keep your eyes open as you read scripture).

13. You can love people by mourning with them when they mourn and celebrating with them when they celebrate. Sitting with them in their time of need, helping them when they are in need, honoring others above yourself, being hospitable, praying for them, not seeking revenge, but forgiving and leaving vengeance to God.

14. The simple gospel(good news) of Jesus is where we once were separated from God because of sin, Jesus has reconciled us to God once again through His death and resurrection. Because of Jesus' sacrifice, our sins are paid for; He did what we could never do: live in perfection and fulfill the law of God. Due to this sacrifice and act of love, we can be connected to God again in a relationship. All that is required of us is to accept and profess that Jesus is Lord(the Son of God) and Savior(sent to save us from the death we deserve because of our sins by dying on the cross and defeating death by rising from the dead three days

late) by faith and live for Him thereafter via His Holy Spirit. See John 3:16-18 and Romans 6:23 for more visuals of the gospel made simple to understand and share..

Shine On!

1. The woman cheated on her husband and was caught.

2. They were ready to stone her.

3. No, they knew what the law of Moses said.

4. Jesus said, "let anyone who is without sin be the first to throw a stone at her." So, essentially, Jesus said, sure, you can, but only if you've never sinned.

5. They all walked away because they knew they each had sin in their lives. (Romans 3:23)

6. Jesus.

7. Jesus was the only one remaining, therefore this shows that He was without sin. Being that Jesus had never sinned, He was the only person who could, in good conscience and without any guilt, throw stones at the woman. However, He didn't. Instead Jesus said he would not condemn her, but urged her to go and sin no more. Jesus extended mercy rather than enforcing the law.

8. Jesus.

9. Life.

10. The law required humans to follow God's law perfectly to be in a good relationship with Him, but because our flesh is weak and imperfect, this was like holding a relationship together with duct tape. It was an impossible task for humans to fulfill. However, Jesus fulfilled the law and righteous requirement for us by living perfectly, dying in our place, and rising from the dead to defeat death once and for all. Once we've accepted, believed, and confessed Jesus as Lord and Savior and received His Holy Spirit, we then have the SAME Spirit that worked in Jesus to help us live righteously in a relationship with God. Through repentance, surrender, and living by God's Spirit, we can live life abundantly and full of light. What Jesus did was revolutionary and gave us the ability to do what was impossible: be made right with God from the inside out. That's good news!.

11. By belonging to Jesus - by placing your faith in Him, repenting when you mess up, surrendering your ways to be like Him, and asking for Him to give you His Spirit because you will then have the Spirit of God, the Holy Spirit, within you (Galatians 5:16-18, 24-25).

12. Sin is the darkness of the world, which is the power of Satan and is evil in the eyes of God. Because of sin, those who live in this darkness will earn eternal death and punishment in Hell.

13. Let it shine so that others will see!

14. If you claim to have the light but walk in darkness, you are living a lie and don't have a genuine relationship with God.

15. Possible answers: To allow your light to shine can be summed up with what Paul says in Acts 26:20: Allow your deeds to show your internal decision to follow Jesus. Do what is pleasing in the Lord's sight. However, other specific things mentioned in the other scripture as details to that broad statement: Let go of the sins that would easily make you fall back into old ways and instead focus on Jesus. Stay alert and sober-minded, keep your faith and salvation, encourage other believers, honor leaders, live peacefully, share the gospel with others, be patient, do good to others, be joyful, pray consistently, be thankful, don't stifle (restrain/hold back) the Holy Spirit, don't scoff (mock) at prophecies, hold onto the truth and what's good, stay away from evil, and praise and worship God!

16. Eternal life with God!

17. To fear man and love the praises of men over God, causing you to deny Jesus in front of others or remain silent about Him. You could also hide your light by succumbing to the sins of a group of people rather than setting yourself apart.

18. Knowing yourself and what you're able to withstand, you may have to distance yourself as you all are on two different paths. Imagine trying to walk with a person down a path that splits. You must either part ways or pick a path to go down together.

APRIL

Time with God

1. To hold firmly to; to cleave to

2. If someone is devoted to a sport, they will practice often, research new techniques, talk to other people in the sport to hear what they do and spend lots of time on it. I watched a documentary about Crossfit people who are trying to be titled the fittest in the world, and they all state how they wake up, eat right, train, and repeat each day. They are incredibly focused and determined.

3. To be devoted to God is to stay in God's word, actively being a part of a community of believers, partaking in communion to remember the sacrifice of Jesus, and praying. In doing each of these things, we are to do them faithfully as though we are running in a race striving after a prize, including us dying to our flesh and using self-control while readily taking on the trials that will come in following Jesus. Although it will be tough, the prize we will receive, if we do not give up, is eternal life with our Lord and Savior, the King of Kings, where we are an heir to his Heavenly Kingdom as sons and daughters.

4. Jesus says that we will be able to recognize a false prophet(someone who isn't of God) by their "fruits"- aka what their lives look like in public and private, how they live, and what they say. If their lives aren't glorifying God, then we know they are not God's people. However, these scriptures also suggest that we'll know God's people by their good fruits. These people will be those who do the will of God and follow what His Word says.

5. It's important to read the Bible and spend time with God because without doing that, we wouldn't know what God's will is for our lives. The Bible also teaches us, disciplines us, and trains us to live righteously so that we, who have accepted Jesus as Lord, are equipped in our new lives. The greatest thing of all is that we get to know who God is through reading His scriptures.

6.

Thessalonians	Bereans	Athenians
- Some Jews were persuaded and followed Jesus. - A large number of Greeks joined as well. - Quite a few prominent women joined too. - Other Jews were jealous and started a riot and brought believers before the court because they heard Paul and Silas speaking of Jesus as King, but Caesar was supposed to be the only king. - The Jews that didn't believe went to Berea to stir up trouble because people were believing.	- Noble in character - Received the message of Jesus readily and eagerly - They searched the scriptures they had (old testament) each day to make sure what Paul and Silas said was correct and true. - Many believed - A few prominent Greek women AND men believed.	- Had idols everywhere - They were religious but had no true guidance. - They asked questions and wanted to hear what Paul had to say on the "new idea." - Ignorant to who they were worshipping, they worshipped a nameless god. - Paul told them who the one true God of the world was - They had poets who mentioned them as being "offspring" of God, but they built idols to represent him just as the Israelites did in Exodus 32:1-4 - Some mocked Paul and didn't believe in the resurrection of Jesus. - Some were intrigued and wanted to know more and became followers. - Prominent Greeks followed
All of Them		
- Paul and Silas went to each city to share the gospel. - People believed the gospel message Paul and Silas taught. - Greek women believed - People with power in Greece believed!		

7. The Bereans were more devoted because they fact-checked Paul and searched the scriptures daily! They eagerly listened and wanted to know more. The Athenians were a close second, in my opinion, as they were open to listening, and they had questions, unlike many of the Thessalonicans.

8. We can be more like the Bereans by not only listening to sermons preached each Sunday but taking the time to read the scriptures ourselves on our own time during the week! It's vital for us to fact-check because some preachers could be lying or misinterpreting scripture. If we live like the devoted Bereans, we will study God's word ourselves.

9. Jesus consistently served and helped others. After being amongst a great crowd and doing mighty miracles and teaching, He still made time to get away and alone with God and pray. Jesus was in the temple listening to the teachers, asking questions, and sharing His insight as a young 12-year-old.

10. Those who are devoted to God (constantly seeking Him) can expect their prayers to be answered as they know and pray the will of God. They are delivered (freed from all manners of sin as they consistently repent) and protected because God watches over them closely. They are radiant, shameless, and are blessed. They lack nothing (this doesn't mean materialistically, as someone who is devoted to God can be poor physically. However, their perspective, understanding, and trust that God provides keep them from worrying, and they are content like Paul, Phil 4:11-19), and there is no condemnation.

Let's make it personal: Part 2

Sample answer: I often use the excuse of being tired or just allowing laziness to cause me to not get in the presence of God, but seeing how devoted Jesus was to pray after a long day of doing miracles and teaching, I can make sure I take the time to seek God as well. I love how investigative young Jesus was; He asked questions, shared His insight, and enjoyed being in the house of the Lord. I can do this more by once again fighting laziness and getting into the word daily, asking questions of my leaders, and sharing my insights with others. I also love the devotion of the Bereans. They were investigative and searched the scriptures for themselves to be assured that they were being told the truth, and they had great faith. I can apply this to my life by not only listening to the sermon my pastor preaches on Sunday, but I can study those scriptures myself and be sure to apply them.

One Way

1. The narrow gate. The road through the narrow gate is difficult, and few people find it.

2. The wide gate.

3. The wide gate that leads to Hell is most popular because verse 13 says that there are "many who enter by it."

4. Living a life of sexual sin (sexual immorality), worshipping idols (idolatry), cheating on your husband/wife (adultery), homosexuality, thieves (stealing), greediness, drunkards/ drunkenness(people who get drunk), slandering (abusive), swindling (people who cheat people of things), impurity, debauchery/lust, evil desires, anger, fits of rage, malice (malicious behavior), dirty language, lying (falsehood/living a lie), selfish ambition (selfishness), dissension, division, envy, orgies (wild parties), sorcery (practicing witchcraft), hatred (hostility), jealousy, and quarreling/discord.

5. There are MANY sins we can live our lives doing that will lead us to Hell. So, the gate is wide because

Answer Key

there are many options on this path.

6. To be made holy and right with God by calling on the name of Jesus Christ and by the Holy Spirit cleansing us. Jesus is the only way to God!

7. There's only one way to get to God through accepting Jesus. There are two if you're including allowing the Holy Spirit to enter your life as an option, but this is only after you have accepted Jesus as Lord and Savior (Acts 2:38). Compared to the many ways to get to Hell, there's only one way to God.

8. Openly declare with your mouth (say) that Jesus is Lord AND believe in your heart that God indeed did raise Jesus from the dead (resurrection). You must put your trust in God. Scripture says that by doing that, you will never be disgraced (put to shame; earn eternal death). you will never be disgraced(put to shame; earn eternal death). Ultimately, you must see, know, believe, and confess that Jesus is the Son of God and is thus the chosen one to save the world

Finished Work

Prophecy	Fulfillment
Micah 5:2 The ruler of Israel would be born in Bethlehem.	Luke 2:4-7 Mary gave birth to Jesus in Bethlehem.
Zechariah 9:9 The King would come riding on a donkey.	John 12:12-16 Jesus rode on a young donkey entering Jerusalem.
Psalm 22:18 Clothes are divided and gambled for.	John 19:24 The Roman soldiers decided who would get Jesus' clothes by throwing dice.
Exodus 12:46 (Read Exodus 12:7,12-14 to better understand what the Passover is) By law, the Passover lamb's bones could not be broken.	John 19:31-36 (Read John 1:29 and 1 Corinthians 5:7 to understand Jesus as a lamb) Although the legs of the others that were crucified with Jesus were broken, Jesus' were not.
Zechariah 12:10 They will look on the one they have pierced and mourn.	John 19:34-37 The soldiers pierced Jesus' side.

1. Jesus tore the veil that was separating God and man. Through Jesus, we have been reconciled to God again and can freely come before Him and have a relationship with Him. Jesus was the perfect sacrificial lamb needed to fulfill God's requirements due to our sins.

2. "It is finished!"

3. Jesus gave His life to purchase our freedom from the slavery of sin. So, the debt of sin has been "paid in full." We're now able to come boldly before the throne of God and be in His presence on our own with Jesus as our representation/lawyer.

your salvation?	(See Ephesians 2:8 and Isaiah 1:18-20) You have been saved by grace and will inherit eternal life.	your past?	(See Romans 6:5-7) Your old self is dead, crucified, and is no longer who you are.
your identity?	(See Ephesians 2:18-19 and Romans 8:16-17) Child of God and heir of His coming kingdom!	your present?	(See Romans 6:1-2 and Ephesians 4:22-24) You are now able to live freely, no longer a slave to sin; renew your mind and put on the newness of Christ.
your authority?	(See Luke 10:17-20) You have power and authority over every demon and manifestation of Satan/darkness.	your future?	(See Colossians 3:3-4 and Revelation 22:12) When Jesus returns, you will rise in glory with Him and reap the rewards He has for you according to your life.

5. Receive Jesus and become a child of God, all else will follow after this as God leads you down a path towards intimacy with Him. Jesus has done the work, you just have to receive.

Deeply Loved

1. Elijah believed in God's word and was obedient to Him. Elijah was full of the power of God, faith, bold, encouraged, and sure of God. He knew when called on God, He would respond. God was faithful to His word and did as He said. He also responded to Elijah's prayer and shamed the prophets of other gods.

2. Where Elijah was once running by the power of God in victory, fear consumed him and he no longer remembered God's love or power, and now he was running away in fear. Elijah was also humbled during this time. Asking God to take his life, his faith was shot and he wasn't able to recover. God however stuck beside Elijah and extended his loving hand of care, giving him instructions to stay alive; He cared about Elijah's wellbeing and didn't give up on Elijah. God still honored him, spoke to him, and encouraged him through this time of testing and trial. God wasn't loud, He whispered to Elijah during this time.

3. God never left Elijah's side. He was gentle and kind, understanding and patient with Elijah even though he was being difficult and not believing His power. God however didn't kill Jezebel to help Elijah get out of this time of suffering. I think this is because Elijah didn't ask Him to and she wasn't the true source of torture/suffering, it was Elijah's fear that was the real torturer and source of suffering. God's love he kept extending to Elijah during this time of suffering was meant to dispel the fear and get Elijah back on track. If Elijah would've come to his senses, He could've continued to be used by God and would've grown deeper in love and knowledge of God. He would have a new testimony of

God's ability to carry him. May we learn from Elijah and run to God during times of suffering rather than running away. Ask God what the suffering is meant to expose in you and surrender it to God.

4. God declares His love for His bride(the church) out loud and unashamedly, He disciplines us, He doesn't turn us away because of our sin, He looks on us with compassion and desires us to be healed, He sits with sinners that we would be saved. He promised to never leave His disciples or forsake them. They won't be abandoned by Him. Although they deserved to be cast aside because of their carelessness and rebellion, God looked at Israel like a parent who loves their baby, He longed for them and provided a way out, He had compassion, and He relented, not allowing His anger to consume them. He also chose them and set them apart to be one of His although He didn't do the same for others. He also loved them by keeping His promise to His people. Oh, what great love He has and wants to show us.

5. Being that the Ephesians foundation was in Christ because they believed in Him and had a relationship with Him, they operated in love. Paul also shows that God's love is wider, longer, higher, and deeper than we think, but it can be grasped by all who are the "Lord's holy people" (believers). Lastly, Paul also shows us that God can do much more than we could even fathom because of His Holy Spirit that lives within us (which was given to us out of love).

6. The trials help us to grow by developing perseverance, character, and hope.

7. God is with us in the midst of those trials because we have the Holy Spirit.

8. For us to have the Holy Spirit, Jesus had to die.

9. God showed us His love for us by sacrificing His Son, Jesus, while we were enemies of Him. While we couldn't care less about God, He cared enough about us to send His Son to die on our behalf. THAT'S LOVE.

10. God wanted us to be reconciled to Him. He wanted us to be one with Him again.

11. The Israelites are described as rebellious, evildoers, and corrupt children who turned their backs on God. They were heavily disciplined but still stuck in their ways, desolate, and barren. They were making sacrifices to God, but He was displeased by them because they were meaningless. They were covered in sin.

12. God was willing to help them be cleansed. God was ready to give them another chance to get it right if they were obedient.

13. Our response is to love God above all else. Also to love and forgive others. To live as Jesus did, being kind and compassionate even to those who persecute us, not holding grudges, but living peaceably no matter how people treat us. This is Christ's way, if we fail to do this, we will perish in the end.

14. God continually offers the opportunity for repentance and for the people to turn from their wicked ways.

15. Feel or express sincere regret or remorse about one's wrongdoing or sin.

16. To bring back; going back to; to turn.

17. To change one's mind or purpose.

MAY

Pray Without Ceasing

1. In the scriptures we see the following things mentioned in prayer (there are more, as you study scripture this list will grow) declarations of who God is, needs and desires are expressed, repentance and asking for forgiveness, pleading for help (ie for strength to endure through temptation), deliverance, and for the Holy Spirit to be given.

2. There can be many more answers, these are just examples: Some things I learned are that persistence in prayer is vital for a breakthrough, and because of Jesus, I can speak to and address God as my Father, speaking directly to Him as though I'm directly in front of Him before the throne.

Testimony

1. They may have assumed that severe trials and suffering come only because someone committed a particular sin.

2. Jesus informs them that it isn't because of sin, but simply that God could be glorified through it.

3. Praise and worship (God); describe or represent as admirable.

4. Using His saliva and dirt from the ground, Jesus made clay to put over the man's eyes.

5. If the man hadn't obeyed Jesus' instruction to wash in the Pool of Siloam, he probably wouldn't have been healed.

6. The blind man spoke up and shared his story with the people asking about his transformation. God was glorified because he gave credit to Jesus for healing him from a handicap that he had since childbirth.

7. Possible answers: Loved the most by his father, youngest son, honest, and had prophetic dreams; he was a bit arrogant, and immature as well..

8. They were jealous of Joseph.

9. Joseph was sold to various people, but Potiphar, an Egyptian officer, was the most influential/ powerful.

10. God was with Joseph in the midst of his circumstances, and Joseph consistently found favor with Pharoah. So much so that he ended up holding the second-highest position in Egypt.

11. Joseph gave his family food to endure the famine, supplies for their journey back home to Canaan, and he instructed the servants to give them back their money, so it was all free of charge.

12. Although his brothers intended to harm him and plotted for his demise, God turned it around for his good. God knew beforehand what was needed to provide for Joseph's family (the Israelites). It was through the initial suffering of Joseph being sold into slavery that God made a way for his family to

be provided for during the great famine with land and food. He also developed Joseph's character and maturity through it; Joseph was more humble, meek, and submitted to God by the end of his life.

13. God is loving, will fight for His people, and uphold His people through trouble. He will vindicate those wrongly accused.

14. They both have the power to triumph over the schemes of Satan.

15. By sharing your unique testimony, you can keep it real and personal with people who are investigating Christ by showing him/her that God really is who He says He is.

16. Suffering is to be expected especially for followers of Jesus, as Jesus forewarned us in His world that we WOULD have trials. The trials allow us to share in the suffering Jesus went through and share in His joy upon His return if we don't give up. We can have peace. because God will not leave us in a state of suffering forever.

See God, Experience God

1. Although there are many "gods" and idols, there is only one true God who is actively operating in the lives of His people. Foreign gods can't compare.

2. God parted the ocean for the Israelites to walk safely through a place where there seemed to be no path and they were stuck between a rock (the sea before them) and a hard place (Pharaoh's army behind them). God not only allowed them to walk through safely, but He also trapped their enemies.

3. Jesus told the waves to be still and they did. The once tumultuous sea became peaceful and still.

4. They were afraid, in awe, and marveled at the works of Jesus.

5. Jesus has been present and active in the earth since before the beginning and created the earth in unity with God the Father and Spirit. Jesus is simply God in the flesh and thus all of creation yields to Him.

6. Although we cannot see God physically in His body, we can see evidence of Him clearly in what He has created. Every day we wake up is a miracle of God. Think about it, we are currently floating in space on a rock covered with water that does not overtake the land (except in disaster) that is the perfect distance from the sun. Each day we live, we are living because a muscle made of tissue and cells is "beating" and pumping blood around our bodies(our heart) and a different set of tissues are sending electrical currents through our bodies telling them to do things(our brain), we are walking miracles living because God said so.

7. They thought of themselves to be wiser, so they made idols of the things that God made. They worshiped the created, not the Creator; they made their own gods rather than allowing those things to point them to the One true God of Heaven naturally.

8. God is a jealous God and says to put no other god before Him. It infuriates Him, we see this in the Old Testament & the New Testament.

9. God is both near and far. He is there in the small moments and details, but He also sees and knows the big picture and can see everything. So much so that no one can hide from God. He is the Author and Finisher, but He's also in the details of your story as well.

10. Yes, he cares deeply. So much so that He's willing to carry your burdens, your anxious thoughts, and everything plaguing your mind. All of it, He's willing to carry and takeaway if you'd give it to Him.

11. Many possible answers. Just be sure to focus on what God said, did, and what character traits you notice. Write those things down.

12. Job responded to God in humility, awe, and repentance

Snatched Thoughts

1. Thoughts.

2. Your thoughts. You can easily lie with your words, but your true self is what lies within you in your thoughts and heart. This concept makes Mark 7:6 more understandable: "Jesus replied, 'You hypocrites! Isaiah was right when he prophesied about you, for he wrote, 'These people honor me with their lips, but their hearts are far from me.'"

3. Fear because of the threats of Jezebel to take his life.

4. Lord God All-Powerful; Lord Almighty

5. It is evident that in those moments Elijah was having a hard time believing God was actually All-Powerful as here he is hiding in a cave from a mere human.

6. Elijah was replaced by a successor named Elisha whom God told him to appoint.

7. Setting your mind on things above (eternal) and not earthly, thinking about things that are true, honorable, right, and pure.

8. Not guarding your eyes (gates); what you allow yourself to consume will flow from you.

9. They are not of this world. Your weapons are the Sword of the Spirit (the word of God) and prayer in the name of Jesus, whom all authority has been given (Matthew 28:18).

10. Take those thoughts captive and make them obedient to Christ.

11. Possible answers: Grab hold of, seize, capture, overcome, and take possession of

JUNE

God Knows

1. Joseph's dreams meant that he would be a ruler and his family would bow to him at some point.

2. Joseph's brothers were jealous of their father's love for Joseph and they didn't like the outcome of

Answer Key

his God-given dreams. They didn't believe and didn't want to submit to what Joseph's prophetic dream meant of him being ruler over them.

3. Bewildered, betrayed, alone, and afraid.

4. Joseph went through the Midianite and Ishmaelites and was finally sold to Potiphar, one of Pharaoh's top officials.

5. No, scripture tells us that God was with Joseph, and, because of this, Joseph prospered with God at his side.

6. Joseph found favor with Potiphar and he trusted Joseph so much that he was promoted to being an attendant. Thus he was put in charge of Potiphar's household and all that he owned.

7. Joseph was being elevated in status over time. We can slowly but surely see God's plans unfolding as Joseph was in charge of all of Potiphar's possessions in a role of great leadership and responsibility.

8. Joseph took his role seriously and sternly told Potiphar's wife no because he honored his master and would not sin against God by sleeping with her.

9. Potiphar's wife lied and said Joseph came onto her and fled the scene upon her screaming for help. Being that she lied to her husband, Potiphar was angry and put Joseph in jail. Based on Potiphar's wife scheming, lying, and deceitful actions, this was an act of Satan.

> Selah Moment: (Sample answer) I would feel incredibly lonely and confused. I would probably want to give up on God because so many bad things were happening to me, even though I'd been faithful.

10. God was right there with him.

11. No.

12. Joseph was favored by the prison warden and was put in charge of all of those in prison. Although caused by unjustifiable circumstances, Joseph was yet again put in a role of great leadership and responsibility thus showing God's plan for elevating Joseph was still in motion and proving God was still in control.

13. Joseph met the cupbearer and the baker of the king of Egypt, Pharaoh.

14. Interpret dreams.

15. During his time in jail, he used his gift of interpreting dreams to interpret the cupbearer and baker's dreams. However, you can also see that Joseph was desperate to get out of jail as he told them not to forget him when they got back to Pharaoh.

16. God put Joseph around people who were connected to the highest authority in Egypt. He was also in a role of leadership yet again which was God's plan for his life.

17. He expressed that it wasn't by his own power, but through God that Pharaoh would get an interpretation

of his dream.

18. Joseph was summoned and was able to interpret the dream that no one else in Pharaoh's counsel could. As a result of noticing Joseph's wisdom because of the Spirit of God moving in his life, Pharaoh placed him over his house and thus all of Egypt. Only Pharaoh himself was over him. During this time he was married and had children. Joseph also set up and enacted a process for Egypt to be sure to thrive during the prophesied years of famine that was coming.

19. Joseph was in the highest place of power that he could be in Egypt.

20. Due to the famine in Canaan, Joseph's brothers had to come to Egypt to get grain. Being that Joseph was the man in charge of the operations as governor, they bowed to him upon arrival to make their request. In Joseph's dream, the various piles of grain bowed to Joseph's pile of grain, and his brothers ended up bowing down to him. Jacob, Joseph's father, also came to him as well which was in the dream as well.

21. NOPE!

22. The entire time

> *Selah Moment: (Possible Answer) Although Joseph's brothers and Potiphar's wife had evil intentions planned for him, God's power was greater. No man could change the course God had already set. Although God allowed Joseph to go through many trials, His plans for Joseph never changed because God is not a liar, and He does not change His mind about matters of His people, this encourages me to be hopeful and keep my faith in God and stay the course.*

23. Man cannot curse what God has blessed. God does not lie and His word cannot be revoked and He will forever be with His people.

24. This principle and these attributes of God were prevalent in Joseph's life because although his family and Potiphar's wife tried to thwart the plans of God, they could not prevail. God's will was done and His word came to pass.

25. Although Adonijah tried to force himself onto the throne, the only voice that mattered and had true authority was King David's. By King David's decree, Solomon was named king.

26. The decrees of the King were what came to pass, not the decisions or schemes of the enemy or man alone. Thus showing God's decrees are what end up being set in place because He is supreme and in control.

27. This is important to take note of because you can use it to wage war against the enemy so that you don't lose faith when trials come against you. When you know what God said you have a strong sword of the spirit to use and hold onto, keeping you steadfast and not giving up.

Answer Key

Overflow

1.
   a. Hope

   b. Joy and peace

2.
   a. Trust in God

   b. Possible answer: Believing in Jesus, negating your own understanding to believe God's, having faith and obeying God as you feel led.

3.
   a. For them(us) to overflow with hope.

   b. The Holy Spirit

3.
   a. The Holy Spirit will expose the truth of sin, righteousness, and judgment. He prophesies, informs, directs, and glorifies Jesus. The Holy Spirit is also a great symbol of hope because Jesus promised to send Him after He left the earth. This promise was first fulfilled in Acts 2:1-13. Jesus left this earth to prepare a place for you in Heaven (John 14:1-7), and thus, the Holy Spirit is a guarantee that Jesus is alive and will be back. Therefore, with the deposit of the Holy Spirit, you can have great hope in Jesus Christ's return in due time.

   b. The Holy Spirit is an advocate, helper, and comforter (stated in various versions of John 16:7)

5. Possible answer: The more you trust in God, the more joy and peace you can have. And it is through trusting in God that you'll have hope by way of the Holy Spirit being within you! Trust in God always.

Resist

1. Satan desired to be above God, he wanted to make himself like God (the Most High), and thus, he was cast out of Heaven for his pride.

2. Satan deceived Eve and twisted God's words causing Eve to question what God said and look at the situation (of not eating from the tree) differently.

3. Yet again, Satan twisted God's words and made promises to Jesus. He tried to put himself in God's shoes, promising Jesus various things that contradicted what God said. In the process of twisting God's words, Satan also challenged Jesus' character and identity.

4. Satan is crafty, deceptive, on the prowl looking for culprits to devour, a thief, and a murderer of faith. He is angry because his time is short before the Kingdom of God comes in all of its righteousness, glory, and splendor.

5. First, you must submit yourself to God (surrender and give Him your life) and resist (stand firm against, withstand) the devil. By resisting, God says the enemy will flee!

6. To withstand, to exert force in opposition; oppose, to set yourself against someone, repel, or to go in the opposite direction of and pull away from. When defining this word I saw a vision of someone pulling away from a dangerous person who had their arm; that's a visual you can have to go along with this when thinking of resisting Satan.

7. You can resist by staying alert, keeping your faith, living according to the word of God by obeying it, and spiritually putting on the full armor of God.

8. Belt of truth, the breastplate of righteousness, keep your feet fitted with readiness to share the gospel (Romans 10:15), the shield of faith, and the helmet of salvation.

9. The offensive weapons are the sword of the Spirit, which is the word of God, and praying in the Spirit (asking the Holy Spirit what you should pray; praying in tongues if you have that gift). Rather than just praying from your mind, pray from your heart and ask God to help you, relying on the Holy Spirit to fill your prayers with meaning (Romans 8:26). By also using the authority God has given you in prayer, you are also able to command demons to flee in Jesus' name due to your salvation. Lastly, you have the Holy Spirit interceding on your behalf as well! Meaning God Himself is interceding on your behalf.

> *Important note: Although you have authority over Satan because of Jesus, tread lightly when dealing with casting out demons. Be sure to talk to a mentor or someone well versed in this area for proper ways to handle this side of the spiritual world.*

10. They both responded with the words God said. However, there were differences:

Eve:

*She conversed with Satan

*She considered Satan's words, pondered on them

*Her eyes agreed with Satan and her desire to know more peaked

*Insecurity won, she didn't know who she was in the eyes of God

Jesus:

*He responded with the word of God and nothing else! No further conversation was had beyond that

*Jesus was sure of Himself and didn't defend Himself against the accusations against His identity (ie He didn't say "Yes I am the Son of God"); He knew he didn't need to prove Himself to Satan.

*Jesus rebuked Satan (Note: we do not rebuke Satan, but the Lord God can, in our fight/Eve's fight(in this example) against Satan, Eve could've said, "The Lord rebuke you satan".

11. Although Eve knew what God said, she continued to dialogue with Satan. She pondered on and considered what he was saying, forfeiting what God had made clear before. Thus, her eyes glimmered

and she saw the fruit in a different light. Due to Satan's words, she now desired the benefit of having the wisdom of God rather than obeying His commands because Satan enticed her to believe she could have more than what she had. Pride, deception, and greed are essentially what caused Eve to fall into sin as she began to put her own thoughts and desires before God's as she considered the enemy's words.

12. Each time Satan offered Jesus tremendous and mighty things or tempted Him to do various deeds, Jesus responded with the word of God as He said, "it is written" and proceeded to quote Old Testament scripture. For every temptation Satan threw at Him, Jesus had scripture to go against it. Not only did Jesus speak the word of God, as Eve did this as well, but Jesus acted on it and stood firm. He saw God's word as final and there was no questioning it.

13. God will not let you be tempted beyond what you can bear and He will provide an escape route so that you can endure and make it out without giving in.

Choose this Day

1. Jesus told him to let his fishing nets down into the deep water to catch some fish.

2. Jesus is completely submitted to God and only speaks what He says.

3. Based on Jesus' track record and character, it shows that whatever He says, you can be assured that it's a fact and must be obeyed. Thus, since Jesus told Simon to cast his nets into the deep ocean, he would be wise to listen because Jesus must know something Simon doesn't.

4. Simon was doubtful because they'd been fishing all night and hadn't caught anything.

5. Possible answer: Being that Jesus asked him to do something that went against everything he knew as a fishermen, I'm sure it was tough because it didn't make logical sense to Simon, especially after failing so many other times prior.

6. He obliges to what Jesus said because Jesus, his Master, said so, and he trusted Him.

7. After obeying Jesus, they caught so many fish that the nets began to break!

8. Simon saw the magnificence of God and was repentant. He also didn't feel worthy of being in Jesus' presence because what happened that day was nothing short of a miracle, and he felt undeserving.

9. Simon was more submitted to Jesus. Seeing the fruits of Jesus' power opened his eyes to the might, sovereignty, provision, and goodness of Jesus.

10. No. If anything, Simon probably thought it wouldn't work in his favor. So, he simply had to have faith and trust what Jesus instructed him to do.

11. Jesus says he would be a fisher of men. Simon would make many disciples and aid in bringing many people into the Kingdom. Even to this day, disciples have been added to Simon's Heavenly account as his life is still a testament to the faithfulness of God, and it was through Simon (Peter) that the first church began after Jesus ascended (Matthew 16:18, Acts 2:1-41).

12. Through Jesus, God will transform you into exactly who you're supposed to be. Ultimately, the work He's begun in you will continue until it comes to completion in Heaven by His power working in you now; sanctification.

13. God desires that all people would believe in His Son and not perish, He desires for people of every nation to be standing before His throne in the end praising and being with Him as He planned so long ago.

14. God desires for all believers to use the gifts He's given them to strengthen the Church and make disciples. He also desires for us(the Church) to be unified so that the world would see us and know Him, that we'd be able to overcome Satan, and He wants us to know we are loved by Him and last but not least, He desires for us to be with Him and He with us!

15. The word of God(the Bible), His Holy Spirit(the Helper), various leaders(prophets, pastors, teachers, apostles, and evangelists) gifted by God, community(fellowship with other believers), salvation, and access to God in prayer.

JULY

Peace in Chaos

1. Believers gain access to an abundance of grace through their knowledge and understanding of who God and Jesus are.

2. They were afraid and panicked.

3. Jesus was sleeping peacefully.

4. Possible answer: Jesus' knowledge of God was so in-depth and in tune that He knew He had nothing to worry about, and thus He could be at peace during the storm.

5. Jesus rebuked them for their lack of faith in Him.

6. Jesus had been doing many miracles and showing His great power and authority, so they should've been able to have faith that Jesus could get them out of that predicament.

7. They could have experienced the same peace and rest as Jesus during the storm.

8. They knew Him on a deeper level and were in awe that He had such power and authority. So, although they didn't have great faith, they were still able to get to know Jesus even more as they endured the trial.

9. Definitely, as scripture says, what the enemy meant for evil, God will turn around for our good. Although the disciples lacked faith, God was able to use that moment to show his might! The disciples were able to see Jesus in a new light and see His character and authority in action.

10. Jesus warned them of the coming chaos they would experience as they would be separated from each other and Him. Jesus also warned them of the trials they would soon face.

11. Jesus warned them in order to prepare them ahead of time. By doing this, Jesus was showing His prophetic and all-knowing nature. Thus, when it came to pass, the disciples would remember Jesus said it first, and they'd continue to believe and keep their faith.

12. Peace comes from Jesus. Jesus told the disciples that peace would be found in Him and then says that there would be trials, which suggests that finding peace in Jesus doesn't remove the trials but adds God to the mix. By finding peace in Jesus, you'd still endure, but you'd also have a confidant to help and carry you through it.

13. In verse 17, Jesus promises to rescue Paul from both the Jews and Gentiles. In verse 24, an angel appeared and told him that he'd stand on trial in front of Caesar.

14. He shook it off.

15. Paul was able to have peace because he trusted in the words God told him prior! He knew he'd have to stand before Caesar, and that hadn't happened yet, so Paul was sure that he'd make it through.

16. This should be encouraging because contrary to what some believe, just because you have given your life to Christ doesn't mean - poof - all of your trials and problems disappear. With this evidence from today, believers everywhere can be encouraged that they have the ultimate weapons and sources of peace (the name of Jesus, God's word, and the presence of God via the Holy Spirit) to help them through every storm, trial, mess, or ounce of chaos.

Let's make it personal

God promises to prosper you and give you hope and a great future. God also promised that He is doing a new thing and will provide a way for you. Ultimately, Jesus has gone to prepare a place for you to dwell with Him forever when the good and proper time comes.

Lean Not

1. Trust in the Lord with all your heart and lean not on your own understanding; in all your ways submit to Him, and He will make your paths straight.

Selah moment: Trust means to have confidence in, to be bold and secure, sure, to fear nothing for oneself; to throw yourself or your cares on someone; to throw in the face(of God) Acknowledge means to know, to see with your eyes or mind, to know by experience, to make known, to declare

2. Trust in the Lord with ALL your heart.

3. By not leaning on your own understanding of things, submitting everything you do to God, not thinking you know it all, fearing God, and turning away from evil (anything against God), then you can trust God fully.

4. God is all-knowing, all-seeing, and all-understanding.

5. Having knowledge of everything.

6. God.

7. Proverbs 3:5 tells you to trust in the Lord and to not rely on yourself. It is important that you follow these commands because God knows everything, not you, so He is the BEST choice to follow. Although you may think you know what's best for you, you're not all-knowing like God, so you'd be selling yourself short if you didn't lean on Him for answers. To trust in God is like choosing to use Google for a research project versus only relying on the information you currently have in your brain. Google would help you take home that A+ every time. This is the same with God. By trusting in the all-knowing God, you'll be guided down every path meant for you, and you will be successful because God is with you leading the way.

8. By trusting God, you can expect God to bring clarity to your life and show you the paths to take. You can also expect God to do more for you than you would've ever asked or thought of.

9. Naturally, you can plan and develop ideas for where you're going in life, but God ultimately has control and will determine what's best. If you are wise, you will trust those steps He shows because He is all-knowing, and thus, his plans will always be greater than yours.

10. God is a loving, caring, sacrificial, faithful, and generous Father. With such character, He is completely trustworthy and will always come through according to His will and way that is best.

Get Up!

	Mark 10:46-52	John 5:1-15	Mark 5:35-43
What was needed?	Bartimaeus was blind, so he needed sight. He also asked that Jesus would have mercy on him.	An invalid (a disabled person) needed healing from the ailment he'd had for 38 years.	Jairus' daughter was sick and in need of good health. She later needed complete restoration to life.
What hindrances were present?	People around him chastised him and were discouraging.	He felt isolated and had no one to help him into the pool believed to heal those who got in.	Jairus' daughter's symptoms worsened and she died. Jairus' friends were in his ear, insinuating it being too late for Jesus to save his daughter who'd died before he could express his need to Jesus in time.

How did the person respond to the hindrances?	Unashamedly, Bartimeus seized the moment. As soon as he heard Jesus was close by, he did all he could to draw His attention. Bartimaeus wasn't worried about what other people thought as he shouted for Jesus. He just wanted his healing and knew all he had to do was get to Jesus.	The invalid made excuses for why he wasn't healed yet. He had been in this disabled state for so long, he probably accepted his "fate" and thus gave up on trying to be healed.	Judging by Jesus' encouragement, he may have been troubled, crying, and was visibly afraid. Jairus had faith and led Jesus to his daughter.
What did Jesus say/ do?	Amongst the large crowd, Jesus heard Bartimaeus' cries. I assume, amongst the crowd, Jesus couldn't see who was shouting his name, so he stopped where He was and told those around him to call for Bartimaeus to come to Him. The same people that chastised Bartimaeus were likely the ones who ended up delivering Jesus' message, "Cheer up! On your feet! He's calling you." Jesus asked him, "what do you want me to do for you?"	Cognizant of the length of time the invalid had been disabled, Jesus saw the man and asked him, "do you want to get well?" In the midst of the man's excuses, Jesus gave him a command, "Get up! Pick up your mat and walk." Jesus then found the man later and told him not to enter back into his old sin patterns.	Jesus silences the hopelessness and doubt of Jairus' friends by telling him not to fear but to have faith and believe. Jesus saw the state of the little girl differently than the common eye. He saw her as being asleep while people at the house saw her as dead. (Why? Maybe because He saw her spirit and they saw her flesh? Or simply because He is God and thus is Alpha and Omega, he saw her as what was to come.) Jesus had the room filled only with those full of faith: Peter, James, John, and the girl's parents. While in the room, Jesus told the little girl to "get up!" The faith of her father saved her life.

How did the person respond to Jesus?	Upon Jesus' call for Bartimaeus to come to Him, he was of good courage and proudly got up and went forward. When he was finally face-to-face with Jesus, he was open and honest and full of faith, telling Jesus, "Rabbi, I want to see." He then received his sight and followed Jesus.	The man was completely healed! Although it broke the law of customs on the Sabbath, the man obeyed Jesus by picking up his mat and walking away from the place he resided for 38 years as an invalid.	The little girl woke up and was raised from the dead.
What was the outcome?	His faith healed him. He got new sight and followed Jesus.	The man was made well.	The girl was raised from her "sleep".

You be You, Let God be God

	Isaiah 9:6	Psalm 139:1-10	Job 9:4-10	Matthew 6:26-30	Ephesians 3:20
Characteristics of God you notice	Power is His. He can bear much. His(Jesus) name is and thus He is the "Wonderful Counselor", He is the "Prince of Peace", He is the "Mighty God", and He is the "Everlasting Father"	God intimately knows you and knows everything you do. He is everywhere and sticks by your side. He is your guide	God is wiser than the wisest, and He is more powerful than anyone. He commands things to be so on earth, and they are so, and He performs miracles, signs, and wonders endlessly!	God knows your every need; He provides for those needs, and He values you!	God is able to do far more than any human could ever fathom and He has placed His power within you via His Holy Spirit.

Let's make it personal: Part 1

Possible answer: As Job said in Job 40:1-5 and as Paul suggests in Ephesians 3:20, as a human, you are limited in your abilities and understanding compared to the Almighty God. Although you may be able to make grand decisions and can control certain areas of your life, without God, those abilities are not possible and can be taken away. On the contrary, God is unlimited in his abilities and will always be more powerful, wise, and present. Such attributes cannot be stripped from Him nor duplicated by anyone. Jesus is the Alpha and the Omega (Revelation 1:8), the beginning, end, and everything in between. He has been here since the beginning of creation (John 1:1), so it is best practice to take heed and submit unto him for proper guidance because, with Jesus, you are safest and set up for greatness as you trust in Him.

Possible answer: Without God and His Word, you are wandering down a dark path because it is like a lamp and light unto your path (Psalm 119:105). So by taking heed and following through with what God says in His word, through people He may use to speak into your life, or via circumstances you go through, the path you are on is illuminated, and you are headed towards everlasting life if you choose to submit and follow Him. Without God's guidance and light, you are headed to destruction, demise, and damnation. Jesus makes it very clear in John 8:42-47 that you truly only have two options in life: hearing from God and doing things God's way as sons of obedience or doing things the enemy's way as sons of disobedience - aka sons of Satan(Yes, doing things your way and not regarding God, is choosing the latter option).

Although this answer is a personal one, here's one of the CBJ reviewer's response to help you think through this question: "I sometimes think I know what's best for me, and I question what God is doing. I like to know everything before I do anything, and that's just not the way God works. I'm learning He won't give you step seven before you've done step one. I've also acted as if I'm Lord (God) over my time when I move slowly and act like I have all the time in the world to get moving in doing what God has told me to do.

The reality of time is that I don't control it, and it's running out; for tomorrow isn't promised, and Jesus is coming.

	Proverbs 3:5-6	Matthew 6:31-34	Hebrews 11:6	Mark 12:28-34	Philippians 4:6
I will stay in my lane by...	Trusting in the Lord and NOT relying on my own knowledge and understanding.	Seeking God first and foremost and NOT worrying.	Having faith and approaching God with the belief in His existence and His abilities.	Loving God and loving your neighbor (all humans) Note: Loving God means obeying His commands, thus you must read His word to know them	Praying and do NOT being anxious.

Let's make it personal: Part 2

Sample answers:

-Before you do anything in the morning, pray and thank God

-Meditate on scriptures AND apply them

-Consult God with every decision (pray, pray, pray!)

-Be intentional about trusting rather than questioning God (immediate, faith-filled obedience)

-Be intentional about loving others (encouraging them, giving things to them, serving them, etc.)

> "REJOICE always, PRAY continually, GIVE thanks in all circumstances; for this is God's WILL for you in Christ Jesus."
>
> 1 Thessalonians 5:16-18 (NIV)

AUGUST
Order over Chaos

1. No. God has planned all things in advance. God was intentional to use each day for creating all things in their proper order. He also knew who Jeremiah was before his existence, and planned for him to be set apart as a prophet. It didn't just happen at random! God planned for the Israelites to prosper, have hope, and an equitable future despite their excile. It didn't just happen out of nowhere when they arrived in Canaan and eventually into glory in Heaven.

2. Each time, Jesus shows that He is aware of the time and order in which He was to do something.

He knew His purpose, and He knew how long He had to achieve it. Jesus also shows that His all-knowing (omniscient) power is what allows Him to know the timing and order in which things were to be done here on Earth. Jesus also even knew the capacity of His disciples in what they could handle, so He only told them what they could carry in that time.

Pause here and be reminded today that Jesus is coming back for His bride (the church, the people who have accepted Him and placed their faith in Him) soon and very soon.

3. Through King Solomon, God has shown us that everything has a purpose, and everything must go through a specific time period in life; it's just a matter of when. Nevertheless, the times (seasons) will change, and you must be ready to respond accordingly and not give up!

4. They were able to understand the times; aka discern the seasons.

> Selah Moment: (Possible answer) They were able to know what Israel was to do during the war(s).

5. Esther was in a position to help save the Jews from being persecuted. If she weren't able to see the times she was living in and didn't accept this calling on her life, she wouldn't have been able to save a nation! It is also important to note what Mordecai said, "for if you remain silent at this time, relief and deliverance for the Jews will arise from another place." So by paying attention to the times and rising to the occasion, Esther would be choosing to accept God's will as He very well could've used someone else. If she didn't want to be the one to be used by God, Esther was replaceable as God's will would prevail nevertheless.

6. The time is coming for Jesus to return to judge the world. If people's lives are not in order (having not repented and given their lives to Jesus by that time), he/she will be doomed to eternal destruction and separation from God.

7. Going and making disciples!

8. Eternal separation from God; Hell.

9. His Holy Spirit, the Word of God, and our religious leaders (preachers, teachers, and prophets of God)

10. By drawing closer to God through living according to the scriptures, which comes by reading and obeying the word of God, you can have more significant order in your life. It is also vital that you pray daily! Lastly, you know you best, so choose methods of organizing your thoughts, life, and time with God by journaling, writing things down, recording your thoughts and revelations, etc.

11. If you're trusting in God fully, there will be a peace that surpasses all understanding (Proverbs 3:5-6). The decision will also align with God's word!

Run the Race

1. The quality or fact of being determined; continuing to exist; persistence

2. Commitment, dedication, continuing even when times get tough, purpose for accomplishing the task, a goal to be accomplished, belief, faith, vision (seeing the bigger picture), motivation, discipline, and rest.

3. The race to the finish line of sitting before the throne of God, making our way to Heaven via our relationship journey (race) with Jesus.

4. Jesus forewarned us that in this world (crooked and perverse world, Phil 2:15), we'd have trials. Our flesh is weaker than our spirit, so we are more susceptible to fall into temptation because the enemy is prowling around looking for his next victim to tempt and lure into sin.

5. Everyone has access and opportunity to win and make it, but not everyone will. Only those who call on the name of the Lord and keep God's commands will be saved.

6. The reward is eternal life with God!

7. By standing firm, owning that you have victory in Christ and do not have to give in to temptation, repenting of your sins daily, having actions that align with your faith, and loving others deeply, you can

run with endurance.

8. By taking captive your thoughts (stopping thoughts that are not like Christ) and thinking about things that are true, honorable, lovely, noble, and admirable (Philippians 4:8), thus allowing your mind to be renewed. Through these steps, not only will you physically be in the act of working for the Lord, but you will also be actively transforming into who God knows you to be. Praying honest prayers unto God, asking Him to show you where you fall short and need improvement will keep you humble and in a constant state of seeking growth and depth in your relationship with God. Lastly, by worshiping God not only in actions and knowledge but in spirit and truly connecting with God on a more intimate level from your heart over time.

9. The fullness of God.

10. "Let us not become weary in doing good, for at the proper time we will reap a harvest if we do not give up."

Scripture Dissection: The Love of God

1. The Lord, God Almighty! (Yahweh, El Shaddai; Exodus 6:3). The Creator of the Heavens and the Earth.

2. The people/families of Israel.

> *Selah (pause) Moment:*
> *"Chose"*
> *"Chosen"*

3. "Ahabah" means having affection for

4. "Everlasting" means lasting forever or a very long time. "Olam" means time out of mind, without end, long duration.

5. "Mashak"; To pull or guide in a certain direction.

6. His love for His people and desire to be reconciled with them

> *Selah moment:*
>
> *He sent His Son to bear the nails on the cross on our behalf while we were enemies of His, not listening, not taking heed, and not repenting. Thank you, God, for your faithfulness.*

7. "checed" meaning: goodness and favor; redemption from troubles/enemies; preservation of life.

8. Jeremiah 31:1-14 has a theme of God restoring His people in the future. Thus, Jeremiah 31:3 suggests why God plans to bring about such restoration and how. The answers are clear:

God wants to restore His people's lives because He loves His people, and he draws them in with His goodness and special consideration of each person as He knows each one by name.

Answer Key

Crafty with Purpose

1. The ability to generate, create, or discover new ideas.

2. Having a high level of skill, passion, and experience in a given area (Tom Popomaronis, 2016)

3. Control gained by enforcing obedience or order, orderly or prescribed conduct or pattern of behavior

4. Son of Jesse, a Bethlehemite (from Bethlehem), musician, brave, warrior, well-versed, good looking, a shepherd (takes care of and tends to sheep), he was victoruous in battle, anointed by God, a skillful player of the lyre(harp), and the Lord was with Him.

5. Strong, fighter (covered in armor that weighed 5,000 silver pieces, his sword weighed more than 600 pieces of silver), from Gath, twice as tall as most men (close to 10 ft tall). The Philistines looked to him and catered to him (someone carried his shield), and he was arrogant.

6. He belittled their army and spoke highly of him being a Philistine. He also told them the battle would be different; it simply needed to be one person who would fight and kill him, and whoever won the fight would have the other as a servant.

7. Intimidation and belittling.

8. The Israelites were scared as Goliath would ask for someone to battle him day and night for forty days!!!

9. David was not a part of Saul's army; only Jesse's oldest sons were. David spent his time feeding his father's sheep as a shepherd.

10. David had righteous anger against Goliath because he, an "uncircumcised Philistine" and thus not a man of God, kept speaking down to the army of God, the Israelites. David also wanted to know what the reward would be for the one who killed Goliath, thus showing that he was thinking about fighting him.

11. He decided to fight Goliath.

12. Being that David was a shepherd, he had to fight off a lion and a bear to save his sheep, and thus, he had a tactic that he'd used many times before that moment of being before Goliath. Most importantly, he knew that God was with him and would protect him.

13. David told Saul that he couldn't wear all of the extra armor because he wasn't used to that. He simply went with what he knew: his shepherd's staff, a sling, five stones, and faith in the Lord God. With just one stone slung by David, slew Goliath.

14. Using stones and a slingshot to fight when people commonly used swords and armor.

15. David had to fight off various animals while protecting his father's sheep, so he got to practice. David was also a man of great faith, so he must have spent a lot of time with God as well.

16. David learned the skill and trade of shepherding which included protecting the sheep and he was

also skilled at playing the lyre. David's intimacy and faith in God were also learned/gained through His discipline in seeking after the heart of God. David was not only skilled at protecting sheep and playing the lyre but He was also anointed by God due to his intimacy with Him. David was a skilled man who was intimate with God..

17. Without David's faith and intimacy with God, none of the results would've been possible, the Lord moved behind everything David did. From the music note played to the small stone thrown; because God put His power, might, and Spirit on them, they caused great and mighty things to happen: Saul was delivered and Goliath was defeated. (Author sidenote: This motivates me to know God deeper, it wasn't only the skill, might, or willpower of David that brought Him victory, it was God! Want to defeat giants in your life? Yes, grow in skills and have practical tools, but ultimately you must know God and He must know you). Without having much practice with the lyre, David would not have been known for playing well in the eyes of man and thus he wouldn't have been summoned to serve the king. Without David's skill in protecting sheep, David would not have been equipped for battle physically causing Israel to be without and leaving Goliath a victory. Although God could've and would've raised someone else to be victorious for Israel and do these things, David's legacy(the family line of the Messiah) wouldn't be what it is.

18. No. David constantly mentioned that it was God that would (and did) deliver him.

SEPTEMBER

Plans, Plans, Plans!

1a. All things are meaningless in this life vs. the only meaningful things in life are to live to please God

1b. Fearing the Lord and living for Him is the best way to live as we will be judged in the end; all things will come to the light

2. James states that your life is like a mist that is here for a little while and then vanishes; meaning, your life is short in the grand scheme of God's plan of eternity.

3. Operate from what the Lord is willing because He is the only definite, immovable, and secure thing in your life.

4. They would both agree on the fact that life has no real purpose without God and is meaningless if it doesn't rely on His way/plans.

Also, take note that a meaningful life is a life that is lived LOVING God (with all of our heart, mind, soul, and strength) and being LOVED by Him. It is also best lived when we take that love and put it into action in service to God especially by LOVING OUR NEIGHBOR as we love ourselves. Apart from these two things, life will be dull and meaningless. Life is shorter than we think and more profound than we know. We must consult God on what we are to do with our lives; otherwise, it is a waste. God is eternal, but our mortal bodies are not. The will of God and the love of God is vitally important.

5. Paul makes it clear that the things we can see with our eyes here on Earth are temporary, fleeting, and will eventually wear away. Things that we cannot see, things in the realm of the spirit, will remain (God, Jesus, and the Holy Spirit). Thus, we are better off having faith in God than in our own plans that are moveable. This also shows that our relationship with God must be more than skin deep. We cannot have

Answer Key

surface-level relationships with God, where it is mainly centered around works alone. God cares more about what is unseen - the matters of the heart! God desires intimacy from each of us.

6. Jesus warns against things done to be seen and with selfish or impure motives

7. The things built with Christ as the foundation, with the proper motives, and heart are the things that will last. The things that transform what is unseen(people's spirit, heart, and soul), things that are done without selfish motive, and matters of applying our faith (ie. giving, praying, fasting, trusting God, sitting with Jesus, and knowing Him, servanthood, discipling and doing life with people according to the ways of Jesus, and loving others well) are all things that will have eternal value.

8. Planning humbly, with Christ at the foundation, with His leadership and motives, trusting God, allowing Him to dictate, and committing your ways to Him is the only guaranteed way for our plans to be successful. *Disclaimer: The outcome may not always be what you thought or envisioned, but it will be best and for your good(Romans 8:28).

9. God is most focused on the state of your soul and the souls of others, which is transformed through a relationship with Him as you seek after Him. Therefore, God cares most that you get to know Him personally and have a relationship with Him through Jesus and then help others do the same. Thus, what you do to advance the Kingdom of Heaven by multiplying its population via forms of discipleship, evangelism, outreach, and other matters for Christ carry more weight than doing things for your glory or that only last here on Earth.

10. It's very important to know God intimately to first hear Him clearly and receive plans from Him, but also to hear complete instructions. David had plans for the temple from God, but he wasn't to build it, God told Him to give it to his son to build. If David had built the temple although he had all of the plans from the Holy Spirit, he would've been in disobedience.

Let's make it personal:

Activity #2-

Mainly focused on what's in front of you and feels good	(Intentional about the future and what's right)
Prefer physical blessings from God	(Prefer intimacy with God)
Majority of your daily activities focus on God and the gospel in some way	Majority of your daily activities focus on worldly things
Working on things you want to do with no regard of others or God	(Working on things God has called you to even if it's not what you prefer)
Focus more on appearance and possessions	(Focus more on someone's soul and heart)
Use your gifts to benefit others	(Use your gifts to benefit others)
Rarely ever help those in need	(Intentional about helping those in need)

Broken Jars

1. To repair something that is broken or damaged.

2. The Israelites were exiled, separated from their home, brokenhearted, and wounded (probably mentally, spiritually, and physically).

3. God was able to build those exiled Israelites back up into a powerful nation that was once exiled and abandoned, and He is able to mend (heal) and bring things back together. Ultimately, God is able to do anything, for He is mighty in power, and He understands all things (including the things that we go through). All in all, God can mend any and everything!

4.

	Brokenness	Mended
Isaiah 61:1	People were captives	They would have freedom
Isaiah 61:2 & 3	People were mourning	They would be comforted and have the "oil of joy"
Isaiah 61:3	People were run down, ashes	Traded ashes for beauty
Isaiah 61:4	There were devastated places	These places would be
Isaiah 61:7	People who were in shame and disgraced	They would receive a double portion, inheritance, and everlasting joy

5. A thorn is a problem one struggles with continuously, thus making them imperfect. In the words of Paul, it is also a "messenger of Satan."

6. It allowed Paul to be in such a position that would cause him to turn to God in the midst of his weakness, in need of God's power to help him make it through. God wants us to be in a relationship with Him and acknowledge and ask Him for help. It's not to allow us to be tortured, but to help us stay submitted - Paul, the man who wrote much of the New Testament, included.

7. To keep us from thinking too highly of ourselves and becoming conceited or arrogant.

8. Turn to God consistently for help and strength.

9. Jesus says prostitutes and tax collectors, people who have immense sin and brokenness would attain the kingdom of God before the chief priests and religious leaders because they heard the words of God, accepted them, and repented, but the religious people did not.

Answer Key

10.

	Describe the person before he/she encountered God.	How did God intervene/respond?	Describe the person after he/she encountered God.
Mary Magdalene: Read Luke 8:1-3 and Mark 16:9-11	Possessed by seven demons	Jesus encountered her and delivered her from the demons	Mary followed Jesus, helped fund his ministry and was the first person Jesus revealed Himself to upon resurrecting from the dead.
Zaccheus: Read Luke 19:1-10	A rich tax collector who likely cheated people and was harsh towards others	Jesus spent time with Him and went to his home	He gave half of his possessions to the poor and vowed to pay back four times the amount he cheated anyone out of.
People of Nineveh: **Read Jonah 1:1-2 and Jonah 3** Note: Nineveh is in modern-day Iraq	They were a very wicked nation	God sent Jonah, a prophet, to preach against them and warn them of their coming destruction	The king and peoples fasted and repented! They turned to God and God relented from destroying them.

11. God has to allow His light to shine in our hearts by us coming to know, understand, and receive His glory, power, and Holy Spirit through Jesus' death and resurrection (aka giving our lives to Christ).

12. Knowledge of the good news/the gospel (our ability to know God fully and be in a relationship with Him); salvation. The great mystery of the Old Testament revelaed in the flesh (John 1:1)!

13. We are unworthy, weak, and our flesh can fail (Matthew 26:41).

14. God did this to prove that He is all-powerful. If God can transform and use the most unlikely people with a debilitating handicap(sin) to spread His message and "turn the world upside down" (Acts 17:6), then there are no ifs, ands, nor buts about the fact that God is a miracle worker and has operated and worked through us by His power. Thus, showing He is real and is connected with us. He gets the glory as He proves His surpassing greatness. God is the G.O.A.T forreal! To give a visual, God using us broken vessels to accomplish His will is like turning a team full of rookies into Olympic champions in one season; what a Coach!

15. Jesus says the remedy is to watch for the enemy's tactics, be on the lookout, stay awake and acknowledge when the enemy is working and follow that up with prayer.

Tell Your Story

1. Paul says, "we know and prophesy in part," which means we don't see and speak the whole picture. God just gives portions.

2. We will see in full on the day of Christ's return, and we are made whole.

3. According to the scriptures, it was through the blood of the lamb (Jesus' sacrifice on the cross) and the word of their (the angels) testimony that defeated Satan!

4. To record or witness; evidence given, a report

5. The power of Jesus is expressed in His compassion for a woman that is far from holy and He speaks prophetically to her. After He revealed Himself to her as the Messiah, she used her testimony of how Jesus spoke into her life to tell others in her town about Him. This led to people coming and seeing about Him and they too believed because of their encounter with Him. Jesus' power is also expressed in Him delivering a man of many demons. After he was delivered, Jesus likely told His disciples to give the man one of their tunics as the man was clothed after being delivered, this also shows Jesus' love and compassion. Although the man wanted to come with Jesus, Jesus ordered Him to stay in his town and testify of what Jesus did for Him and many heard and were amazed.

6. Your testimony is a simple, easy, and personal way to show people through experiential evidence your reasoning for why you follow Jesus.

Ablaze

1. "This is why I remind you to fan into flames the spiritual gift God gave you when I laid my hands on you. For God has not given us a spirit of fear and timidity, but of power, love, and self-discipline."

2. To stir up and keep ablaze, to remind yourself of the gift that is within you as a believer.

3. The Holy Spirit.

4. FIRE!

5. The Holy Spirit gives you power, love, self-control, wisdom, understanding, counsel, might, knowledge, and fear of the Lord. The ability to discern, prophesy, heal, do miraculous works, speak in different tongues, and interpret those tongues all come from the Holy Spirit. The Holy Spirit gives you joy, peace, long-suffering, gentleness, goodness, faith, meekness, and the ability to speak before men on behalf of God as well.

6.

Hebrews 10:24-25	Jude 1:20-21	I Samuel 30:6-8	Romans 12:6-8	Psalm 42:5-6	John 4:31-34	Joshua 1:8 and Psalm 48:9
Encouraging other brothers/sisters in Christ; gathering with other believers	Praying in the Spirit; remain in God's love, abide with Him & obeying the Lord's commands	Lean on the Lord in times of trouble, cry out to Him; seek Him for wisdom about all things	Use the gift(s) of the Holy Spirit that God has given you; make use of the gifts, put them into practice	Remember what God has done; speak the truth of Jesus to yourself, speak the scriptures; HOPE IN GOD!	Do the will of God; accomplish His work	Meditate on the word of God and His love for you

OCTOBER

Vision

1. The Chaldeans (Babylonians). They were merciless enemies of the Israelites, fierce, often overtook others dwelling places, they were feared and dreaded individuals, and had experienced soldiers amongst them.

2. Habakkuk was desperate for answers and a plan. He did not understand why God was allowing the enemy to prevail and He wanted to know how they could overcome.

3. It was important because it was a prophecy (vision/knowledge from God of what was to come), and clarity was required so that it could be passed on, and when others heard it, they'd listen and understand.

4. God gave Habakkuk a vision of the end of Babylonian reign and rule. God shows him that they will get what they have earned because of their wicked deeds. At this appointed time, the knowledge of God's glory (honor and reputation) will cover the entire Earth! Everyone will know who God is.

5. They would all crumble and succumb to the iron nation.

6. The Kingdom of God

7. King Nebuchadnezzar went insane as God prophesied and when he came to his senses he was humbled and believed in the Holy God of Israel. His son sadly also fell into the same sins and was ultimately destroyed taking the Babylonian empire down with him.

8. Judgment and the fall of Satan and everyone who followed him on earth.

9. Satan and his demons.

10. God desires for us all to repent and be saved.

11. God provided us with Jesus as the sacrifice for our salvation if we'd trust and believe in Him.

12.

	What was the vision?	How was the provision made?
Exodus 35:4-35 and Exodus 36:1-7	A sanctuary (tabernacle) was to be built unto God.	The Lord stirred hearts to give and raised up laborers to accomplish the task. They ended up with more than enough to fund the vision.
Nehemiah 1:1-11 and Nehemiah 2:1-8	The walls of Jerusalem needed to be rebuilt.	Nehemiah knew the right people to ask. The king wrote a letter on Nehemiah's behalf for the governors to provide the materials for his every need.
2 Samuel 7:1-13, 1 Kings 3:3-14, and 1 Kings 5:2-18	David desired to build a temple (house) for the Lord to dwell in.	God said it wasn't for David to build but his son would. God later blessed Solomon with immense wealth due to his humility, thus providing for the project of building the temple.

Obey

1. God told Saul to destroy the Amalek people and animals for opposing the Israelites.

2. Saul and his soldiers captured the King and did not kill him. They also kept the best of the animals that they could find.

3. Saul said they'd be sacrificing the animals unto God.

4. King Saul was addressed and punished, thus showing that God expects the follow-through of instructions to fall on leadership. Those in leadership must be upstanding, bold, submitted to God, deliver the decrees of God, and assure they are done. As my pastor says, everything rises and falls on leadership.

5. God values obedience over sacrifice.

6. No, although in our eyes, witchcraft would be a heinous sin, Samuel states that even rebellion (disobedience) is just as sinful, thus showing that anything done in God's sight that doesn't align with Him is all equally as wrong.

7. His position as king of Israel.

8. These people will experience the wrath of God that is soon to come.

9. Sons of disobedience

Selah moment: Caleb believed and obeyed God fully. This allowed him to enter into the promised land and set his descendants up for greatness.

10. She traveled seeking after Elisha for his help because he'd prophesied that she'd have a son.

11. Elisha instructed Gehazi to take his staff and lay it on the boy's face.

12. Yes, he fulfilled what Elisha instructed him to do.

13. No, the boy was still dead.

14. Elisha prayed and then laid on the boy's dead body twice. After the second time, the boy sneezed, and his eyes opened. He was alive!

15. Elijah stretched out on the dead boy's body three times and prayed to God, and the boy was revived.

16. Elisha likely followed the example set by Elijah. He obeyed what Elijah had taught him.

17. Naaman had leprosy, which is a disease that causes bumps and discoloration on the skin.

18. Elisha, a true prophet in Israel.

19. Elisha told him to go and wash himself seven times in the Jordan River, and his leprosy would be cured.

20. He was upset as he was prideful about Elisha not coming outside to greet him, and he thought Elisha would simply "wave his hand over his leprosy" and pray to God to heal his leprosy. Naaman was also upset that he'd have to go into the Jordan River because he thought the rivers in Damascus were better (he was bourgeois--bougie- because the Jordan River was dirtier than other rivers).

21. No. He wasn't going to follow through with what Elisha instructed.

22. His officers, the people closest to him, talked some sense into him.

23. Naaman was healed entirely, and his skin was as healthy as a child's.

24. Those who hear the word of God and obey it are blessed!

Altogether Beautiful

1. You are altogether beautiful, my love; there is no flaw in you.

2. Solomon sees his wife as beautiful and flawless.

3. Jesus died on the cross to make the Church spotless. So, under the covering of Jesus, God sees us as spotless and holy in His sight.

4.

	Read Genesis 17:1-19 Person: Abram & Sarai	Read Matthew 16:16-19 Person: Simon	Read Isaiah 62 People: Israel
How did God identify the person? What did God call this person? (Hint: Pay attention to the meaning of their names)	Abraham (father of many nations) Sara(princess)	Peter (rock; Jesus would build His church upon Peter's leadership)	Hephsivah & Bulah (delighted in and married), sought after, and holy)
When did God give the person this name, before or after they became it?	Before	Before	Before
BELIEVING God and having FAITH was/is required of each of the people you've read about in order for them to BECOME who God called them to be! James says that As James and the writer of Hebrews shows us, FAITH IS FOLLOWED BY ACTION. So...			
What act of faith was/is required of the person/people to live up to the name?	Circumcising the males and laying with his wife, thus believing the words of God.	Enduring through trials and failures, letting go of his own ways and taking on the ways of God, and boldly speaking the word of God those God showed him.	Repenting and turning back to God; believing in the Messiah

5. Children of God; sons/daughters of Abraham

6. Repent, have faith in Jesus, be born again by being baptized by the Holy Spirit and water

The Great Escape

1. Those who are righteous, do not walk down the path of the wicked, keep proper company, and yet meditate on the word of God day and night.

2. God is holy and Jesus is righteous. You can become holy and righteous by having faith and surrendering your life to Him.

3. By seeking God, hiding the word of God in our heart, and living a life that mirrors the word of God.

4. Evil desires which are rooted in sin.

5. Through accepting God's call to salvation because of our knowledge of Jesus' death, burial, and resurrection.

6. Adding goodness to your faith, knowledge, self-control, perseverance, godliness, mutual affection, and genuine love for others.

7. To be effective and productive (Matthew 28:19) in our relationships with Jesus, those things are essential.

8.

Refresh your memory on the attributes that you should be growing in (2 Peter 1:5-7)
Don't follow the desires of your flesh and honor authority
Live a holy and godly life
Guard yourself from false beliefs and unsound doctrine
Grow in grace and the knowledge of Jesus

9.

The Apostles teachings (for us, this looks like reading the word of God, the Holy Bible)
Fellowship (being with their community)
Partaking in the Lord's Supper (communion)
Praying

Coming together and helping each other and those in need

10. Therefore, let anyone who THINKS that he STANDS take heed lest he FALL. No TEMPTATION has overtaken you that is not COMMON to man. God is FAITHFUL, and he will not let you be TEMPTED beyond your ability, but with the temptation, he will also PROVIDE the way of ESCAPE, that you may be able to endure it.

NOVEMBER

Deeply Rooted

1.

	What was his job?	What offering did he bring to God?	How did God respond to his offering?
Cain	Worked the soil; farmer, agriculture	Some of the crops that he'd grown	God did not look with favor; disappointed
Abel	Kept the flocks; maybe a shepherd	Fat from the firstborn of the flock	God was pleased and looked with favor

2. Cain was angry and visibly saddened.

3. Cain did not listen to God's corrections and chose to murder his brother.

4. Anger, because God favored Abel's offering over his. Cain was also disobedient to God's standards, but his brother was righteous in his actions, so that may have created envy in his heart.

5. Cain was cursed because of his actions, when he tended to the ground(farmed/gardened, the first job of Adam) it would no longer grow crops for him, he was also a restless wanderer on the earth. (Cross reference) I notice that Cain's consequences were similar to the curses placed upon his parents, Adam and Eve: he too was put out of the land given to him and gardening was made difficult because he followed in the footsteps of sinning against God like his parents did. As for Cain's family, Lamech (Cain's son) followed in his footsteps by murdering a man. A cycle of sin and consequences was in effect in this family line. NOTE: Generational curses don't have to carry on, they can be broken, see Ezekiel 18!

God is With You

1. An uncultivated, uninhabited, and inhospitable region. One could expect a wilderness to be prickly, tough terrain, a strenuous path, and "the road less traveled."

2. The Philistines were an aggressive group of people and enemies of the Israelites.

3. Although taking the path through the Philistines' land would've been quicker, God chose to lead the Israelites through the wilderness to get to the promised land.

4. God knew if the Israelites went through the land of the aggressive Philistines, the Israelites would deal with war and would want to turn around and go back to Egypt as opposed to pressing on. So, to keep them from giving up too quickly, He led them the longer route. He led them through the wilderness to protect them and their promise.

5. God was with them every step of the way through the wilderness and led them by a pillar of cloud during the day and a pillar of fire during the night.

6. So that when He protected the Israelites from Pharaoh, He would get the glory.

7. When they saw Pharaoh's army in the distance, they were fearful, complained, questioned Moses for leading them out of Egypt, panicked, and assumed the worst was to come via death in the wilderness.

8. Moses encouraged them not to be afraid, stand firm, and trust God to show up and fight on their behalf. All they had to do was be silent before God.

9. God told Moses to use the staff that he'd been given to split the sea so that the Israelites could walk on dry ground.

10. Possibly because Moses was looking to God to show up but hadn't used the tool(s) God had already given him.

11. The sea separated and divided into two allowing the Israelites to walk through on the dry ground.

12. Yes, and their enemies were crushed.

13. They sang a song of praise unto God, telling of His goodness and what He'd done for them.

14.

	Where were the Israelites?	What was needed?	What did the Israelites do?	What did Moses do?	What did God do?
Exodus 15:22-27	The wilderness of Shur, Marah	Drinkable water	Complained/grumbled to Moses about their lack of water to drink.	Cried out/prayed to God for a solution	Showed Moses a log to throw into the water, making the water of Marah sweet and drinkable. God also led them to a place with plenty of water.
Exodus 16:1-18	Wilderness of Sin	Food to eat	Complained/grumbled about their hunger; they also reminisced on their past of being able to eat during their captivity	Listened to God for His way out and delivered the message to the Israelites	Provided meat at night via quail and bread in the morning from the dew
Exodus 17:1-6	Rephidim	Water	Argued with Moses about being thirsty and yet again complained about leaving Egypt	Cried out to God for advice on what to do with the Israelites	Provided water when Moses struck a rock with his staff

15. When we cry out to God, He makes a way for us, even in the dry, barren land of wilderness.

16. If you endure the times of suffering properly(with God, not complaining, but turning to Him for help), you can come out on the other side full of so much. You can gain a new understanding and depth of God's word and ways, greater endurance in your faith, fortified character, increased hope in God and communion with His Holy Spirit, a new depth unlocked of your knowledge of God's love for you, you'll be able to encourage and strengthen others who eventually go through tough times, you will have shared in the death and life of Jesus, you will know and experience the God of all comfort and compassion ultimately drawing you closer to Him and refining you along the way.

17. The hope you can have as you endure is that this time of suffering through the dry wilderness isn't pointless, you're going somewhere with God in tow. During these moments/seasons, you can also have hope that the God of all comfort and compassion is with you, the Holy Spirit that brings life and prophecy is within you(if you've asked God for it), and knowing that trouble won't last always, but glory is at the end of it all.

18. This scripture encourages us to use common sense and be wise, if a situation seems to have danger, it is not wise to take that option for the sake of suffering. Be wise and hide yourself from said danger, it is not wise to choose suffering for yourself when other options are available. It doesn't make you more holy

to take the harder path for the sake of taking it. God presenting and taking you down a way of suffering vs. you unwisely choosing it or blindly walking into it are different. (An example of this would be if Moses still took the Israelites the way of the Philistines despite God's warning, yes the Israelites still struggled in the wilderness, but it was in the will of God and wisely taken.) Be vigilant and be wise! This doesn't mean be anxious and over plan to avoid danger, pain, and suffering, just be wise and keep your eyes open as you journey with God.

Don't Tap Out

1.

	What actions describe our enemy, Satan?
Luke 22:31-32	Wants to sift God's people like wheat; tear them apart; ruin them. We can also see that Satan is on a leash when it comes to followers of Jesus as he had to ask God to touch His people.
John 8:44	The devil is the father of lies! He's a master of it, lying is his craft, his native language, and skill! He's also a murderer.
1 Peter 5:8	Satan is waiting, lurking, and prowling on a search for someone to devour.

2. Jesus prayed that Peter's faith would not fail.

3. Satan is after your faith!

> Selah Moment:
>
> Consider trials as "pure joy"!
>
> Tested faith
>
> Trials and tested faith produce perseverance and maturity in your walk with God.

4. To be alert and sober-minded, meaning to be watchful for tricks and schemes of the enemy that would try and trip you up and be self-disciplined when those moments arise.

5. Three.

6. Jesus responded with, "it is written."

7. The word of God!

8. Jesus was tempted three times, but using the word of God, He won each battle. It's clear that the word of God is powerful (Hebrews 4:12) and worked because, in the end, Satan fled.

9. Various answers are possible. By allowing Jesus to be tempted, we have a Savior and a God who has been through and conquered what we go through daily living in this sinful world, in which Satan has

dominion. This step was necessary for Jesus to prepare and equip Him for the journey ahead within His ministry; to qualify Jesus as one who could indeed defeat Hell and the stain of sin (Ephesians 4:6-8), and give us an example of how to fight in this world. We have an empathetic God who can never be defeated.

10.

	Describe the problem the person had.	What reason did he/she have to tap out and give up?	Instead of tapping out, what did he/she do instead?	What was the outcome?
Matthew 15:21-28	A Canaanite woman needed a miracle for her daughter, but at first, Jesus denied helping her.	Jesus denied her help at first.	The Canaanite woman persisted and showed Jesus that she was humble, eager, and had great faith by stating that she'd accept even just the crumbs of the "children's bread."	Her daughter was healed.
Mark 10:46-52	Bartimeus was blind and wanted to get the chance to be healed by Jesus.	Everyone around him was telling him to stop and be silent.	Bartimeus cried out louder and all the more to get Jesus' attention.	Bartimeus got Jesus' attention, and his sight was restored.
Luke 8:42-48 and Mark 5:24-34	A woman who suffered from constant bleeding for 12 years could not be cured.	There were big crowds around Jesus, so she couldn't get the opportunity to talk to Jesus.	With faith in her heart, the woman reached for Jesus' garment and touched it.	She was healed!

11. Apostasy will happen before Jesus returns, the great rebellion, the abandonment of the faith by professed Christians.

12. Possible answer: Seeing trials as a joy and opportunities to grow closer to God, solidifying your faith in Him so that when times get even darker in the world, your faith will stand the tests to come! Endurance is your portion, stamina, resilience, and firm faith will be produced. Answers also depend on the revelation God gives you in the scriptures. You must apply them. I don't want you to fall away, but your heavenly Father doesn't want this even more!

13. The full armor of God.

14. We are instructed to put on the full armor of God because it will enable us to stand firm against Satan's schemes and resist him.

15. Belt of truth, body armor/breastplate of righteousness, shoes of peace to preach the good news, shield of faith, helmet of salvation, sword of the Spirit(word of God), and praying in the Spirit

16. A rich harvest in gaining eternal life and being reunited with God, and increased faith in Him!

17. I(Jesus) have told you these things, so that in me you may have peace. In this world, you will have trouble. But take heart! I have overcome the world." John 16:33

"You, dear children, are from God and have overcome them because the one who is in you is greater than the one who is in the world." 1 John 4:4

18. Jesus didn't tap out because He chose to surrender to the will of God instead of his own flesh. He also knew His purpose in being on the earth. So instead of choosing comfort, He endured the necessary suffering to accomplish the mission at hand: redeem humanity by bridging the gap between God and man!!!

Unreliable Faith

1. Jesus told Peter to "come" out onto the water.

2. Peter got out of the boat and walked on the water towards Jesus.

3. No, we can assume that Jesus was simply standing on the water waiting for Peter to come to Him.

4. Peter began to look at the wind and circumstances around him and began to sink.

5. Possible answer: Peter may have begun to sink because he allowed his fear to be greater than his faith, being that his focus shifted from Jesus and turned to his circumstances.

6. Jesus reached out to Peter and caught him.

7. Jesus said he had little faith and doubted.

8. The scripture says that Jesus immediately took Peter's hand. Therefore, although He was silent and may have seemed far away from Peter, He was actually close by and ready to help when truly needed.

9

	How was the person tested?	How did the person respond?	What did this test expose about the person?	Did the person pass or fail the test?	Where was God during it all?
Read Genesis 3 Adam & Eve	The serpent tempted Eve to eat from the tree God said not to eat from	Adam ate the fruit given Eve was deceived and fell into temptation	Adam's lack of leadership and belief in God's word Eve's covetousness in her heart and unbelief in God's word	FAILED	Somewhere else in the garden but His eyes were on them

Read Genesis 22 Abraham	God told Abraham to offer Isaac as a sacrifice	Abraham obeyed and took Isaac to the mountain to sacrifice him	Abraham's submission to God; willing to obey at all costs	PASSED	In Heaven, but His eyes were on Abraham
Read Mark 4:35-41 Jesus' Disciples	A storm came as they were traveling by sea	They were afraid and accused Jesus of not caring for them	The disciples' lack of faith in the Jesus and their lack of knowing Jesus' heart	FAILED	Jesus was literally with them, sleeping on the boat; God the Father watched in heaven
Read Acts 2:12-41 Peter	People accused the disciples of being drunk with wine	Peter stood up boldly, correcting the mockers and shared truth	People acceptance of what Jesus called Him to do; feed His sheep the Word of God	PASSED	Within Him by the Holy Spirit; God watched from heaven

10. God is near and will hold our hands. I know this because of God's character and how He dealt with Israel.

11. You will receive the crown of life, which is symbolic of eternal life with God. So, do not be dismayed while you are going through a test or trial, but rejoice all the more and allow the Holy Spirit within you to lead and guide you.

12. Jesus promised them that during a time of testing before men, the Holy Spirit would teach them how to respond in that very moment!

DECEMBER

Pressed

1. "We are hard-pressed on every side, but not crushed; perplexed, but not in despair; persecuted, but not abandoned; struck down, but not destroyed."

2. Possible answer: As believers, Paul and those in ministry with him went through many trials and troubles, but it never stopped their great commission, and though their flesh took a beating, their spirit was alive because God was with them. Nothing that came against them was able to destroy them, their faith, nor their closeness to God.

3. To be made right with God and have life, you must die to your fleshly desires/sin nature by symbolically crucifying it, surrendering your life to God, and choosing to be a living sacrifice. By "picking up your cross," you are accepting the trials that come with following Jesus, but through that acceptance, you also are receiving eternal life as He was raised from the dead and back to life. In due time, so shall we who

choose to die to our flesh here on Earth - we will be raised to life with God in eternity.

4. It's through believers' sacrifice of their flesh as we mobilize and share the gospel that others can be freed and live.

5. Yes, the consolation is that Christians are victorious because Christ is in us via the Holy Spirit, who is greater than he (Satan) that is in the world and is against us. We (Christians) also have hope that on the day of Christ's return, we will enter into glory along with those who we disciple and share the gospel with, and they receive. So, although trials suck and are uncomfortable, we are more than conquerors, for if God is for us, who can be against us and prevail?

6. Diamonds undergo immense heat and pressure amongst other rocks deep inside of Earth to be produced.

7. Olives are crushed to make a paste and then are pressed to separate the oil from the paste.

8. Stay on guard, stay awake, watch, and pray! Jesus prayed and aligned Himself with the will of God so He was able to endure His time of greatest pressure.

9. Stay on guard: see, perceive, discern, to look at. (Strong's 991)

Watch: to be alert, vigilant, and keep awake (Strong's 1127)

Pray: ask God to provide and worship Him (Strong's 4336)

10. Possible answer: Being that this didn't happen, these answers are just inferences. Had Peter been alert and praying when Jesus was, he likely wouldn't have been so frantic or taken by surprise when the betrayer and army came. He would've been ready to respond appropriately rather than based on his flesh.

Blank Canvas...Clean Slate

1. The wickedness, violence, and evil of the human heart, thoughts, and actions.

2. God decided to flood the earth to wipe it clean of the human race and essentially start over with humanity.

3. To cleanse it of the wickedness and evil people of the time.

4. God promised to never again destroy all of life by flooding waters. This covenant was sealed with the rainbow in the sky as a reminder of God's promise/covenant.

5. They had to sacrifice an animal that was spotless and had nothing wrong with it.

6. To be the ultimate sacrifice for us to be reconciled to God and save the world.

7. No!

8. On the last day.

9. Sin, which leads to death (Hell and eternal separation from God).

10. There is no condemnation for those who are in Christ Jesus

11. I must know Jesus, put my faith in Him, and commit my life to following Him and living by His Spirit.

12. He humbled himself, came to his senses, and realized at his father's house he'd be provided for, even as a servant.

13. To change one's mind or purpose about something; to turn away from something; to be remorseful over.

14. When the son acknowledged that he sinned and made his decision to get up and go back to his father's house in verse 20.

15. His father accepted him with open arms and celebrated his return home.

16. His father ran to him when he saw his son up the road; it just required the son to repent, turn away from his sins/past life, and come home!

Selah moment:
Possible answers-
- Probably not.
- He would've stayed in his guilt and shame, would've struggled unnecessarily, and missed out on what his father was ready to offer him.

17. God invites and is waiting for his people to return to Him and "settle the matter" of sin and wickedness within the hearts and lives of His people. He desires to cleanse us from our sins and turn them white as snow. All He requires is that we must turn to Him and obey.

Worth the Wait

1. Stay where one is or delay action until a particular time or until something else happens; remain in readiness for some purpose; wait, or look eagerly for.

2. Someone or something having power, authority, or influence; a master or ruler; Jehovah = 'the existing One', the proper name of the one true God; Yahweh

3. To stay where you are and delay action until Yahweh, the one true God, who has all authority and power, says to go and make things happen or until He allows them to happen on His own.

4. God promised to make Abram into a great nation and that his offspring would be plentiful. God also promised Abram to give the land of Canaan to said offspring.

5. 75 years old.

6. No, they didn't because Sarai wasn't able to conceive children.

7. Abram was obedient and moved when God said so, built an altar (a place to pray, worship, and offer sacrifices unto God), and continued to work and grow in wealth. And as God instructed, He walked around

the land that God was giving him, admiring it and getting to know it.

> Selah Moment:
> • Obey God
> • Pray about what you're waiting on
> • Continue to work while you're waiting
> • Get to know more about what you're waiting on

(For example: if you're waiting to be married, obey God's word for keeping yourself pure and whatever else He may instruct you to do. Pray about your future marriage, continue to work on your faith and relationship with God, knowing yourself, and progressing in the areas God has given you during your singleness, and learn about marriage and God's purpose for it. Marriage is just an example; you insert whatever you're waiting for into those remarks).

8. Abram began to worry and question God because he didn't have any children and didn't know if He could be sure that he'd gain possession of the promises of God.

9. God reassured him. an

10. No.

11. Ten years

12. Sarai suggested that Abram sleep with her slave, Hagar, and they'd have children through her.

13. Hagar became pregnant with a son, Ishmael. During this pregnancy, Hagar grew to despise her master, Sarai. Thus, Sarai mistreated Hagar, and she fled. Upon fleeing, Hagar encountered the angel of the Lord, who assured her that God heard her and that she'd have many descendants, and her son would be hostile towards his other brothers. Additional fact: Ishmael's descendants were known as the Ishmaelites and chose to fight against God and His people, the Israelites (Psalm 83:1-8).

14. 86 years old

15. 99 years old

16. Every male had to be circumcised as a sign of the covenant(an agreement, like a contract) between Abraham and God; otherwise, they'd be cut off from the people for breaking this covenant.

17. God says that He will give her a son and kings will come from her!

18. Sarah was 90 years old, and he was nearly 100 years old, so he didn't believe them having a son would be possible.

19. Isaac

20. He obeyed God's orders of circumcising all the offspring of his as God told him to.

Answer Key

21. God made good on His promise and gave Sarah a son, and they named him Isaac. At eight days old, Abraham circumcised him.

22. 100 years old.

23. 100 - 75 = 25 years of waiting

24. We are waiting for the day of Christ's return, the day of the Lord when the old heavens and earth will officially pass away and the new will come. The glory of God and righteousness will only live on from that day forward.

25. It hasn't come to pass because God wants many to be saved. This waiting period is for us to choose to repent and turn back to Him by following Jesus and living for Him. God loves the entire world, therefore He doesn't take pleasure in our demise, He wants us to choose Him, so He's given us time to do so..

26. 1000 years to God is merely like a day and one day like 1000 years depending on His purposes. So what seems long to us, is short to Him and what would appear to be short to us can be long. Here's a fun additional thought: we know that per the book of Genesis, the world and everything in it (man, plants, animals, etc) was made in 6 days, but if 1 day in the eyes of God is like 1000, maybe this process took 6,000 years. I don't know if this is true, it's just a pondering of mine.

27. They brought oil for their lamps and rested when they needed it.

28. They rested as well, but didn't have enough oil to make it through the night, so they missed out on the wedding banquet(Heaven)

29. "But seek first his kingdom and his righteousness, and all these things will be given to you as well. Therefore do not worry about tomorrow, for tomorrow will worry about itself. Each day has enough trouble of its own." (NIV)

30. Seeking first the kingdom of God above all worldly things by pursuing Jesus, resisting pressures to fall away, and living holy and godly lives.

Chosen by the King!

1. The people of Israel, the children of Israel, the Israelites (three different names for the same group of people).

2. They are people who are holy, chosen, and God's treasured possessions.

3. Destroy them, make no treaties with them of peace, show no mercy, they could not marry them, break down their items of worship to other gods, and burn their idols. They were essentially to have nothing to do with them and destroy all things related to them for them not to be swayed by their way of living. This also applies to us currently in not being unequally yoked in a relationship with unbelievers.

4. God chose them because they were small in number and thus God would get the glory from their victory and because God made promises to their ancestors Abraham and Isaac.

Selah Moment: To be chosen for God's team on that day, you had to be a female of Abraham's lineage through Isaac or a circumcised male of Abraham's lineage through Isaac and keep the laws of God.

5. He was used to not eating meat due to Jewish traditions/commands set before Jesus coming.

6. God told Him not to deem something as impure that He has made clean.

7. It was unlawful for Jews and Gentiles to engage with each other, but Peter went against this because of the vision and instruction God gave him before his arrival.

8. God was showing Him that both Jew and Gentile (non-Jews) are welcome in the faith. No longer was it just for those of Jewish descent. The Israelites were no longer the only ones who could receive God's grace and favor of salvation.

9. The special people he invited didn't want to come. They were too preoccupied with their work and dwellings and denied the invitation.

10. Any and every one!

11. He was not dressed in wedding attire.

12. Those who are appropriately dressed! This means those who are chosen and accept God's word (invitation) and clothe themselves in righteousness (wedding clothes). So, those who accept Jesus as Lord and live as such via the transformation of their heart because of their faith in Jesus. You can't just live any way you want and say you're a Christian. Although you are no longer under the law but instead under grace (see Appendix A for more info on this shift), your works show evidence of your faith.

13. The Israelites were rebellious and trespassed (offended God with their sin) against God continuously, so He invited everyone to accept His saving grace and salvation in order to come back to Him.

14. The king didn't get a response to His invitation sent to a select few for the wedding of his son, so he opened the wedding up to anyone who wanted to attend. God has done the same with us. He initially only welcomed His chosen people, the Israelites, the Jews, but has now invited us all, Jew and Gentile, to come to be wed to His Son, Jesus (the bridegroom, Luke 5:34-35) as the Church (bride of Christ, Ephesians 5:25-28).

15. God first chose you and called you to be His through a relationship with Jesus.

16. Jesus didn't desire to go to the cross and be separated from God to take on our sin and shame. Still, He chose to lay down His life for us on the cross, thus choosing us and God's will over His emotions and sentiments about dying the painful and torturous death of crucifixion. The victory on the other side of the pain was worth it for Jesus.

17. Be fruitful, love others, and make disciples.

18. "I Am."

19. You are chosen, royal, holy, His special possession, and called out of darkness into His light.

20. Accept it, sing, declare, and proclaim praises unto God, telling others of His goodness and ability to bring them out of the darkness as well.

21. You weren't an afterthought and the Jews aren't now done away with. God did not change His mind about the natural-born children of Abraham through Isaac, they can still be saved. He also had you in mind from the very beginning of time as you were included in the "many nations" God said Abraham would one day be the father of per the prophecy God gave him back in Genesis 17! He just chose to reveal His full plan in His good and perfect timing. God has grafted(or "drafted"(;) you into the family through the death and resurrection of Jesus and your acceptance of Him. When you believed and then received the Holy Spirit, you were adopted into the family of God. That is why you are chosen. Your faith has saved you, this wasn't or couldn't be earned by your birthright or good acts, but freely given by God and willingly accepted by you.

Appendix A:
To Condemn or Not to Condemn?

First and foremost, if Jesus, God in the flesh, doesn't condemn(execute final judgment, establishing guilt, sentencing you to Hell) you at this time, but only disciplines you (Hebrews 12:6), you definitely shouldn't be condemning yourself(remaining in a place of guilt and punishment) so harshly for falling short. You should however repent so that you are in good standing with God before judgment day. This time on earth is a matter of becoming more like Christ, living by His Spirit, and helping others to do the same (2 Peter 3:9). As Paul confessed, you still live in your flesh here on Earth, causing there to be a sin struggle (Romans 7:15-25), thus you will mess up at times. Jesus Himself also said that yor spirit is willing, but your flesh is weak (Matthew 26:41). So do not condemn yourself for messing up; instead, repent and accept God's clean slate. Although there is no condemnation for those who love Jesus and walk according to His Spirit, do not become comfortable with sinning because you know you will be forgiven (Romans 6:1-2), as that's a dangerous place to be since whatever you obey is your master (Romans 6:16).

Appendix B: The Law or Grace?

The purpose of the law was to show all of humanity God's standards, which then reveal our incapability of keeping these standards perfectly (Romans 7:7-13). Whenever they didn't meet the standard set by God in His commandments, that was, and still is, considered sin (in archery, "sin" means you missed the mark; that is echoed here as well, as sin is when we miss the mark of God's glorious standards). Upon sinning and falling short, God required them to sacrifice animals to purify them of their sinful acts (Leviticus 4, Hebrews 9:13). However, the problem was they'd burn sacrifices and offerings and still turn around and live as though there was no law (Isaiah 1:4, 11-13); this is what God calls lawlessness or evildoing in the Bible (Matthew 7:22-23). There was no internal change because of the animal's sacrifice; it was all actions. So, although the law exposed the Israelites of their sin, it didn't transform them and make them right with God completely because the animal sacrifices weren't powerful enough to take away their sins. The great thing is, God is all-knowing and knew that the laws of Moses and animal sacrifices wouldn't fulfill His ultimate plan. He knew there was only one sacrifice that would suffice. God knew there was only one true, lasting, and definite way to make things right and reconcile His people back to Him (because ultimately that's God's greatest desire: us to be with Him). What was that way? Jesus. God Himself, wrapped in flesh (John 14:6).

Jesus wasn't plan B; He was the plan from the beginning - for this was all pre-planned. How do we know this? God says in His word that Jesus was there from the beginning of time before He formed the earth and before Moses and Abraham were even born (John 1:1 and John 8:58). God had planned from the beginning to send Jesus, His only Son, the only person on Earth to come straight from Him (Matthew 1:18-23) into the world. Jesus was sent to be the perfect sacrifice to break the chains of sin and the death it caused through His death and resurrection (rising from the dead) (2 Corinthians 5:21, Hebrews 9:14-15). It is through Jesus' sacrifice that the purpose of the law is completely fulfilled (Matthew 5:17), for we are finally able to fully be made right with God and are freed from the bondage of sin and death (Romans 8:1-2).

How can sin (darkness) and death be transformed? With light and life. How do we get that light and life? From the source Himself, Jesus, the light of the world (John 8:12). Unlike the actions required to keep up the law of Moses, under the law of grace, all that takes is faith and repentance because of God's graciousness and His love that was poured out on us through Jesus (Hebrews 11:6, Ephesians 2:8-9). Upon making that decision, we receive the Spirit of God (The Holy Spirit, also known as the Holy Ghost). Our lives can then be made new because having the Spirit of God inside of us is like having a high-tech GPS/navigation system inside of you, leading and guiding you, making you more sensitive to your actions and decisions. If you yield by dying to yourself and living according to the Holy Spirit inside of you (not according to the flesh you're wrapped in or to the world you're surrounded by), then you will please God (1 John 2:4). But, it starts with faith (Romans 7:5-6, Romans 8:8-11). You must then allow the light of Jesus to shine through you to dispel the sin and darkness that is knocking at your door every waking moment (Romans 7:4, James 4:7). Lastly, it is through your light that others can see and come to know who Jesus is (Matthew 5:16). As a lighthouse leads people to safety, it could be by your light shining brightly that people choose to leave their lives of sin (darkness) and death in exchange for light and eternal life; the light of Christ. So, shine brightly, for you could help save a soul. Selah.

Appendix C: The Trinity

There is a question that has plagued the minds of the Pharisees (Jews) in Jesus' day, it has been a source of debate amongst Christians and people of other religions, and even simply amongst families in Christian households. For centuries the debate has gone on in regards to the question: "Is Jesus God?" This very question of trying to identify Jesus to put Him in a category is one that actually matters a great deal. Is He just a man? Is He God? Is He a prophet? Is He a mixture of it all? Who is Jesus?

Very plainly, simply, and quickly this question can be answered this way: Yes, Jesus is God in the flesh(form of man). He is more than a prophet who speaks the word of God, Jesus IS the word of God(John 1:1-5) and thus He is certainly more than just a man. In John 8:58, Jesus boldly solidified this fact when he said, "very truly I tell you,","before Abraham was born, I Am!" Here, Jesus calls Himself the name of God, "I Am" (see Exodus 3:14) and thus declares that He and God are one. While we're here, the Holy Spirit is God as well and just as Jesus was here before the foundation(beginning) of the earth, so was the Holy Spirit(Genesis 1:2). To see more about how God the Father, Son(Jesus), and Holy Spirit flow as one, read John 16:1-15. There you will see how although the three have different roles and forms, there is no division amongst them, they move and operate as one God. For there is only one true God in all the universe.

In my opinion, that alone is enough to sign off and end the conversation. However, Jesus, knowing all things, knew this was a topic of conversation and the meditation of many people's hearts in His day and he constantly proved Himself. If you read scripture in the New Testament, you'll also quickly find that Jesus also was not afraid to have tough conversations; this topic was no different. Thus, if you'd like more evidence of this truth of Jesus keep reading.

In Matthew 16:13-17, the following happened,

> *"When Jesus came to the region of Caesarea Philippi, he asked his disciples, "Who do people say the Son of Man is?"*
>
> *They replied, "Some say John the Baptist; others say Elijah; and still others, Jeremiah or one of the prophets."*
>
> *"But what about you?" he asked. "Who do you say I am?"*
>
> *Simon Peter answered, "You are the Messiah, the Son of the living God."*
>
> *Jesus replied, "Blessed are you, Simon son of Jonah, for this was not revealed to you by flesh and blood, but by my Father in heaven."*

A few things to note here:

1) Jesus is the Messiah, the Christ, the Anointed one, who God promised to send to save and set captives free(Isaiah 61:1-11, Luke 4:16-21).

2) Jesus claimed God as His Father.

3) God the Father revealed this truth to Simon Peter and that is why he was able to boldly and clearly proclaim that Jesus was the Son of the living God.

In these verses alone we see that Jesus was not just a man nor was He just a prophet. Furthermore, I suggest you read all of John 6, but in a snippet of this chapter in verse 38, we also see that Jesus claimed to have come from heaven when He said, "for I have come down from heaven not to do my will but to do the will of Him who sent me" which is evident as He was not born as mere humans are. He was born of the virgin Mary who never had sex as we can see in Luke 1:26-45.

Jesus didn't stop here and only proclaim to have come from Heaven or to just be God the Father's Son, but He also proclaimed His oneness with God in John 10:30; Jesus said, "I and the Father are one." In those days such an expression of equality with God was punishable by death because blasphemy was held with high regard and some of the Jews exclaimed this as they tried to stone Him to death, but Jesus knowing who He was, confidently stated and operated in His identity, not once, but many times.

Some may now say, "if Jesus is God, how can God die since Jesus died on the cross?" To this point, my first response would be that, that is a great question. Secondly, I believe this question speaks to the power and thoughtfulness of God. He knew the need for there to be three expressions of Himself, one of which being in the form of a man, Jesus, and therefore being able to do and experience all that man is able to do, including the ability to die(Philippians 2:5- 11). Don't forget though, Jesus didn't remain in such a broken and defeated state as on the third day, He rose from the dead, thus ultimately expressing His authority He knew He had(John 10:18), thus showing the supreme and all-powerful nature of God(Matthew 28:1-10).

There you have it, God the Father, God the Son, and God the Holy Spirit(affectionately known as "The Trinity" by the Church) are one and have yet to be defeated. If you're still struggling to believe this, I suggest you pray that God would reveal His truth to you. Lastly, I leave you with these words of Jesus, "even though you do not believe me, believe the works, that you may know and understand that the Father is in me, and I in the Father" (John 10:38).

Selah and Amen.

Appendix D: Deliverance

What is deliverance?

A form of healing in which one is freed(delivered) from demons(fallen angels), also known as evil or unclean spirits.

What is deliverance vs inner healing?

It's important to know that not all issues we face are because we have a demon, some problems are due to soul(mind, will, and emotional) hurts from our upbringing as we've gone through life in a world where sin exists. I once heard a teacher say, "You can't counsel a demon and you can't cast out a wound". Everything we struggle with isn't a demon and thus can't just be cast out; instead, we need strategic exposing, tending to, and replacing with matters of Jesus; this is often called "inner healing". Whereas other things in life do need deliverance if it is indeed a demon.

One Inner healing technique:

TIP: Take your time as you go through this process. Write down your answers to these points to see the process AND/OR have a trusted Christian friend guide you through these. He/she should ask the Lord to show them answers for you too.

- Identify the issue (what are you struggling with?)
- Ask Jesus to show you what's at the root of it.
- Ask Him to show you when it first started.
    - Allow yourself to feel the emotions of that time and express them (ie cry, verbally express how you felt in that time, etc)
    - What thoughts and beliefs did you have and create from this moment?
- Ask God where He was in that moment AND how He felt about it.
    - Matthew 18:6 shows God's heart towards people who abuse and cause His children to stumble in sin.
- Ask God to redeem that moment and show you His desire for you.
    - Ask him for a new way of thinking according to His will; create a new statement to

think instead of your old thoughts.
- When I've done this for myself, God has shown me a picture and even spoken a comforting message to me.
- Make an Isaiah 61:3 trade.

"To appoint unto them that mourn in Zion, to give unto them beauty for ashes, the oil of joy for mourning, the garment of praise for the spirit of heaviness, that they might be called trees of righteousness, the planting of the Lord, that He might be glorified." Isaiah 61:3

- Give the Lord the issue you've been dealing with, surrender it to Him in prayer, and release it as best you can from your heart and mind. You can do this by speaking it.
  - Example: Lord I give you _____ or I release ___ to you..."
- Then ask for and accept the opposite of the issue you've been facing.
  - Example: If you've been struggling with lust, ask for the purity of Christ. If you've been struggling with anger, ask for the love of God to fill you and bring you peace. This is what I call an "Isaiah 61:3 Trade."

Can I deliver someone?

Yes, every disciple of Jesus can cast out demons and thus "deliver" someone. Jesus said so in Mark 6:17, "These signs will accompany those who have believed: in My name, they will cast out demons, they will speak with new tongues." In an atmosphere of complete surrender to God, prayer, and worship, or just being in the presence of a disciple, demons/evil spirits that have been lying dormant within people may expose themselves by speaking through a person, making noises, or causing erratic behaviors through a person. Personally, only in those moments of manifestation will I ever engage in deliverance for someone else or if the Holy Spirit instructs me to in other moments. Thus, my suggestion about delivering others, is to do so wisely and under the inspiration of God.

WARNING: If you are not a disciple of Christ and thus have not accepted and confessed Jesus as Lord and Savior, been filled with His Holy Spirit, and/or if you live a life of unrepentant sin, DO NOT attempt to deliver someone. An example of deliverance gone wrong can be found in Acts 19:11-16,

"And God was doing extraordinary miracles by the hands of Paul, so that even handkerchiefs or aprons that had touched his skin were carried away to the sick, and their diseases left them and the evil spirits came out of them. Then some of the itinerant Jewish exorcists undertook to invoke the name of the Lord Jesus over those who had evil spirits, saying, "I adjure you by the Jesus whom Paul proclaims." Seven sons of a Jewish high priest named Sceva were doing this. But the evil spirit answered them, "Jesus I know, and Paul I recognize, but who are you?" And the man in whom was the evil spirit leaped on them, mastered all

of them, and overpowered them so that they fled out of that house naked and wounded."

Satan and his minions(demons) have power and the only way to overcome them is through one who is greater than him, that person is not you, it's Jesus Christ; the only one who has gone to the pits of hell and taken the power back on our behalf (Revelation 1:18). Thus, without being surrendered to Him and having His authority and power, you cannot do anything against Satan. Repeat after me: I NEED JESUS' AUTHORITY TO OVERCOME SATAN. Said authority is ONLY given to His disciples, especially those who fast and pray (1 John 4:4, Matthew 10:7-8, Matthew 28:18-20, and Matthew 17:21).

How does deliverance happen?

This short study is only meant to express that deliverance is possible and does happen. I suggest you use the following information for yourself if you see the need for deliverance within yourself or if demons manifest themselves in your presence. For more information, please read the Bible and do research on Christian deliverance ministries for more details.

1. Accept Jesus as Lord and Savior and ask God for His Holy Spirit.
   - I can't express this enough, the only authority we can have over satan is from Jesus.

2. Repent, forgive, and release all bitterness.
   - These things are big hindrances to being delivered. You (and/or the person needing deliverance) must repent of sin and let go of it, you must forgive those who have wronged you, and you must release any bitterness towards people or even God that you are holding onto. The demon(evil spirit) is there because, in some way, it has a legal right to be. So cancel those rights by repenting, forgiving, and releasing.
   - You may have to repent on behalf of your family members and ask God to show you if this evil spirit has been passed on generationally or not. Repent of whatever God shows you.

3. Command it to GO in Jesus' name.
   - The best teacher is Jesus Christ Himself, here are a couple of ways He told demons to flee:

     a. "But Jesus rebuked him, saying, "Be silent, and come out of him!" And the unclean spirit, convulsing him and crying out with a loud voice, came out of him." (Mark 1:25-26)

     b. "And He said to them, "Go!" And they came out and went into the pigs; and behold, the whole herd rushed down the steep bank into the sea and drowned in the waters." (Matthew 8:32)

- The first apostles of Christ are also great teachers:

    a. "...And Paul...having turned to the spirit, said, "I command you in the name of Jesus Christ to depart from her!" And it went out at the very hour." (Acts 16:18)

4. Pray AND Urge

- Ask the Holy Spirit to fill them and urge them to sin no more; sin is what gives Satan the legal right to inhabit people or oppress people. We must turn from those ways and turn to Christ, that is true repentance.

    a. "...Behold, thou art made whole. Sin no more, lest a worse thing come unto thee." (John 5:14) - context: invalid man healed

    b. "When an impure spirit comes out of a person, it goes through arid places seeking rest and does not find it. Then it says, 'I will return to the house I left.' When it arrives, it finds the house unoccupied, swept clean, and put in order. Then it goes and takes with it seven other spirits more wicked than itself, and they go in and live there. And the final condition of that person is worse than the first. That is how it will be with this wicked generation." (Matthew 12:43-45)

- Proverbs 26:2 shows us that without having cause for demonic activity to be attached to us, it won't, so we must remain in a repentant state and follow Jesus:

    a. "Like a fluttering sparrow or a darting swallow, an undeserved curse does not come to rest."

If the demon doesn't leave, continue praying and commanding. If after more time it doesn't leave, contact a senior leader (who you know has a lifestyle of fasting and prayer) and ask them to assist. If this isn't possible, pray for the person and you go fast and pray and return at another time(see Matthew 17:14-21). I'll end this with the words of Jesus,

"The seventy-two returned with joy, saying, "Lord, even the demons are subject to us in your name!" And he said to them, "I saw Satan fall like lightning from heaven. Behold, I have given you authority to tread on serpents and scorpions, and over all the power of the enemy, and nothing shall hurt you. Nevertheless, do not rejoice in this, that the spirits are subject to you, but rejoice that your names are written in heaven."

Luke 10:17-20.

Selah.

Appendix E: Evangelism

What is evangelism?

Let's start with studying the word itself, according to the Canadian Encyclopedia, Britannica, and the Blue Letter Bible,

> *Evangelism is an English word derived from the combination of the 2 Greek words* **euangelion** *meaning "good news." During the Roman empire's reign, this word was used for the announcement of the appearance or accession to the throne of the ruler, and* **euangelizomai**, *meaning "to announce, declare, proclaim, bring glad tidings, and to preach."*

Therefore, the word "evangelism" literally, contextually, and spiritually means "to proclaim the good news that the ruler (Jesus) has ascended to the throne." That is what you are doing when you evangelize and share the "good news" aka the "gospel."

What is the good news (gospel) that we are to proclaim?

Ultimately, the good news is that God loved us so much that He paid our debt and defeated the power of darkness (sin, Hell, Satan, and demons) in our lives allowing our sins to be forgiven, freedom, and oneness with Him again.

How did He do this? By physically coming to earth in the form of a man, Jesus (John 1:1, Colossians 2:9), he fought for us by living a sinless life and yet allowed himself to be tortured, died on the cross, and rose from the dead three days after. Through these events, God has offered the entire world forgiveness of their sins and reunification with Him now and in eternity after Jesus returns. (Isaiah 53:5-8)

These acts did three things:

1. Jesus paid our debt

    - Like being fined by police or a judge if we break the law on earth, humanity owes God a lot of fines (more than we could ever pay ourselves) because we break His law every time we sin (publicly or privately) or even think about sinning. From our youth to adulthood, we have evil intentions due to sin and can't follow the law perfectly causing debt to build up. Jesus' death and resurrection paid the debt once and for all, allowing God to forgive our sins if we ask (Genesis 8:21, Romans 5:12, Colossians 2:13-14, and 1 John 1:7-9).

2. Jesus freed us from the law and offers us new life by His Spirit

- We can't obey God's law fully on our own, but because of Jesus, we can now live freely and whole by having the Holy Spirit within us. By living according to the Spirit of God, He offers us new life, righteousness, conviction if/when we sin again (which should lead to repentance), guidance to avoid sin, transformation to be completely done with sin patterns we (or our ancestors) have fallen into, He gives us revelation of God, gifts, ultimate freedom, and so much more (Galatians 3:10-14, Romans 8:1-4, John 15:26, 1 Corinthians 12:1-11, John 3:5-6, John 4:24).

3. Jesus gave us power over sin and Satan

- Being that Jesus literally defeated death on our behalf, by placing our faith in Him and receiving His Spirit, we too can carry this same authority to free ourselves and others from the consequences of death (oppression of demons, sickness, and eternal death by offering them salvation). No longer do we have to be bound to sin or demons, we can be free and operate in authority by the spirit of God in Jesus' name (Romans 6:3-11, Colossians 2:15, Revelation 1:18, Matthew 28:18, Luke 10:17-20, 1 John 4:4).

Because of these things, through faith in Christ alone and receiving the Holy Spirit, we can overcome every sin and struggle and we get to be with God now and eternally in Heaven when the time comes!

Although this is good news, there is some sad news too: Sin and darkness still rule many and Jesus is returning for final judgment to deal with Satan and those who follow him. Anyone who does not put their faith in Jesus will be condemned with Satan and his demons to Hell forever, eternally separated from God. Why? Because their debt will have remained unpaid, their sin will still be ruling them, and their allegiance will still be to the devil and not the one true God. Imagine this: someone writes you a check or tries to send you a money transfer for 1 trillion dollars to pay off the fines and debt you've accumulated. To get this money into your bank account, you must first ACCEPT the payment for it to be deposited into your account. If you don't accept (cash the check/approve the money transfer) the money remains available (until the expiration date), but never impacts your account for you to spend and use as you need. This is what it's like for those who do not accept Jesus.

Jesus wrote us each the biggest check/money transfer of our lives, but if we don't accept Him, it never benefits us. He is readily available to us until the expiration date of our death or the day He returns and judges the earth, whichever comes first. Don't leave His sacrifice on the table, accept Him and awaken others that they have a spiritual check/money transfer of salvation waiting to be cashed in.

How do we accept this salvation check? We accept Jesus through faith and declaration. This looks like admitting we are sinners who need saving and repenting of our sins, believing in our hearts that Jesus is the Son of God who saved us by dying and being raised from the dead paying the debt we owed, and declaring (saying) with our mouth that He is Lord of our lives. We can then ask for God's Holy Spirit to fill us and make us new. Jesus also tells us to be baptized after making this decision to follow Him as a spiritual act of dying to our old ways and being made new by His Spirit.

God loved us so much that He provided the best and only solution to our sin problem, He provided Himself. Let's tell the world.

How do we proclaim the gospel?

Practically you can share the gospel in various ways, but before sharing some methods, I'd like to first point out that this shouldn't be a robotic, one-way or nothing kind of thing and as you grow in this area, the Lord will show you new ways to share too. Jesus instructed us to make disciples, not robotic churchgoers, so evangelism shouldn't be robotic either. Disciples are people who will grow to love God and not only know information about Him. Disciples are also people who desire more than to just escape hell but to also bring heaven to earth through their prayers, witness, and actions. Below are steps I believe will help you to make disciples as you share. Please know that you may not continue in a relationship with some people after sharing with them, but with others you will. Whether you remain in a relationship with them or not, always pray and trust that the seeds you planted will be watered. Also know that ultimately, whether you someone makes Jesus their Lord or not through your witness, it's God that brings the increase and salvation (see 1 Corinthians 3:5-9). Below are some practical points on sharing. I purposefully didn't put numbers and "steps" because as you continue in relationship with people the order of this may shift.

Point A: Connection

The best way I've noticed to make disciples per the scriptures and through personal/observed experiences is through first connecting with the person you're sharing with. Get to know him/her and pray for them. Jesus often reclined at table with people, we should do the same

- Get lunch, a coffee, or a treat together and talk
- Chat with people on the bus/public transport
- Do your favorite hobby amongst a group and talk with people afterward or during

Note: Don't rush beyond this. You may not always share deep revelation at this phase. Be discerning.

Point B: Plant

Share nuggets of the gospel or the whole thing if there's space and the person desires to hear more. Here are some ways you can plant "seeds":

- Anything the Holy Spirit brings to mind as you and the person chat (if you share, be sure to give the Holy Spirit credit; ie, "I believe that God can speak to us through his Holy Spirit and as you shared that, He reminded me of/showed me a picture of/told me to share with you _____. Does that have meaning to you?")
- Something that relates to Jesus and what you know about the person (ie, "When you shared _____, that reminds me of how Jesus _____ in the Bible. Have you ever heard of anything like this?)
- Share a brief testimony about something that connects to them (ie, "...that reminds me of a time in my life when _____[insert brief testimony of what Jesus did for you]. Has anything like this ever happened to you before?")
- Share a scripture that you've been studying or something you've learned recently.
- Ask direct questions: "Have you ever read the Bible? It speaks about ____ as you mentioned," then ask if he/she would like to read it with you some time.
- Pray for healing if they are injured or ill in any way (if they are healed or see any difference, give glory to God and the fact that the kingdom of God has come near them and share the gospel)
- Be a witness by how you live with radical love, kindness, and respect, especially towards an enemy.
- Share the gospel fully via the The Bridge diagram, The PERFECT Model, or The BRB Model (see details for these at the end of this section).

Point C: Pray

In your own solo time with the Lord, pray for the people He's brought into your life. You can ask him/her how you can pray for them(depending on cultures, they may not understand what this means, so you may have to explain) or simply pray according to what the Holy Spirit shares or what you know based on your conversations.

Point D: Repeat

If you get the person's number, work together, or just always see them, keep getting to know them and planting/watering healthily. Resist the urge to rush things, remember, God brings the increase. We must simply be faithful to planting and watering.

If you don't continue you can still pray for them and ask the Lord to send others to bless them.

Why do we share the gospel?

We share the gospel for many reasons, but there are four that stand out to me the most:

1. To prepare people for what's to come. (Revelation 22:12)
2. It is the cure everyone in the world in one way or another is looking for.
3. It's mentioned in both the Old and New Testament as a beautiful act. (Isaiah 52:7 and Romans 10:15)
4. It's a way to partner with God in doing something "bigger than ourselves" and live purposefully.
5. Jesus said to do it.

"Then Jesus came to them and said, "All authority in heaven and on earth has been given to me. Therefore go and make disciples of all nations, baptizing them in the name of the Father and of the Son and of the Holy Spirit, and teaching them to obey everything I have commanded you. And surely I am with you always, to the very end of the age." Matthew 28:18-20

Appendix E: Evangelism

GOSPEL SHARING MODELS:

The Bridge Diagram:

This is a method I learned in college in Campus Outreach and I have never forgotten it. You'll need something to write on and with (depending on where you are when you find yourself needing to share the gospel, this can be pencil and paper, sand and your finger, a napkin and a pen, etc). You'll also need to memorize Romans 6:23, "For the wages of sin is death, but the free gift of God is eternal life in Christ Jesus our Lord" and Romans 10:9, "If you declare with your mouth, "Jesus is Lord," and believe in your heart that God raised him from the dead, you will be saved." Lastly, you'll need to know how to draw the Bridge diagram below and walk someone through each part. You can use the script below to practice, but please feel free to make it your own and ask the Holy Spirit for help and how to share.

For video instructions, search "The MTS Bridge Diagram" on YouTube. Our official YouTube account is @moveandseek. You can also find more resources at www.morethansundayinc.org!

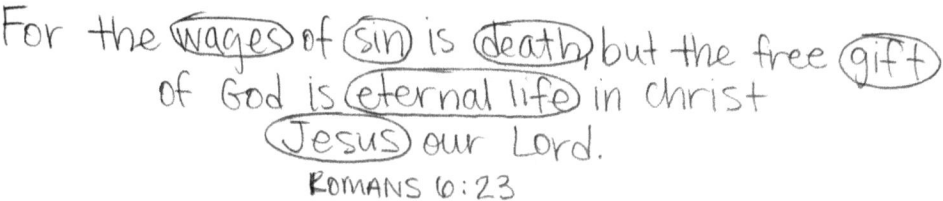

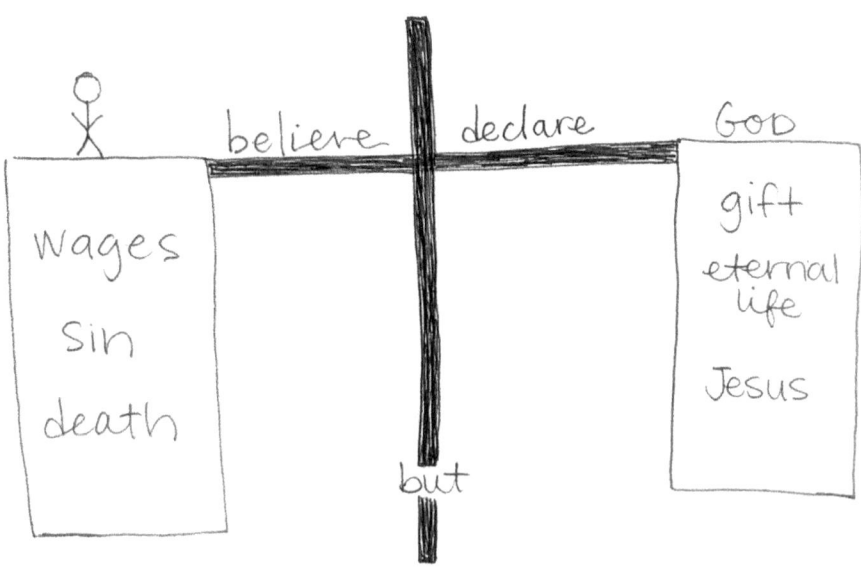

STEP 1: THE GAP

SAY: According to the Bible, at the beginning of human creation, God and man (male/female) were able to live together and everything was so good on earth! But after man chose to sin, it separated them from God and His goodness.

DRAW: Two boxes with a gap in the middle of them.

WRITE: "Man" (or you can draw a stick person if you want) on the top of one box and write "God" on top of the other.

ASK: How do you think man can get reconnected to God? What do you think could be a bridge to reconnect us? (Answers may be: doing good things, feeding the poor, not being a bad person, etc)

STEP 2: THE BRIDGE

SAY: Romans 6:23 tells us all about what happened next.

WRITE and **READ:** "For the wages of sin is death, but the free gift of God is eternal life in Christ Jesus our Lord." -Romans 6:23 (write this at the top or bottom of the page)

SAY: In this verse we see that because of sin (any thought/action that is not perfect according to God), man earns the wage (it's like a paycheck) of death (eternal separation from God).

WRITE: "wages," "sin", and "death" inside of the box under man.

ASK: Have you ever sinned before? (Let them answer, then share how you have as well). Did you know that our sin is what caused us to be separated from God? Did you know that because of the sin in our hearts none of our good actions alone are good enough to reconnect us to God because He's perfect?

SAY: Because of our sin, you and I both deserve and have earned death and that's sad, but there's good news! The next part of the verse says, "but the free gift of God is eternal life in Christ Jesus our Lord." This part of the verse shows us that God gifted us a way to have eternal life and to be with Him again through Jesus.

WRITE: "but" at the bottom of the gap. Then write, "gift," "eternal life," and "Jesus" inside the box under God.

ASK: Did you know that Jesus is God in a human body and because of that, he is called the Son of God? (Let the Holy Spirit lead you to share more here)

SAY: Through Jesus' death on the cross and resurrection (coming back to life) from the dead, God has made a way for us to be reconnected to Him if we want to be.

DRAW: A cross (like a big lowercase "t") in the middle of the gap, connecting man's side to God's side.

ASK: How does that make you feel knowing that God wants you to be with Him? How do you feel knowing that there's a way to get back to God?

STEP 3: CROSSING THE BRIDGE

SAY: Romans 10:9 tells us what we have to do to walk across the bridge Jesus built. It says, "if you declare with your mouth, "Jesus is Lord," and believe in your heart that God raised him from the dead, you will be saved." So it takes believing and declaring (saying) it to be saved.

WRITE: "believe" and "declare" (or "say it") on each side of the cross.

ASK: Do you believe that God sent Jesus to die for your sins and was raised from the dead? If not, do you want to believe? Do you have questions? (Answer them if you can, if not, share your willingness to search for the answer in the bible with them, etc. Be Spirit led)

PRAY: Based on what they say, ask if you can pray for them and ask the Holy Spirit to reveal Himself to them; be sure to listen to hear if God would reveal anything specific for you to share with the person prophetically (He may show you a picture, say a single word, remind you of a scripture, etc). If they choose to make Jesus Lord of their life, have them openly declare it in prayer, telling God themself that he/she believes and wants Jesus to be Lord of their life and asking for forgiveness of their sins (this is repentance).

STEP 4: FOLLOW UP

If the person decides to declare Jesus as Lord of their life, (Yay!) what now? Tell them about the Holy Spirit and baptism. Then, pray and ask the Holy Spirit to fill them and make them new, helping them to walk and live as Jesus would want them to. Encourage them to read scriptures, pray (talk to God about life, thank Him, repent when they mess up, ask for what they need, etc), worship (sing songs about Him and live a life that honors Him), and join a true bible believing church for community and fellowship (if there is no church, you all can read scriptures and eat together if you want). Lastly, ask them if there's anyone in their life they think would want to know about Jesus too. Encourage them to share what they learned with them.

If the person doesn't choose to declare Jesus as Lord, although it may be saddening, know that you've done your part. Offer to stay in touch with them if they'd like and enjoy the rest of your day. Be sure to pray for them in your own time too.

The PERFECT Model:

If you can remember the word "PERFECT" and what each letter means, you can also share the gospel this way. Memorize this acronym and scriptures that align, make it your own by adding your testimony where you see fit, ask the person questions to get them engaged, and ask the Holy Spirit to lead you. Whether you use this model to share the gospel or teach yourself the gospel simply, use it as you desire and as the Spirit leads you. Please don't feel bound to any one way of sharing, just make sure it's biblical.

Perfection: In the beginning, God created the world and everything in it in order to be one with them as a family. It was perfect, full of beauty, there was no death or chaos, and Adam & Eve (everyone's earliest ancestors) dwelled with God in Eden. (Genesis 1-2)

Evil: Unfortunately, Adam & Eve were tempted by Satan and chose to follow his lead instead of obeying God. This is called sin. Because Adam and Eve are our ancestors, their sinful actions affected all of humanity, making sin a part of our natural design. This was horrible for us and the world God created to be one with us in. Adam & Eve choosing to listen to and obey Satan caused God to separate them from Him and the world was cursed with a plague of darkness (sin, war, corruption, evil, and chaos) in a world where Satan and evil spirits had power. (Genesis 3, Isaiah 59:1-2, Genesis 8:21, Romans 3:23)

Requirement: In order for humans to be one with God again, God has a requirement: we have to follow His law perfectly and have pure hearts. If we fail to follow His law, we have to pay with a sacrifice of an animal (a life for a life). If God's standard isn't followed and the payment isn't made, debt would accumulate. If we look at history and even our own lives, we can see how impossible of a task this actually is. It's impossible for us to follow God's law perfectly, and even when people try to follow the law alone, their hearts are still dark, so none of their actions are good enough. Thus, debt is built up quickly and there's not enough animals in the world to sacrifice for the number of times we sin. What are we to do? How can we fulfill God's requirement so we can be in relationship with Him again? (Leviticus 4, Numbers 15, Psalm 24:4, Isaiah 64:6, Galatians 3:10, Romans 6:23, Romans 8:4)

Fulfilled: Knowing all along that humanity would fail and never be able to live up to His standard alone, God was prepared and in the right time, sent Jesus (God in the flesh, born through a virgin named Mary) as a perfect sacrifice for us to fulfill His requirement and offer us forgiveness. Jesus taught us how to live, revealed who God was (Father, Son, and Holy Spirit), what God desires, and was ultimately the perfect sacrifice to fulfill God's "life for a life" policy paying all of humanity's debt once and for all so that we could be forgiven. Just as Adam's choice caused sin (death) to enter all of humanity, Jesus caused life to be available for all of humanity who chooses to call on His name to be saved. (Colossians 1:15-17, Romans 8:3-5, Romans 5:12, John 1:1, Isaiah 53:4-7)

Encounter & **E**valuate: God is steadily seeking after us, desiring for us to choose Him. Once we realize this and encounter Him, we can truly evaluate our lives to see our need for Him. Through believing that Jesus is the son of God who died and rose from the dead, declaring with our mouth that Jesus is Lord of your life, repenting (seeing our need for him and apologizing for doing things our own way), and asking for His Holy Spirit to give us new life and power from God as we are born again, transformed, and receive a new heart, we are saved. It's also important to be baptized in water too! (John 6:44, 2 Peter 3:9, John 3:16, Romans 10:9, Matthew 28:19)

If we choose to ignore God and not evaluate our lives, we must know that Jesus is returning and will judge the world and Satan. Those who do not put their trust in Jesus alone will be condemned with Satan and his demons. (Revelation 22:12, John 3:18-20, Matthew 25:41)

Continue: After accepting Jesus, we are to continue in a relationship with God, praying, worshiping in song and living lives according to Jesus' truth, meditating on the Scriptures, being in community, and repenting where needed. (Acts 2:42, Colossians 2:6, John 3:21, Romans 8:1-11)

Tell: Tell someone the gospel and share who Jesus is with others. Ask God to open your eyes to opportunities and to lead you to them.

The BRB Model

Remember the words: Believe, Receive, Repent, and Become AND Memorize John 1:12-13 and Matthew 4:17

"But to all who did receive him (Jesus), who believed in his name (Jesus), he gave the right to become children of God, who were born, not of blood nor of the will of the fl esh nor of the will of man, but of God." John 1:12-13 (ESV) "From that time Jesus began to preach, saying, "Repent, for the kingdom of heaven is at hand." Matthew 4:17 (ESV)

To be saved, you must BELIEVE by faith in who Jesus is (the Son of God who was sent from Heaven to die and come back to life from the dead), RECEIVE Jesus as Lord of your life (make Him the ruler of your life) by declaring with your mouth that He is Lord, and REPENTING (apologizing and turning back to God) of your sin when you mess up. Then, you will BECOME a child of God as you are born again upon asking and receiving His Holy Spirit, living accordingly thereafter.

Appendix F: Fasting

What is fasting?

Fasting is defined as "to afflict one's soul" as mentioned in Isaiah 58:3. If you look at the Hebrew definition of "afflict", "soul", and biblical examples of fasting, you will find the fasting means to weaken one's will, appetites, emotions, passions, and one's living being(body) unto God by abstaining from food. This is also known as "humbling yourself before God."

Who fasted in the Bible?

There are many examples of people fasting in the Bible in both the Old and New Testament, I will reference them throughout this study. Here are a few: Jesus (Matthew 4:1-2), Moses (Exodus 24:15-18), Daniel (Daniel 10:1-14), Esther (Esther 4:10-16), Ezra (Ezra 8:21-23), and John the Baptist and Jesus' disciples (Matthew 9:14–15). Take some time to read each of these passages for your understanding.

Is fasting required for salvation? When should I fast?

Repentance and faith in Jesus (belief that Jesus died and rose from the grave while also confessing His Sonship and Lordship, followed by works to show your faith) is all that is required for salvation. So, no, fasting isn't required for you to be saved, but if you have the opportunity, go for it, for it has great strength, purpose, and power connected to it! In Matthew 6:16, Jesus also said "WHEN you fast..." not "IF you fast..." so this shows He intends for us to fast during our lives and journey with Him. Here are some examples of when people fasted:

- Jesus fasted before starting His public ministry, the Holy Spirit led Him into the wilderness to fast.
- Esther & other Jews fasted in a time of great trouble and she desired favor from the Lord before going before the king unannounced.
- Daniel fasted as he desired to understand the meaning of an intense message sent to him so he humbled himself before God to seek the answer and help.
- Moses fasted while appearing before God for guidance and instruction for the Israelites.
- Ezra fasted to seek God for safety in their travels.
- Jesus' disciples would fast after Jesus had died and resurrected as they longed for His return, but they didn't fast while He was with them.

No matter who was fasting, they all had the commonality of fasting to humble themselves before God! A good spiritual discipline I've learned is to dedicate one day a week to fasting and praying from morning to evening(sunrise to sunset).

How long should I fast?

Biblically, people fasted anywhere from 1 day to 40 days. So, pray and ask the Holy Spirit to show you how long you should fast.

What should I fast?

Fasting is a means of denying your flesh and thus humbling yourself before God. In most of the accounts presented in this study and the others throughout the Bible, biblical fasts were when people abstained from all food and sometimes drink as well. Ask the Holy Spirit to reveal how you should fast. He's always our most helpful source! Depending on the purpose of your various fasts, you may sense that God would lead you to fast in different ways.

Why should you fast?

"Yet even now," declares the LORD, "return to me with all your heart, with fasting, with weeping, and with mourning..." Joel 2:12

- God tells the people to RETURN to Him, He then says HOW to return to Him, through FASTING. So fasting is a means of consecration, dedicating yourself to//returning to God! When God says he desires us to mourn, He is saying He wants us to be sorrowful because of our sins! He wants our hearts to break for the things that break His heart! So in essence, similar to mourning the death of a loved one, we are mourning the death that tries to consume us within like lust, unforgiveness, envy, sexual immorality, drunkenness, homosexuality, etc. In acceptance of Jesus, fasting, and prayer, we are taking a stand against sin and kicking it out as we return to God in a big way.

"And he said unto them, This kind can come forth by nothing but by prayer and fasting." Mark 9:29 KJV (Mark 9:14-29 for full context)

- Fasting brings about greater authority as you intentionally connect yourself to God and rid yourself of your fleshly desires. While fasting we are totally reliant on God as we deny ourselves, so He can move and operate through us more freely! During this time, we also show Satan and every demon from Hell whose side we are on, thus giving them no room to operate and instead they must respond to God in us and be evicted. My pastor has said before, "Where there is great anointing you know there was great sacrifice", fasting and seeking the Lord with your whole heart is a part of such sacrifice.

"When I shut up the heavens so that there is no rain, or command locusts to devour the land or send a plague among my people, if my people, who are called by my name, will humble themselves and pray and seek my face and turn from their wicked ways, then I will hear from heaven, and I will forgive their sin and will heal their land. Now my eyes will be open and my ears attentive to the prayers offered in this place." 2 Chronicles 7:13-15

- Fasting humbles you before God and draws you into a place of repentance and surrender to Him. God gets your attention and you're able to connect with Him and show your desire for His company, aid, and attention. His ear is also more attentive to you in those times too as you intentionally turn from sin and seek Him.

Fasting etiquette, how should you fast?

"[Fasting] without prayer, it's just a diet". ~Somebody

- As you see in 2 Chronicles 7:13-15 above, fasting and prayer(connecting with God, seeking and being in His presence) always go together in the scriptures, so if you only abstain from food but don't seek God more intentionally during this time, it's useless and you're not fasting at that point, you're simply dieting.

"When you fast, do not look somber as the hypocrites do, for they disfigure their faces to show others they are fasting. Truly I tell you, they have received their reward in full. But when you fast, put oil on your head and wash your face, so that it will not be obvious to others that you are fasting, but only to your Father, who is unseen; and your Father, who sees what is done in secret, will reward you." Matthew 6:16-18

- Don't fast to showboat or make people think you're so spiritual or to get the praise of people, for God says that, those praises will be the end of your reward! Thus making your time of fasting obsolete and useless all because your heart behind why you were fasting wasn't pure!
- As you're willingly denying your flesh, the enemy is likely going to tempt you in various ways! Be it with food you've committed to stay away from or with pressures that make you want to act ungodly. When you're tempted, find the way out! For God promised we wouldn't be tempted beyond what we could bear and He'll always provide a way out(1 Corinthians 10:13). Take it! Many times when fasting that week just magically becomes the week where people want to give free food or there's a potluck at the workplace, resist and lean on God to make it through.
- When you feel ready to complain, sulk, or give in, choose to rejoice and thank God. Pick a Bible verse to memorize(Isaiah 26:3 is a good verse you can start with) while you're fasting and in times of struggling during your fast, recite it, pray it, and thank God for

who He is. Cry out to God about the things you are struggling with and release them to Him, repent where needed!

Homework: Read Isaiah 58 for God's desires when you fast! Take time now to ask God about when your next fast should be.

YEARLONG CHRONOLOGICAL BIBLE READING PLAN		Created on: biblereadingplangenerator.com			
Jan-1	Gen 1-3	Feb-1		Mar-1	
Jan-2	Gen 4-7	Feb-2	Ex 11-14	Mar-2	Num 34-36; Deut 1
Jan-3	Gen 8-11	Feb-3	Ex 15-18	Mar-3	Deut 2-5
Jan-4		Feb-4	Ex 19-21	Mar-4	Deut 6-9
Jan-5	Job 1-4	Feb-5	Ex 22-25	Mar-5	Deut 10-12
Jan-6	Job 5-7	Feb-6	Ex 26-29	Mar-6	Deut 13-16
Jan-7	Job 8-11	Feb-7	Ex 30-33	Mar-7	Deut 17-20
Jan-8	Job 12-15	Feb-8		Mar-8	
Jan-9	Job 16-19	Feb-9	Ex 34-37	Mar-9	Deut 21-24
Jan-10	Job 20-23	Feb-10	Ex 38-40	Mar-10	Deut 25-28
Jan-11		Feb-11	Lev 1-4	Mar-11	Deut 29-31
Jan-12	Job 24-26	Feb-12	Lev 5-8	Mar-12	Deut 32-34; Ps 91
Jan-13	Job 27-30	Feb-13	Lev 9-12	Mar-13	Josh 1-4
Jan-14	Job 31-34	Feb-14	Lev 13-16	Mar-14	Josh 5-8
Jan-15	Job 35-38	Feb-15		Mar-15	
Jan-16	Job 39-42	Feb-16	Lev 17-19	Mar-16	Josh 9-12
Jan-17	Gen 12-14	Feb-17	Lev 20-23	Mar-17	Josh 13-15
Jan-18		Feb-18	Lev 24-27	Mar-18	Josh 16-19
Jan-19	Gen 15-18	Feb-19	Num 1-4	Mar-19	Josh 20-23
Jan-20	Gen 19-22	Feb-20	Num 5-8	Mar-20	Josh 24; Jdg 1-3
Jan-21	Gen 23-26	Feb-21	Num 9-11	Mar-21	Jdg 4-7
Jan-22	Gen 27-30	Feb-22		Mar-22	
Jan-23	Gen 31-33	Feb-23	Num 12-15	Mar-23	Jdg 8-10
Jan-24	Gen 34-37	Feb-24	Ps 90; Num 16-18	Mar-24	Jdg 11-14
Jan-25		Feb-25	Num 19-22	Mar-25	Jdg 15-18
Jan-26	Gen 38-41	Feb-25	Num 23-26	Mar-26	Jdg 19-21; Rut 1
Jan-27	Gen 42-45	Feb-27	Num 27-29	Mar-27	Rut 2-4; 1 Sa 1
Jan-28	Gen 46-49	Feb-28	Num 30-33	Mar-28	1 Sa 2-4
Jan-29	Gen 50; Ex 1-2			Mar-29	
Jan-30	Ex 3-6			Mar-30	1 Sa 5-8

Jan-31	Ex 7-10			Mar-31	1 Sa 9-12
Apr-1	1 Sa 13-16	May-1	Ps 68, 89, 96, 100	Jun-1	1 Kgs 2; Ps 37, 71
Apr-2	1 Sa 17-20	May-2	Ps 101, 105, 132	Jun-2	Ps 94, 119; 1 Kgs 3-4
Apr-3	Ps 11, 59; 1 Sa 21	May-3		Jun-3	2 Chr 1; Ps 72; Sos 1-2
Apr-4	1 Sa 22-24; Ps 7	May-4	2 Sa 6-7; 1 Chr 17; Ps 25	Jun-4	Sos 3-6
Apr-5		May-5	Ps 29, 33, 36, 39	Jun-5	Sos 7-8; Pro 1-2
Apr-6	Ps 27, 31, 34, 52	May-6	2 Sa 8-9; 1 Chr 18; Ps 50	Jun-6	Pro 3-5
Apr-7	Ps 56, 120, 140-141	May-7	Ps 53, 60, 75; 2 Sa 10	Jun-7	
Apr-8	Ps 142; 1 Sa 25-27	May-8	1 Chr 19; Ps 20, 65	Jun-8	Pro 6-9
Apr-9	Ps 17, 35, 54	May-9	Ps 66-67, 69-70	Jun-9	Pro 10-13
Apr-10	Ps 63; 1 Sa 28-30	May-10		Jun-10	Pro 14-17
Apr-11	1 Sa 31; Ps 18, 121, 123	May-11	2 Sa 11-12; 1 Chr 20; Ps 32	Jun-11	Pro 18-21
Apr-12		May-12	Ps 51, 86, 122; 2 Sa 13	Jun-12	Pro 22-24
Apr-13	Ps 124-125, 128-129	May-13	2 Sa 14-15; Ps 3-4	Jun-13	1 Kgs 5-6; 2 Chr 2-3
Apr-14	Ps 130; 2 Sa 1-3	May-14	Ps 12-13, 28	Jun-14	
Apr-15	2 Sa 4; Ps 6, 8	May-15	Ps 55; 2 Sa 16-18	Jun-15	1 Kgs 7; 2 Chr 4; 1 Kgs 8; 2 Chr 5
Apr-16	Ps 9-10 14, 16	May-16	Ps 26, 40, 58, 61	Jun-16	2 Chr 6-7; Ps 136, 134
Apr-17	Ps 19, 21; 1 Chr 1-2	May-17		Jun-17	Ps 146-149
Apr-18	Ps 43-45, 49	May-18	Ps 62, 64; 2 Sa 19-20	Jun-18	Ps 150; 1 Kgs 9; 2 Chr 8
Apr-19		May-19	2 Sa 21; Ps 5, 38, 41	Jun-19	Pro 25-28
Apr-20	Ps 84-85, 87; 1 Chr 3	May-20	Ps 42; 2 Sa 22-23	Jun-20	Pro 29; Ecc 1-3
Apr-21	1 Chr 4-5; Ps 73	May-21	Ps 57, 95, 97-98	Jun-21	
Apr-22	Ps 77-78; 1 Chr 6; Ps 81	May-22	Ps 99; 2 Sa 24; 1 Chr 21-22	Jun-22	Ecc 4-7
Apr-23	Ps 88, 92-93; 1 Chr 7	May-23	Ps 30, 108-110	Jun-23	Ecc 8-11
Apr-24	1 Chr 8-10; Ps 102	May-24		Jun-24	Ecc 12; 1 Kgs 10-11
Apr-25	Ps 103-104; 2 Sa 5; 1 Chr 11	May-25	1 Chr 23-25; Ps 131	Jun-25	2 Chr 9; Pro 30-31; 1 Kgs 12
Apr-26		May-26	Ps 138-139, 143	Jun-26	1 Kgs 13-14; 2 Chr 10-11
Apr-27	1 Chr 12; Ps 133, 106	May-27	Ps 144-145; 1 Chr 26-27	Jun-27	2 Chr 12; 1 Kgs 15; 2 Chr 13-14
Apr-28	Ps 107; 1 Chr 13-15	May-28	1 Chr 28-29; Ps 127, 111	Jun-28	
Apr-29	1 Chr 16; Ps 1-2, 15	May-29	Ps 112-115	Jun-29	2 Chr 15-16; 1 Kgs 16; 2 Chr 17
Apr-30	Ps 22-24, 47	May-30	Ps 116-118; 1 Kgs 1	Jun-30	1 Kgs 17-19
		May-31			

Jul-1	1 Kgs 20-22; 2 Chr 18	Aug-1	Isa 31-34	Sep-1	2 Chr 36; Hab 1-2
Jul-2	2 Chr 19-22	Aug-2		Sep-2	Hab 3; Jer 41-43
Jul-3	2 Chr 23; Oba; Ps 82-83	Aug-3	Isa 35-37	Sep-3	Jer 44-47
Jul-4	2 Kgs 1-3	Aug-4	Isa 38-39; Ps 76; Isa 40	Sep-4	Jer 48-51
Jul-5		Aug-5	Isa 41-44	Sep-5	Jer 52; Lam 1-3
Jul-6	2 Kgs 4-7	Aug-6	Isa 45-48	Sep-6	
Jul-7	2 Kgs 8-11	Aug-7	2 Kgs 19; Ps 46, 80, 135	Sep-7	Lam 4-5; Eze 1
Jul-8	2 Kgs 12-13; 2 Chr 24; 2 Kgs 14	Aug-8	Isa 49-51	Sep-8	Eze 2-5
Jul-9	2 Chr 25; Jon 1-3	Aug-9		Sep-9	Eze 6-9
Jul-10	Jon 4; 2 Kgs 15; 2 Chr 26	Aug-10	Isa 52-55	Sep-10	Eze 10-13
Jul-11	Isa 1-4	Aug-11	Isa 56-59	Sep-11	Eze 14-17
Jul-12		Aug-12	Isa 60-63	Sep-12	Eze 18-20
Jul-13	Isa 5-8	Aug-13	Isa 64-66; 2 Kgs 20	Sep-13	
Jul-14	Amo 1-4	Aug-14	2 Kgs 21; 2 Chr 32-33	Sep-14	Eze 21-24
Jul-15	Amo 5-8	Aug-15	Nah 1-3; 2 Kgs 22	Sep-15	Eze 25-28
Jul-16	Amo 9; 2 Chr 27; Isa 9	Aug-16		Sep-16	Eze 29-32
Jul-17	Isa 10-12; Mic 1	Aug-17	2 Kgs 23; 2 Chr 34-35; Zep 1	Sep-17	Eze 33-36
Jul-18	Mic 2-5	Aug-18	Zep 2-3; Jer 1-2	Sep-18	Eze 37-39
Jul-19		Aug-19	Jer 3-6	Sep-19	Eze 40-43
Jul-20	Mic 6-7; 2 Chr 28; 2 Kgs 16	Aug-20	Jer 7-9	Sep-20	
Jul-21	2 Kgs 17; Isa 13-15	Aug-21	Jer 10-13	Sep-21	Eze 44-47
Jul-22	Isa 16-18	Aug-22	Jer 14-17	Sep-22	Eze 48; Joe 1-3
Jul-23	Isa 19-22	Aug-23		Sep-23	Dan 1-4
Jul-24	Isa 23-26	Aug-24	Jer 18-21	Sep-24	Dan 5-7
Jul-25	Isa 27; 2 Kgs 18; 2 Chr 29-30	Aug-25	Jer 22-25	Sep-25	Dan 8-11
Jul-26		Aug-26	Jer 26-28	Sep-26	Dan 12; Ezr 1-3
Jul-27	2 Chr 31; Ps 48; Hos 1-2	Aug-27	Jer 29-32	Sep-27	
Jul-28	Hos 3-5	Aug-28	Jer 33-36	Sep-28	Ezr 4-6; Ps 137
Jul-29	Hos 6-9	Aug-29	Jer 37-40	Sep-29	Hag 1-2; Zec 1-2
Jul-30	Hos 10-13	Aug-30		Sep-30	Zec 3-5
Jul-31	Hos 14; Isa 28-30	Aug-31	Ps 74, 79; 2 Kgs 24-25		

Oct-1	Zec 6-9	Nov-1		Dec-1	Rom 2-5
Oct-2	Zec 10-13	Nov-2	John 12; Mat 22; Mk 12; Mat 23	Dec-2	Rom 6-9
Oct-3	Zec 14; Est 1-3	Nov-3	Luk 20-21; Mk 13; Mat 24	Dec-3	Rom 10-12
Oct-4		Nov-4	Mat 25-26; Mk 14	Dec-4	Rom 13-16
Oct-5	Est 4-7	Nov-5	Luk 22; John 13-15	Dec-5	Acts 20-23
Oct-6	Est 8-10	Nov-6	John 16-17; Mat 27; Mk 15	Dec-6	
Oct-7	Ezr 7-10	Nov-7	Luk 23; John 18-19; Mat 28	Dec-7	Acts 24-27
Oct-8	Neh 1-4	Nov-8		Dec-8	Acts 28; Col 1-3
Oct-9	Neh 5-8	Nov-9	Mk 16; Luk 24; John 20-21	Dec-9	Col 4; Phlm; Eph 1
Oct-10	Neh 9-12	Nov-10	Acts 1-3	Dec-10	Eph 2-5
Oct-11		Nov-11	Acts 4-7	Dec-11	Eph 6; Phil 1-3
Oct-12	Neh 13; Ps 126; Mal 1	Nov-12	Acts 8-11	Dec-12	Phil 4; 1 Ti 1-3
Oct-13	Mal 2-4; Luk 1	Nov-13	Acts 12-14; Jam 1	Dec-13	
Oct-14	John 1; Mat 1; Luk 2; Mat 2	Nov-14	Jam 2-5	Dec-14	1 Ti 4-6; Tit 1
Oct-15	Mat 3; Mk 1; Luk 3; Mat 4	Nov-15		Dec-15	Tit 2-3; 1 Pe 1
Oct-16	Luk 4-5; John 2-3	Nov-16	Acts 15-16; Gal 1	Dec-16	1 Pe 2-5
Oct-17	John 4; Mat 8; Mk 2	Nov-17	Gal 2-5	Dec-17	Heb 1-4
Oct-18		Nov-18	Gal 6; Acts 17; 1 Th 1-2	Dec-18	Heb 5-8
Oct-19	John 5; Mat 12; Mk 3; Luk 6	Nov-19	1 Th 3-5; 2 Th 1	Dec-19	Heb 9-12
Oct-20	Mat 5-7, 9	Nov-20	2 Th 2-3; Acts 18-19	Dec-20	
Oct-21	Luk 7; Mat 11; Luk 11; Mat 13	Nov-21	1 Co 1-3	Dec-21	Heb 13; 2 Ti 1-2
Oct-22	Luk 8; Mk 4-5; Mat 10	Nov-22		Dec-22	2 Ti 3-4; 2 Pe 1-2
Oct-23	Mat 14; Mk 6; Luk 9	Nov-23	1 Co 4-7	Dec-23	2 Pe 3; Jude; 1 Jn 1-2
Oct-24	John 6; Mat 15; Mk 7; Mat 16	Nov-24	1 Co 8-11	Dec-24	1 Jn 3-5; 2 Jn
Oct-25		Nov-25	1 Co 12-15	Dec-25	3 Jn; Rev 1-3
Oct-26	Mk 8; Mat 17; Mk 9; Mat 18	Nov-26	1 Co 16; 2 Co 1-3	Dec-26	Rev 4-6
Oct-27	John 7-10	Nov-27	2 Co 4-6	Dec-27	
Oct-28	Luk 10, 12-14	Nov-28	2 Co 7-10	Dec-28	Rev 7-10
Oct-29	Luk 15-17	Nov-29		Dec-29	Rev 11-14
Oct-30	John 11; Luk 18; Mat 19; Mk 10	Nov-30	2 Co 11-13; Rom 1	Dec-30	Rev 15-18
Oct-31	Mat 20-21; Luk 19; Mk 11			Dec-31	Rev 19-22

BIBLIOGRAPHY

The Canadian Encyclopedia. Evangelism and Evangelicals. Accessed March 20, 2025. https://www.thecanadianencyclopedia.ca/en/article/evangelism-and-evangelicals

Encyclopaedia Britannica. Biblical Literature: Form Criticism. Accessed March 20, 2025. https://www.britannica.com/topic/biblical-literature/Form-criticism.

Blue Letter Bible. Greek Lexicon: Strong's G2097 – εὐαγγελίζω (euangelizō). Accessed March 20, 2025. https://www.blueletterbible.org/lexicon/g2097/kjv/tr/0-1/.

Efron, Zac. "Down to Earth," Netflix, 2020

"Home." GotQuestions.org, Got Questions Ministries, 10 Mar. 2005, www.gotquestions.org/BC-AD.html.

Isbouts, Jean-Pierre. "We May Now Know Which Egyptian Pharaoh Challenged Moses." National Geographic, 22 Jan. 2019, www.nationalgeographic.com/culture/people-in-the-bible/pharaoh-king-punished-god/.

McDowell, Dr. Josh D, and Dr. Clay Jones. "The Bibliographical Test ." Josh, 13 Aug. 2014, www.josh.org/wp-content/uploads/Bibliographical-Test-Update-08.13.14.pdf.

Peterson, Jonathan. "The Bible Explained with Infographics: An Interview with Karen Sawrey." Bible Gateway Blog, 13 Mar. 2018, www.biblegateway.com/blog/2019/03/the-bible-explained-with-infographics-an-interview-with-karen-sawrey/.

"Prophecies of Jesus." GotQuestions.org, Got Questions Ministries, 5 Nov. 2019, www.gotquestions.org/prophecies-of-Jesus.html.

Ramos, Art. "Early Jericho." Ancient History Encyclopedia, Ancient History Encyclopedia, 19 Sept. 2016, www.ancient.eu/article/951/early-jericho/.

Ratner, Paul. "How Old Is the Bible?" Big Think, Big Think, 5 Oct. 2018, bigthink.com/paul-ratner/how-old-is-the-bible.

Rattini, Kristin Baird. "Who Was Ramses II?" National Geographic , 13 May 2019, www.nationalgeographic.com/culture/people/reference/ramses-ii/.

Reinsch, Warren. "Merneptah Stele: Proving Israel's 3,200-Year Existence." Watch Jerusalem, 26 Oct. 2018, watchjerusalem.co.il/446-merneptah-stele-proving-israels-3200-year-existence.

Sawrey, Karen. The Infographic Bible: Visualising the Drama of God's Word. William Collins, 2018.

Book Summary

The Coloring Book Journal is a year-long interactive devotional designed to help you slow down, connect with God, and engage with the Bible in a deeper, more creative, and intentional way.

Each month features four weekly devotionals ("journal entries") paired with:

- Scripture references & open-ended questions
- Reflective questions to spark real-life application
- A coloring page or activity to relax your mind as you get creative
- Author commentary throughout and answers at the end of the book to aid your understanding

Whether you're simply investigating, are new to the faith, or ready to reignite your walk with God, this devotional creates space for honest reflection and meaningful conversations with Jesus. Ready to deepen your relationship with God? This devotional is for you!

www.ingramcontent.com/pod-product-compliance
Lightning Source LLC
Chambersburg PA
CBHW061803290426
44109CB00031B/2928